Hands-On Continuous Integration and Delivery

Build and release quality software at scale with Jenkins, Travis CI, and CircleCI

Jean-Marcel Belmont

BIRMINGHAM - MUMBAI

Hands-On Continuous Integration and Delivery

Commissioning Editor: Gebin George
Acquisition Editor: Rohit Rajkumar
Content Development Editor: Ronn Kurien, Devika Battike
Technical Editor: Aditya Khadye
Copy Editor: Safis Editing
Project Coordinator: Jagdish Prabhu
Proofreader: Safis Editing
Indexer: Priyanka Dhadke
Graphics: Tom Scaria
Production Coordinator: Aparna Bhagat

First published: August 2018

Production reference: 1270818

Published by Packt Publishing Ltd.
Livery Place
35 Livery Street
Birmingham
B3 2PB, UK.

ISBN 978-1-78913-048-5

www.packtpub.com

`mapt.io`

Mapt is an online digital library that gives you full access to over 5,000 books and videos, as well as industry leading tools to help you plan your personal development and advance your career. For more information, please visit our website.

Why subscribe?

- Spend less time learning and more time coding with practical eBooks and Videos from over 4,000 industry professionals

- Improve your learning with Skill Plans built especially for you

- Get a free eBook or video every month

- Mapt is fully searchable

- Copy and paste, print, and bookmark content

PacktPub.com

Did you know that Packt offers eBook versions of every book published, with PDF and ePub files available? You can upgrade to the eBook version at `www.PacktPub.com` and as a print book customer, you are entitled to a discount on the eBook copy. Get in touch with us at `service@packtpub.com` for more details.

At `www.PacktPub.com`, you can also read a collection of free technical articles, sign up for a range of free newsletters, and receive exclusive discounts and offers on Packt books and eBooks.

Contributors

About the author

Jean-Marcel Belmont is a software engineer with a passion for automation and continuous integration. He is heavily involved in the open source community and frequently writes workshops on many different software development topics. He maintains a couple of meetup groups where he advocates clean code patterns and software craftsmanship.

I would like to first and foremost thank my loving and patient wife, Christine, my son, Michael, and my daughter, Gabriella, for their support, patience, and encouragement throughout the long process of writing this book. Thanks also to my close friends and family for their encouragement throughout the book.

About the reviewers

Hai Dam works as a DevOps Engineer in Netcompany, Denmark. His DevOps toolchain are Jenkins, CircleCI, ELK, AWS, and Docker.

Craig R Webster has delivered projects for clients of all sizes, ranging from small startups such as Orkell, Picklive and Tee Genius, through Notonthehighstreet, the UK Government, and the BBC. With more than 15 years of experience developing and deploying web applications, delivery pipelines, automation, and hosting platforms, Craig is able to take point on any technical project and ensure it is delivered on time, and on budget.

Packt is searching for authors like you

Table of Contents

Preface

Writing modern software is hard because there are many groups involved in the delivery of software, including developers, QA, operations, product owners, customer support, and sales. There needs to be a process by which the development of the software is done in an automated way as it is being built. The process of continuous integration and continuous delivery will help ensure that the software that you deliver to your end users is of the highest quality and has been through a series of checks in a CI/CD pipeline. In this book, you will learn how to use Jenkins CI and how to write freestyle scripts, plugins, as well as how to use the newer Jenkins 2.0 UI and pipelines. You will learn about Travis CI in terms of the UI, the Travis CLI, advanced logging and debugging techniques, and best practices with Travis CI. You will also learn about Circle CLI in terms of the UI, the Circle CLI, advanced logging and debugging and best practices with CircleCI. Throughout the book we will talk about concepts such as containers, security, and deployment, among others.

Who this book is for

This book is meant for system administrators, QA engineers, DevOps, and site reliability engineers. You should have an understanding of Unix programming, basic programming concepts, and version control systems such as Git.

What this book covers

Chapter 1, *CI/CD with Automated Testing*, introduces the concept of automation and the explains the importance of automation compared to manual processes.

Chapter 2, *Basics of Continuous Integration*, introduces the concept of continuous integration, explains what a software build is, and covers CI build practices.

Chapter 3, *Basics of Continuous Delivery*, introduces the concept of continuous delivery and in particular explains the problem of delivering software, configuration management, deployment pipelines, and scripting.

Chapter 4, *The Business Value of CI/CD*, covers the business value of CI/CD by explaining problems with communication, such as the ability to communicate pain points to team members, sharing responsibilities among team members, knowing your stakeholders, and demonstrating why CI/CD is important.

Chapter 5, *Installation and Basics of Jenkins*, helps you get Jenkins CI installed on Windows, Linux, and macOS OSes. You will also learn how to run Jenkins in a local system and how to manage Jenkins CI.

Chapter 6, *Writing Freestyle Scripts*, covers how to write freestyle scripts in Jenkins and how to configure freestyle scripts in Jenkins, along with adding environment variables and debugging issues in freestyle scripts.

Chapter 7, *Developing Plugins*, explains what a plugin is in software, how to create a Jenkins plugin using Java and Maven, and goes over the Jenkins plugin ecosystem.

Chapter 8, *Building Pipelines with Jenkins*, covers Jenkins 2.0 in detail and explains how to navigate in Jenkins 2.0 (Blue Ocean), and also covers the new pipeline syntax in great detail.

Chapter 9, *Installation and Basics of Travis CI*, introduces you to Travis CI and explains the differences between Travis CI and Jenkins CI. We look at Travis life cycle events and the Travis YML syntax. We also explain how to get started and set up with GitHub.

Chapter 10, *Travis CI CLI Commands and Automation*, shows you how to get the Travis CI CLI installed, explains each command in the CLI in great detail, shows you how to automate tasks in Travis CI, and explains how to use the Travis API.

Chapter 11, *Travis CI UI Logging and Debugging*, explains the Travis Web UI in detail and showcases advanced techniques in logging and debugging in Travis CI.

Chapter 12, *Installation and Basics of CircleCI*, helps you set up CircleCI with Bitbucket and GitHub and shows how to navigate the CircleCI Web UI. We will also explain the CircleCI YML syntax.

Chapter 13, *CircleCI CLI Commands and Automation*, helps you install the CircleCI CLI and explains each command in the CLI. We will also go over workflows in CircleCI and how to use the CircleCI API.

Chapter 14, *CircleCI UI Logging and Debugging*, explains the job log in detail and shows how to debug slow builds in CircleCI. We will also go over logging and troubleshooting techniques in CircleCI.

Chapter 15, *Best Practices*, covers best practices for writing unit tests, integration tests, system tests, acceptance tests in CI/CD, and best practices in password and secret management. We will also go over best practices in deployment.

To get the most out of this book

In order to get the most out of of this book you will need to be familiar with Unix programming concepts such as working with the Bash shell, environment variables, and shell scripting, and understand basic commands in Unix. You should be familiar with the concept of version control and know what is meant by a commit, and you'll need to understand how to use Git in particular. You should know basic programming languages concepts because we will use languages such as Golang, Node.js, and Java, which will work as build languages that we use in or CI/CD pipelines and examples.

This book is OS-agnostic, but you will need access to a Unix environment and commands in order to use some of the concepts in this book. So, if you are using Windows, it may be useful to have Git Bash (`https://git-scm.com/downloads`) and/or the Ubuntu Subsystem installed if possible. You will need to have Git (`https://git-scm.com/downloads`), Docker (`https://docs.docker.com/install/`), Node.js (`https://nodejs.org/en/download/`), Golang (`https://golang.org/dl/`), and Java (`https://java.com/en/download/`) installed in your system. It would be very helpful to have a text editor such as Visual Studio Code (`https://code.visualstudio.com/download`) and a terminal console application.

Download the example code files

You can download the example code files for this book from your account at `www.packtpub.com`. If you purchased this book elsewhere, you can visit `www.packtpub.com/support` and register to have the files emailed directly to you.

You can download the code files by following these steps:

1. Log in or register at `www.packtpub.com`.
2. Select the **SUPPORT** tab.
3. Click on **Code Downloads & Errata**.
4. Enter the name of the book in the **Search** box and follow the onscreen instructions.

Once the file is downloaded, please make sure that you unzip or extract the folder using the latest version of:

- WinRAR/7-Zip for Windows
- Zipeg/iZip/UnRarX for Mac
- 7-Zip/PeaZip for Linux

The code bundle for the book is also hosted on GitHub at `https://github.com/PacktPublishing/Hands-On-Continuous-Integration-and-Delivery` under the README section, where you can find all the links to the code files chapterwise . In case there's an update to the code, the links will be updated on the existing GitHub repository.

We also have other code bundles from our rich catalog of books and videos available at `https://github.com/PacktPublishing/`. Check them out!

Conventions used

There are a number of text conventions used throughout this book.

`CodeInText`: Indicates code words in text, database table names, folder names, filenames, file extensions, pathnames, dummy URLs, user input, and Twitter handles. Here is an example: "Chocolatey installation instructions can be found at `chocolatey.org/install`."

A block of code is set as follows:

```
{
  "@type": "env_vars",
  "@href": "/repo/19721247/env_vars",
  "@representation": "standard",
  "env_vars": [
  ]
}
```

Any command-line input or output is written as follows:

```
Rules updated
Rules updated (v6)
```

Bold: Indicates a new term, an important word, or words that you see onscreen. For example, words in menus or dialog boxes appear in the text like this. Here is an example: "Click **Continue** and make sure to click on the **Agree** button."

 Warnings or important notes appear like this.

 Tips and tricks appear like this.

Get in touch

Feedback from our readers is always welcome.

General feedback: Email `feedback@packtpub.com` and mention the book title in the subject of your message. If you have questions about any aspect of this book, please email us at `questions@packtpub.com`.

Errata: Although we have taken every care to ensure the accuracy of our content, mistakes do happen. If you have found a mistake in this book, we would be grateful if you would report this to us. Please visit `www.packtpub.com/submit-errata`, selecting your book, clicking on the Errata Submission Form link, and entering the details.

Piracy: If you come across any illegal copies of our works in any form on the Internet, we would be grateful if you would provide us with the location address or website name. Please contact us at `copyright@packtpub.com` with a link to the material.

If you are interested in becoming an author: If there is a topic that you have expertise in and you are interested in either writing or contributing to a book, please visit `authors.packtpub.com`.

Reviews

Please leave a review. Once you have read and used this book, why not leave a review on the site that you purchased it from? Potential readers can then see and use your unbiased opinion to make purchase decisions, we at Packt can understand what you think about our products, and our authors can see your feedback on their book. Thank you!

For more information about Packt, please visit `packtpub.com`.

CI/CD with Automated Testing 1

In this book, we will look at the concepts of **continuous integration (CI)** and **continuous delivery (CD)** and apply these concepts using tools such as Jenkins, Travis CI, and CircleCI. There will be many hands-on scripts that we will write, and we will explore real-world CI/CD automation scripts and scenarios. This chapter will help illustrate the concept of automation by explaining the current practices of a fictitious company called Billy Bob's Machine Parts. Billy Bob's Machine Parts has a lot of manual processes in place and there is some tension between **quality assurance (QA)** and the developer team because the software releases are only done by the lead developer and all QA testing is done manually.

The following topics will be covered in this chapter:

- Manual processes – a hypothetical scenario
- Employee frustration
- Introducing automation
- Developer productivity
- Breaking down communication barriers
- Creating an environment of collaboration

Business scenario

This chapter will describe a mock manual process and the flaws inherent in manual testing and manual processes, and will explain how using CI/CD can drastically improve developer productivity. In this scenario, each member has set up a manual set of processes that are quite time consuming to finish. Additionally, the steps have to be done again if QA encounters issues in the latest release version.

We will look at different scenarios across multiple departments in our fictitious company. Some of the scenarios will look at pain points for the developer team, QA team, customer success team, and sales team. We will build up possible scenarios that could occur across these teams, identifying areas that are good candidates for automation and how communication across these teams exposes areas that can be greatly improved with automation.

The following diagram shows a few business scenarios:

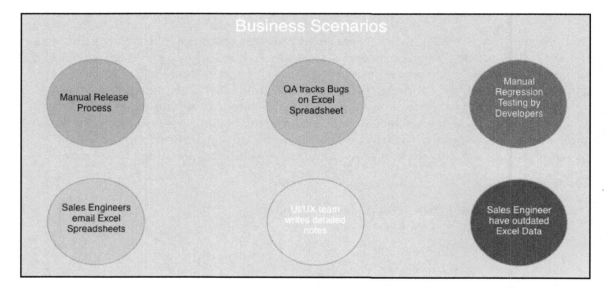

Manual processes – a hypothetical scenario

Betty Sue is part of the QA department at Billy Bob's Machine Parts company. At Billy Bob's Machine Parts company, there is a mid-sized developer team. Eric, the lead developer, starts the manual release process on Thursday morning at the end of a quarter. It takes two days for Eric to finish the release cycle. Unfortunately, he is the only one who can do the release in the developer team. Eric runs all the tests on his local workstation and integrates emergency patches if necessary. Once Eric is done, he emails a ZIP file to Betty Sue in the QA department.

Betty Sue has a couple of QA engineers and starts the manual testing cycle for the new release on Monday morning. Betty notifies Eric that she has already found several issues in the latest release. Betty gets an Excel spreadsheet ready that documents the issues that the latest release has introduced. At the end of the week, Betty has broken down the list of issues with the latest release into critical-, high-, medium-, and low-priority bugs.

 A software bug is a flaw in a software product that is not behaving as intended.

During a release cycle, both Eric and Betty redo each step when issues are addressed. Eric has to repackage all the software components and rerun all of the tests on his local workstation. Betty has to redo the testing cycle because she has to check for regressions and ensure that the latest fixes do not break existing functionality in software components.

Michael, a junior developer on the team, is also doing manual processes. Michael gets a list of issues from Eric and starts working on the more high-priority bugs from the list. Michael tries to address and fix each bug but does not write any regression tests, ensuring that the newer code has not broken existing functionality. When Michael is done, he tells Eric that everything is good on his end. Unfortunately, Eric sees test failures when he runs all the tests on his local workstation. Eric informs Michael that he needs to be more careful while working on fixing issues on the bug list.

Dillon, a member of the QA department, starts testing parts of the new release and tells Betty that there are several issues with the release. He has created a checklist of issues and sends it to Betty. Unfortunately, some of the work that Dillon has done has been duplicated by Betty as they have similar items highlighted in two different checklists. Betty informs Dillon that QA needs to make sure that duplicate work is not being done. Dillon goes back and highlights parts of the release that he will be testing.

Jennifer leads the **customer success team** and gets notified when newer releases are ready to be opened up to customers by the QA department. Jennifer starts preparing videos of the latest release features and consequently asks QA questions about changes in the new release.

Bobby is an experienced member of the customer success team and starts creating videos on the latest features. When the release videos are published to the company blog, QA realizes that some of the videos incorrectly state features that are still in the beta release schedule. Jennifer now quickly scrambles the customer success team and asks QA to clearly mark some features as beta before they are sent to the customer success team.

The sales team has been emailing notes that sales engineers have taken during meetings with prospective clients. Sandy has hand-typed detailed notes about each prospective client and uses an Excel spreadsheet to categorize important sales information. Unfortunately, the sales team emails new changes to Excel spreadsheets to the sales department. Sometimes, confusion ensues because a sales engineer will open an older Excel document and mistakenly give outdated information to other sales engineers.

The UI/UX team tends to work with a lot of mockups and wireframes. Often, during the prototyping phase, UI/UX engineers will embed notes into mockups with transition notes detailing validation states and page interactions. Victor sees a note in one of the wireframes and realizes that there is important page logic embedded in the wireframes. Victor asks the UI/UX team if the notes can be shared with the developer team. The UI/UX team also work with art boards and create ZIP files for each feature work. For instance, Sandy was assigned work on feature x and has been taking detailed notes on the UI interaction for the new page. A lot of work by the UI/UX team tends to be highly visual, and colors mean distinct things. The visual aspect of the work tends to imply certain actions that should occur during phases of UI flow. Developers tend to work with more concrete items so it is not always apparent what natural flows should occur. For instance, if you delete an item, *do you bring up a modal*, which is a little window for confirmation, or *do you just immediately delete an item*? When submitting a form, *does the UI show indications of an error in a certain color and a warning in another color*? *What positions should the validation be placed in*? Sometimes, UI interaction flows are not described in detail and the developers must go back and forth with UI/UX. Documenting why decisions were made in a decision file is important.

Employee frustration

Betty Sue has emailed Victor a list of issues that are categorized by priority. Higher priority issues must be dealt with first, while lower priority issues are dealt with later. Victor gets the list of issues with the newest release and notifies the developer team that they must stop the new feature work they are doing immediately and start fixing the issues with the new release. David, a senior developer on the team, is frustrated because he was in a nice rhythm and now is scrambling to reorient himself with work he did a month ago.

Michael, a junior developer on the team and still new to the codebase, is worried about a higher priority issue that is on the list. Michael scrambles to resolve the higher priority issue but does not think to write any regression test cases. Michael quickly writes a patch for his high-priority ticket and sends his patch to Victor. Victor quickly finds regressions and broken test cases with Michael's patch. Michael did not know that he should write regression test cases to ensure that there is no regressions.

The process of releasing a new patch is not properly documented and newer developers such as Michael frequently create regressions that break existing work. Victor teaches Michael the concept of regression testing and Michael quickly writes a software patch with regression test cases.

Once Victor gets all the new software patches ready, he gets started on a hot-fix release and reruns all the tests on his local machine. Betty gets a new ZIP file with the latest release and starts the manual test processes again. The QA department is manually testing parts of the product, so it is a time-consuming task to test all the parts of the product. Betty has found some more issues with the latest release and sends Victor a smaller list to start working on later in the week.

David is abruptly stopped by Victor and is told to drop his new feature work because the latest changes have defects. David spends the next two hours trying to reorient himself with the issues in the new release. Once confident that he has tracked the issue, he spends the afternoon doing a fix. David notifies Victor that the latest changes are ready to be tested. Victor starts running tests on his workstation and immediately sees that some integration tests are now failing due to the latest changes, and notifies David that these issues must be addressed. David is now frustrated and works late into the evening getting another fix out. The next morning, Victor runs all the tests and everything is passing, so he sends Betty a new ZIP for the latest hot fix. Betty starts the manual testing process the next day and unfortunately finds a couple of small issues again and lets Victor know in the afternoon that there are still some issues with the latest release.

Victor, admittedly frustrated at this moment, huddles all the developers into a room and says no one is to leave until all the issues are addressed. After a long evening stuck in the office, all the latest issues are addressed and Victor lets everyone go home. The next morning, Victor packages up the latest release and emails Betty a new ZIP file. Betty, a little worried after the last test cycle, is pleased that all the bugs have been addressed and gives the QA stamp of approval and lets Victor know that the latest release is ready to go. Both the developer team and the QA team celebrate the end of the work week with a company-sponsored lunch and go home for the weekend.

While QA was testing the hot fix, some of the QA team members had overlapping work. Dillon was frustrated because some his work overlapped work that Betty had done. There is no automation in place in the QA department, so all the work is done manually for each release regardless of whether it is a patch or regular release, and QA must retest all the parts of the UI. Nate, a newer member in the QA team, asks Dillon whether there is a better way to work than doing manual testing but is told that these practices are already in place in the QA department.

Tony, a member of the customer success team, is frustrated with the new release because he spent a lot of time creating new videos for customer X and was told that some of his videos cannot be published and will need to be put in a reserve library. The QA department made a decision at the last moment to halt feature Y but did not communicate this information to the other departments.

Victor, one of the lead sales engineers, is doing a company demonstration and shows an export PDF feature to a prospective client. During the demo, Victor clicks on the export PDF feature and gets a glaring error message. Victor quickly moves to another aspect of the product, saying that this is a temporary glitch and that he will showcase this in another demonstration. Victor finds out that one of the developers made what was supposed to be a simple change in one of the backend services and broke the export PDF feature in the production environment. Victor finds out that the prospective client has decided to go with another software solution and is now visibly distraught because he was counting on this new client to get his end of year bonus.

Samantha, a member of the UI/UX team, is told that one of her mockups is missing a validation flow. Samantha was seeking clarification during the prototyping phase for feature Z and was told that the page did not need any validation, but David has argued that a validation flow is needed. Samantha is visibly distraught and decides to take the day off, and now David is behind schedule for feature Z work:

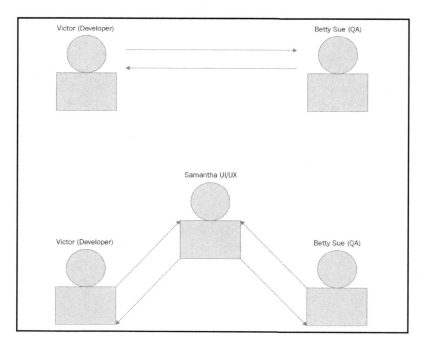

There is two-way communication between Betty Sue from QA and John in the developer team. Communication is of the utmost importance when finding areas to help with automation. As the number of interactions between parties increases, so does the involves parties' awareness of manual processes. Manual processes stay hidden until more parties, such as marketing, sales, customer success, and the developer team, start collaborating more often. Developers are especially suited to finding manual processes, as it not always apparent to non-developers that a process is manual and is capable of being automated.

Introducing automation

Here is an illustration called **Johnny The Automation Bot**, which is used to depict the different departments in a company. Each limb on Johnny represents a different department in a company:

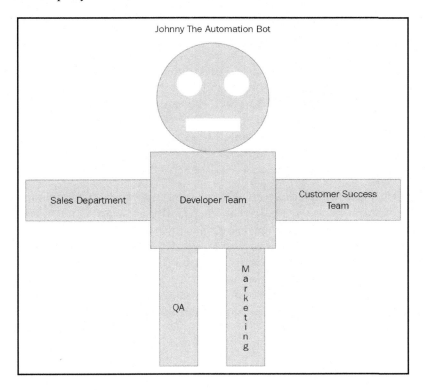

Johnny The Automation Bot is an illustration of the areas that can benefit greatly from automation processes. Automation can be thought of as a procedure or system whereby a machine completes a job that a human would ordinarily do. Automation requires knowing what manual processes are being done, communicating with other departments, and finding what processes are being done manually. CI and CD, as we will see later in the book, are processes that greatly enhance company productivity and processes because they remove developer assumptions and specific environment settings.

 Each limb on Johnny The Automation Bot has an area that is ripe for automation. The sales department is emailing Excel worksheets at the moment to the sales team, and is having a hard time keeping the sales information up to date with changes that other sales engineers are making. Johnny The Automation Bot suggests that the sales engineers have an easy way to upload sales information to a company intranet that can better keep sales information on track. Johnny suggests the developer team writes an Excel integration where the sales engineers can easily upload new sales data to a company intranet. For instance, a menu option that hooks into a company API endpoint could be added that would automatically upload new Excel changes to a company intranet page that has the latest sales information.

The QA department is manually testing the product, and manual testing is a time-consuming and error-prone activity. Johnny suggests that the QA department starts writing acceptance tests using **Selenium WebDriver**. Selenium is a browser automation tool and the QA department can use a language such as Python to write acceptance tests. Johnny says that the advantage of writing automated tests with Selenium is that they can be written once and reused again and again. This will have the added benefit that these tests can be hooked into a CI/CD pipeline, as we will see later in the book.

Betty from the QA department finds out that the customer success team is making a set of videos teaching customers newer features in each build. Customer success is uploading videos through FTP and some of the customer success team spends a large part of their day uploading files. Johnny The Automation Bot suggests that this process be automated through a script. The script should be intuitive enough that any member of the customer success team can run it and it should do the job of uploading and retrying the upload if any network latencies occur during the upload process. Betty shares a script that QA has written that can automate this process and be invoked to run as a background process.

Tony, a member of the customer success team, has now freed hours of work in his work day and can focus on the more important aspects of his job, such as setting customers up for success by creating fantastic videos. Tony has started working with the QA team and is going to start publishing videos and conducting user acceptance tests on parts of the product. QA is now able to better test features because the manual testing has been delegated to the customer success team. QA is focusing on automating the end-to-end test suite with a newer library that will help them write tests faster and, in turn, notify the developer team of broken functionality.

The marketing team has been embedding notes in PowerPoint slides and, at times, the notes are lost or overridden during presentations or company demonstrations. Johnny suggests that the developer team create a script that can convert the PowerPoint slides into markdown and that the markdown files can then be version controlled because markdown is just text files. This will have the added bonus that marketing can share information with the sales team to create more illustrative charts.

Victor has come to the realization that manual processes are destroying productivity and that manual processes have distinct disadvantages. Victor could introduce an automated system in the release cycle that be run be run by any developer in the team through a one-click deployment button. Instead of running all of the tests on a local workstation like Victor is currently doing, each software build can be pushed to a version control system such as GitHub, and all of the tests can be run on a CI environment, such as Jenkins, and developers can be notified automatically whether tests are passing or failing. Bruce, for example, is a newer developer on the team who can quickly read the developer documentation and start doing the next release with little or no guidance. Johnny The Automation Bot gives a big thumbs up for this practice.

Betty also has an opportunity to automate the manual testing process. Using a tool such as **BrowserStack**, Betty can write a series of testing scripts that test each part of the product. Within an hour, Betty can run a suite of acceptance tests in a testing environment and let Victor know the latest issues in the release. Victor can start assigning issues to the developer team and start writing regression test cases that ensure that there is no regressions in the current build. Victor, confident that the latest changes work as intended, can point Betty to a new URL where she can download the latest software release. Johnny The Automation Bot points out that the older practice of creating a ZIP file and emailing it was not a good practice because it requires an extra step each time and can be error prone if the wrong ZIP file is sent. Johnny suggests that the QA department has a dedicated URL where all the latest releases live, and that each release be versioned and state specific information such as a hotfix. For example, the latest hotfix could be `v5.1.0-hotfix 1`, and so, for each hotfix, the QA department would have a compressed file that has latest build and a specifier, such as hotfix. If this build was a regular build, then it could be named `v5.1.0`.

Victor finds out that the QA department has a Browser Stack account. Browser Stack provides access to an entire suite of browsers and mobile clients, and this can help automate the load testing of the UI. Load testing is being done with a custom server that the developer team uses for special scenarios, such as load testing. Johnny The Automation Bot suggests either using services like Browser Stack or having a custom service that can provision the necessary resources to conduct load testing.

Victor finds out that the QA team is having issues testing an email service written by the developer team. Johnny The Automation Bot suggests that the developer team make sure that QA has any scripts that can help work with the email service. Victor tells Betty that the new email service is proxying to the **SendGrid** service and that the developer team has already written a series of scripts that QA can use. The scripts help write a test email and can help QA test what happens under failure conditions.

The UI/UX team is uploading mockups to **Sketch**—Sketch is a prototyping tool—and embedding notes about possible validation states and flows in a page. The notes are extremely detailed and can be quite helpful to the developer team when starting feature work in company sprints. Johnny The Automation Bot suggests that the development team writes a plugin that can help the UI/UX team easily share this information. Victor decides to create a Sketch plugin that creates a PDF with the embedded notes that the UI/UX team can email to the developer team when the prototyping is done. This plugin is easy to install for the UI/UX team because all they have to do is double-click the file and it automatically installs the plugin. Access to the PDF and the embedded notes will help the developers understand use cases and UI flows for the newer feature.

Vincent, a lead sales engineer, has communicated to the developer team that he needs to be informed of process changes in the product, especially when talking to prospective clients about newer features on the company roadmap. Johnny The Automation Bot suggests that the developer team utilize the Git commit log which has detailed information about the latest feature changes. Victor has written a script that scrapes the Git commit log and writes a nice markdown document with all the latest feature work. In turn, the customer success team can work with the developer team and use the markdown file to create a nice blog entry on the company blog detailing all the latest features.

There is a common theme here. Communication between departments is the key to both finding manual processes and creating partnerships that help automate processes. Automation cannot occur unless manual processes are known and, at times, the only way for automation to take place is for specific pain points to be communicated by other departments.

Let's reiterate some of the processes that were automated and enhanced by open collaboration. Victor helped QA automate an email-testing service issue by providing the scripts that the developer team created. QA helped customer success automate a video-uploading task by sharing a script that uploads the video and that has retry logic. The sales department expressed a need to have better visibility on newer features of the product; this caused the developer team to write a script that grabs information from the Git commit log to produce a markdown file, which the customer success team uses to write a nice blog entry in the company blog. The UI/UX team now has a plugin integrated into their Sketch application where they can simply click a button to generate a PDF document with notes taken during the prototype phase, which in turn helps the developer team work on newer features. The developer team finds out that QA is using a tool called BrowserStack and starts using it to conduct load testing on the product. The marketing team now has versioned copies of the marketing PowerPoint slides and is now sharing this information to the sales team to create newer charts for company demonstrations.

The UI/UX team has decided to create a style guide where developers can go for common UI patterns in the software product. The UI/UX team discovered that many different styles were being used in different pages, which was leading to confusion for a lot of customers. For instance, the Parts Supply page has a big blue save button on one page and a red cancel button, but on the Supplier Details page there is a big red save button and a blue cancel button. Customers are clicking the wrong buttons because the UI is not using colors universally. Sometimes, a page uses a confirmation modal to add and delete an item; other times, there is no confirmation modal. The UI/UX team has started working on the style guide and on creating a special URL in the company intranet where the live style guide will reside. The intent is to explicitly create and list all the usable hex colors for the page, design all the buttons in the product, and decide how a form should look and behave on the pages.

Also, there will be a special widget page that has the HTML markup and styling embedded for all the specialized widgets in the product:

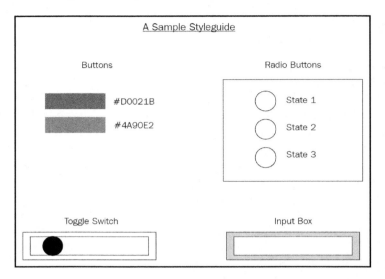

This style guide has hexadecimal color values and has embedded some HTML elements and a toggle switch, which is a specialized widget that has an off state and an on state. The intent of the style guide is for the developers to be able to simply right-click and copy both the HTML markup and the CSS, and to establish a uniform UI presentation. This is a form of automation because developers can simply reuse existing markup and styles and not have to manually create HTML and custom styles where uniformity is best used. Any time users of a product have to guess what to do, you surely invite disaster.

Developer productivity

Since Victor implemented a CI/CD pipeline into the the build, many time-consuming activities are now relegated to an automated pipeline. Whenever software is pushed upstream to a **version control system** (**vcs**), such as Git, an automated build is triggered in Jenkins that runs all of the unit and integration tests. A developer can quickly know whether the code that they wrote has introduced a defect. Remember that Victor had to incorporate all the software patches and manually run all of the tests on his local workstation. This was tedious, time-consuming, and unnecessary.

Since all software is pushed upstream, Victor has set up a code cutoff date for the release branch and has started versioning the software release binaries so that QA can more clearly delineate each build. Victor is immediately more effective as he can start delegating the release cycle to other developers in the team. Any issues encountered in the release cycle can be documented in the release by any developer. Victor now has more time to start planning for the next software cycle and mentoring junior developers in the team. David is now pleased because he can push his latest changes to source control and have all the tests run in a CI environment and be more confident that his changes work as intended.

Betty has set up an entire suite of acceptance tests that check each part of the software product. Any regressions in the product immediately surface in the CI environment and all of the tests can be run daily. The tests that QA are running are more time-consuming and resource intensive than the developer team's tests because they are end-to-end tests, but the advantage for the QA team is that all of the tests are run daily and QA gets a nightly report that details any test failures. Betty has written a collection of page objects that help other members in the QA team reuse other testing scripts and reduce testing cycles. Betty now has time in the QA cycle to mentor newer members in the QA department on testing practices and how to properly mark issues for the developer team so that they know where the issue is in the latest release:

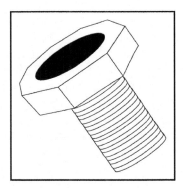

The bolt here symbolizes processes in place; in this case, the release processes that are in need of automation.

David can now start helping Victor to mentor junior developers in the team, and the developer team has started doing a lunch-and-learn series whereby other developers can share knowledge throughout the team. The developer team quickly realizes that these lunch-and-learn sessions are also applicable to the QA department. In one of the lunch-and-learn sessions, QA proposes a change to the developer team about coordinating releases between QA and the developer team. Through this partnership, the release cycle shrinks from a week-long process to a 3-hour process. The developer team rotates the release work so that each developer in the team can learn how to do a release. The developer on duty makes sure that QA has a build available for QA to start testing with, and this build can be triggered automatically using a CI system, such as Jenkins, Travis, or CircleCI. In these CI environments, you can set build triggers that run at a specified date and time. The QA department notifies the developer team of any regressions in the release, and whenever the developer team is ready to push up a hot fix, the build is clearly delineated with the following pattern—`vMAJOR.MINOR.PATH-[hotfix]-[0-9]*`. For the sake of clarity, here is an example—`v6.0.0-hotfix-1`. This delineates major version `6`, minor version `0`, patch version `0`, and hot fix number `1`. This naming scheme is helpful to the QA department in differentiating regular builds with `hotfix` builds.

The customer success team has communicated to the developer team that some customers are having issues working with the Billy Bob's Machine Parts **Application Programming Interface (API)** service. The customer success team asks the developer team whether there is any way to help on board newer third-party API consumers. To clarify, an API consumer is someone who is consuming/using an existing API, whereas an API provider is the one who maintains the actual API service; so in this regard, Billy Bob's Machine Part is the API provider that provides a running API for third-party developers to use. The developer team tells the customer success team that they have been meaning to create a developer portal, which would help the API consumers easily work with the API. The developer team has had a hard time convincing upper management of the value of a developer portal, however, because no one has asked for this specific feature. The customer success team quickly convinces upper management that a developer portal would be a tremendous asset for Billy Bob's Machine Parts API consumers and that API consumers can start building nice dashboards using data from the API service.

In one of the developer meetings, it is discovered that the marketing team is using Google Docs to share documents, but that it is hard to find the uploads because you have to know what you are looking for. Victor quickly realizes that the developer team can help build a company intranet where the sales and marketing teams can share data in a more coherent manner. After a couple of months, the company intranet is exposed and the sales and marketing teams excitedly mention that the company intranet has helped them automate document sharing processes and that many meetings in the past between sales and marketing suffered countless wasted hours trying to find certain documents. The company intranet exposed a filtering mechanism whereby documents can be quickly found using a tag system. Another feature that the company intranet has enabled is the ability for the sales and marketing teams to edit the shared documents.

The sales team now has a great tool to utilize with the company blog, presenting new product features. Victor can now look at the company blog to find out the latest features in the product. This has all been enabled because of the script that Victor wrote that scrapes the Git commit log for commit messages, which in turn publishes a nice markdown file. The script is used on each release and has a listing of all the items worked on, and the developer team sends the newly created markdown file to the customer success team, and they in turn write a nice blog entry that discusses all the details of the latest release based on this markdown file.

The QA team started working on a ticket where a part limit causes a specific UI bug. In particular, if a customer has over 10,000 part listings on a product detail page, then the product detail page crashes with no helpful indication of what occurred. The developer team discovered that the QA team was manually creating new products in the new product page. The developer team helped the QA team by making QA aware of an admin endpoint that creates voicemails programmatically. The developer team helped write a script that generated new parts programmatically and thus saved the QA team from doing the time-consuming task of creating parts manually.

Breaking down communication barriers

In order for automation to take place, communication barriers must be broken down between teams. At times, different parties can think they are on the same page but in reality they are talking about different things.

It is important for the channels of communication to be open in order to combat misunderstandings:

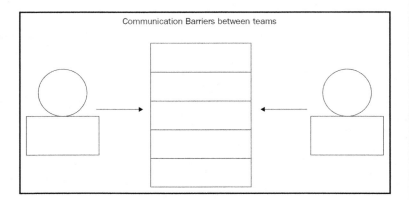

Interestingly, there is still more room for automation within the release cycle. Victor asks Betty about some of the acceptance tests that are in source control. Victor realizes that he could integrate the acceptance tests into a CI environment and create a secondary build where all of the acceptance tests are run each night and get QA would get a report detailing the latest failures each morning. The QA could then review the failing acceptance tests each morning and notify the developer team that feature x has broken—for example, the Parts Supply page—and that the developer working on this newer feature needs to recheck the new business logic.

David starts talking to the UI/UX team and finds that there is a bottleneck between newly exposed API endpoints and the construction of newer pages. The frontend developers are mocking out data in these pages and are constantly surprised by unexpected JSON payloads. The frontend developers are sometimes waiting for weeks for the API endpoint to be published, and instead of sitting by idly, they start mocking out data. This has the unintended consequence that they start assuming what the data model will look like, which in turn makes changing the page more difficult. David lets Victor know that there are tools that exist that can quickly scaffold a data model for an endpoint and give the frontend developers the current data model for an API endpoint. David starts using Swagger, which is an API design framework, as a tool for building newer APIs in the API service. Swagger helps reduce the friction between the developer team and the UI/UX team that was unnecessarily caused because the UI/UX team was waiting on the data model. Jason, a senior UI/UX developer, can now quickly start working on building newer pages because he knows exactly what type of payload to expect from newer API endpoints.

Amanda, a member of the QA team, has started working with the customer success team about load testing and user acceptance testing. Acceptance tests have been added during the user acceptance testing cycle that expose areas where UI/UX can be improved in the core product. The customer success team now has the added responsibility of testing newer pages and exposing possible UI issues. Acceptance tests are good for testing happy path scenarios, meaning when everything is done as expected, but user acceptance testing can expose unintuitive workflows in a UI. Larry, for example, started testing a newer filter feature in the Parts Supply page and discovered that in order for the filtering to start working you need to click on a checkbox. Larry asks QA why filtering cannot be done by default and why a checkbox is necessary; the developers then start working on adding filtering by default:

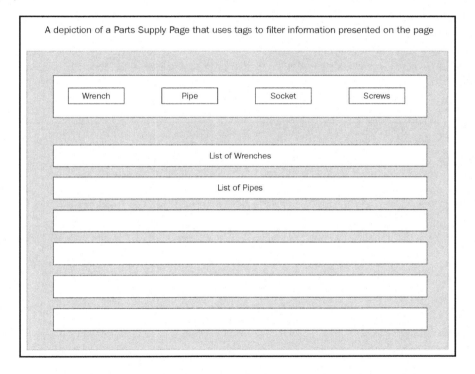

A depiction of a Parts Supply Page that uses tags to filter information presented on the page

| Wrench | Pipe | Socket | Screws |

List of Wrenches

List of Pipes

The diagram depicts no checkbox but simply a page that uses an input box and, whenever a user types *Enter*, comma, or *Tab*, a new filter is applied and then the page is filtered automatically. If there are no results to display, then the text **No Results Found** is shown.

Justin, a member of the customer success team, asks Francis, a member of the QA team, whether he can borrow a video of a newer feature that was tested by the QA department. Justin realizes that the QA team has an extremely valuable set of videos that the customer success team can utilize to teach customers how to use the newest features. Francis creates an internal portal for the customer success team to use when newer videos are released from the QA department. The customer success team has been creating onboarding videos for newer customers and has designed a knowledge portal that explains how to set up, for instance, a newer Parts Supply page.

The sales team has been emailing notes to personal email accounts on discussions with clients and prospective leads. Victor discovers that Harry, a sales manager, recently lost some valuable notes because he accidentally deleted notes he took while having lunch with a prospective client. Victor tells Harry that there is a new company intranet and that there is a projects page that has cards that you can create, so the sales team can create a sales deck for each prospective client. Harry creates a new sales deck for a prospective client and shares it with Jim, the chief sales executive. Jim expresses great excitement because he also realizes that the company intranet can be used to create charts as well. Jim uses the following chart to showcase the latest sales leads to the chief sales executive:

Client X	Client Y	Client Z
Lorem Ipsum is simply dummy text of the printing and typesetting industry. Lorem Ipsum has been the industry's standard dummy text ever since the 1500s, when an unknown printer took a galley of type and scrambled it to make a type specimen book. It has survived not only five centuries, but also the leap into electronic typesetting, remaining essentially unchanged.	Lorem Ipsum is simply dummy text of the printing and typesetting industry. Lorem Ipsum has been the industry's standard dummy text ever since the 1500s, when an unknown printer took a galley of type and scrambled it to make a type specimen book. It has survived not only five centuries, but also the leap into electronic typesetting, remaining essentially unchanged.	Lorem Ipsum is simply dummy text of the printing and typesetting industry. Lorem Ipsum has been the industry's standard dummy text ever since the 1500s, when an unknown printer took a galley of type and scrambled it to make a type specimen book. It has survived not only five centuries, but also the leap into electronic typesetting, remaining essentially unchanged.

The sales team can create a project deck for each prospective client. The company intranet is helping integrate more teams within the company because team members are breaking down communication barriers.

The developer team has discovered that the customer success team has been using the UI for processes that are quite time consuming and error prone. Victor, the lead developer, sets an initiative to create a **Command Line Interface (CLI)** that the customer success team can use to automate many parts of their current workflow that have manual processes. The developer team explains how the CLI can save countless hours for the customer success team and that it can also help API consumers work better with the API service. The CLI can be used to quickly seed the UI with important page data. As each new release might expose newer endpoints, an initiative is created by the developer team to add additional commands to the CLI that work with newer API endpoints.

The CLI application will work in tandem with the developer portal initiative and will boost API consumer adoption. Along with this, the developer team decides to start an initiative on a **Software Development Kit (SDK)** that API consumers can utilize to work with the API. An SDK can greatly improve and enhance third-party adoption of an API provider and therefore increase API adoption. The SDK is especially useful because developers and QA work with different programming languages. The developers of the machine parts API are working with the Golang programming language while QA is utilizing Python for most of their work. The SDK will support many programming languages and will help API consumers get up and running quickly because they can pick a language of their choice to work with the API service.

In order for manual processes to be automated, there must be communication between different groups within an organization. There are bound to be manual processes throughout teams in an organization. The development leadership, the QA leadership, the customer success leadership, and the UI/UX leadership start meeting once a month to discuss newer practices and start finding other manual process within the company that are in need of automation.

Manual processes are not inherently bad, and **user acceptance testing (UAT)** is still effectively done in companies and can help expose issues that automated tests will not find. UAT is especially helpful to test edge-case scenarios that automated tests at times will not uncover, as the example shown earlier demonstrated, where the customer success team tested a newer feature and discovered that the Parts Details page only enabled filtering if a checkbox was checked.

Marketing, sales, and customer success teams often utilize spreadsheet applications, such as a Excel, to compute numbers, and presentation applications, such as PowerPoint, to create charts. Often, the numbers that are calculated in an Excel spreadsheet are saved in revisions, but members in a team must email copies to other team members. Developers can request that the marketing, sales, and customer success teams export values in Excel in **comma-separated value (CSV)** form, which is a text file and much easier to work with. This has the added value that the company intranet can use data visualization tools to create fancy HTML charts and presentations. A library such as D3 can be utilized to create many different types of visualizations that are quite powerful.

Creating an environment of collaboration

In order for teams to start collaborating and openly discussing issues, there must exist a spirit of openness. It is too easy for teams to be siloed, meaning that they are disconnected from what other teams are doing. The developer team can just as easily choose to stay disconnected from the QA department. The issue with this is that communication is the most important element to expose manual processes between teams. Without communication, teams will independently work on items that they deem important.

Social activities where different teams participate together can help break barriers and establish a friendly environment. Often, developers like going to conferences simply for the social aspect of interacting with other developers, and there is often a hallway track, where developers stand outside and simply talk to each other instead of attending active sessions in a conference.

Companies can sponsor social activities and help appoint representatives in different teams who help break the ice between teams. For instance, at a company bowling event, people may be intentionally put into different teams than they are used to working with. A small bowling team can be comprised of a developer, a customer success team member, a QA team member, a marketing team member, and a sales team member. This can inspire a working relationship where the team members get to know each other and communicate openly about issues they are encountering outside of the company event.

The Billy Bob Machine Parts company scheduled a baseball event and Victor, the lead developer, and Betty, the lead QA member, worked together with several marketing team members, sales team members, and customer success team members. Two teams were formed for the baseball event and a company barbecue was scheduled after the game so people could eat together and have conversations.

Another way to encourage active collaboration is to alter company floor plans to be more open. Many software companies have been adopting open floor plans because they remove natural divisions that cubicles create among people. The idea is that if you have an open floor plan, you are much more likely to approach different teams because you can easily walk up to different people and not feel like you are invading their space.

Summary

Communication is the key to finding manual processes, and it is important to find manual processes in order to automate these manual processes. Manual processes tend to be error prone and time consuming, as we illustrated with the various business scenarios. That's where automation, such as implementing a CI build and writing scripts to automate manual processes, comes in. Developers and QA can help develop automation scripts that can benefit many different departments, such as sales, marketing, and customer success. In this chapter, you have learned about the benefits of automation over manual processes and the value of open communication.

In the next chapter, we will learn about the basics of CI.

Questions

1. What is a manual process?
2. What is automation?
3. Why is it important to open up communication between departments?
4. What does CI/CD stand for?
5. Why are automation scripts useful?
6. What is the value of a company intranet?
7. Why should other departments share data?

Further reading

To get more of an introduction to CI and to use a popular CI/CD tool, consider reading *Learning Continuous Integration with Jenkins – Second Edition* (https://www.amazon.com/dp/1788479351/), by *Packt Publishing*.

2
Basics of Continuous Integration

This chapter will help introduce the concept of **continuous integration** (**CI**) and will help set up the foundation of the CI/CD concepts that we will explore in the later chapters. It is important to understand what a CI build is intended for as these concepts transcend any given CI/CD tool that you may use. CI is important because it helps keep a codebase healthy and helps developers keep a software system running independently of any particular developer machine. A CI build enforces independence of software components and local environment configuration. The CI build should be decoupled from any one developer configuration and should be able to be repeatable and isolated in terms of state. Each build that is run should in essence be independent, as this guarantees that a software system is working correctly.

The following topics will be covered in this chapter:

- What is CI?
- The value of CI
- Mitigating risks by utilizing CI
- Software builds at source code check-in
- Small builds and large build breakdown
- CI build practices

Technical requirements

This chapter only assumes a cursory understanding of version control systems but the reader should at least understand what configuration files are, and have a basic understanding of programming. We will briefly look at an example makefile and there will be some code snippets in the chapter.

We will look at several code examples in this chapter, including an API Workshop (`https://github.com/jbelmont/api-workshop`) where we will explain a Makefile and a Demo Application (`https://github.com/jbelmont/advanced-tech-in-wilmington-react-app`) that uses React/Node.js/Express.js/RethinkDB, and we will also showcase a `gulp.js` script file.

What is CI?

CI is essentially a software engineering task where source code is both merged and tested on a mainline trunk. A CI task can do any multitude of tasks, including testing software components and deploying software components. The act of CI is essentially prescriptive and is an act that can be performed by any developer, system administrator, or operations personnel. Continuous integration is continuous because a developer can be continuously integrating software components while developing software.

What is a software build anyway?

A software build is more than just a compilation step. A software build can consist of a compilation step, a testing phase, a code inspection phase, and a deployment phase. A software build can act as a kind of verification step that checks that your software is working as a cohesive unit. Statically compiled languages, such as Golang and C++, often have build tools that generate a binary. For example, a Golang build command, such as `go build`, will both generate a statically compiled binary and run linting on the codebase. Other languages, such as JavaScript, can use a tool such as `gulp.js/grunt.js` to do what are considered build steps, such as **minification**—converting multiple JavaScript source files into one file—and **uglification**, which strips the comments and any whitespace of a source file, as well as linting and running test runners.

CI process steps in a nutshell

A developer can commit code to a **version control projects** (**VCP**) system, such as GitHub and GitLab. The CI server can either poll the repository for changes or the CI server can be configured to trigger a software build via a WebHook. We will look at this later with Jenkins, Travis, and Circle CI. The CI server will then get the latest software revision from the VCP system and can then execute a build script that integrates the software system. The CI server should generate feedback that emails build results upon a build failure to specified project members. The CI server will continuously poll for changes or will respond from a configured WebHook.

The value of CI

CI is valuable for many reasons. First and foremost, a CI build is valuable because it can reduce risks, and the health of your software becomes measurable. CI helps reduce developer assumptions. A CI environment should not rely on environment variables, nor rely on certain configuration files that are set on any one person's machine.

The CI build should be built cleanly and independently from each developer's local machine and a CI build should be decoupled from any local environment. If a developer says that a build works on his/her machine but other developers cannot run the same exact code, then you know that a build may not be functioning properly. A CI build can help with such issues because the CI build is decoupled from any given developer's setup and environment variables and behaves independently of them.

A CI build should reduce repetitive manual processes and the CI build process should run the same way on every build. A CI build process might consist of a compilation step, a test phase, and a report-generation phase. The CI build process should run every time a developer pushes a commit to a version control system such as Git, subversion, and mercurial. The CI build should free up developers to work on higher value work and should reduce possible mistakes that are done by repetitive manual processes.

A good CI build should help generate deployable software anytime and anywhere. A CI build should enable project visibility and should establish confidence in your software with the development team. Developers can rest assured that a CI build will catch issues with code changes more so than when a build is run locally.

Mitigating risks by utilizing CI

CI can help mitigate risks that are prevalent in software builds, such as *it works in my machine* syndrome. CI also helps unify integration points of failure, such as database logic as well as a host of other types of issues.

But it works on my machine!

A common thread among developers is where a software build works on one developer's machine but does not work on another developer's machine. Each developer's machine should mirror—as closely as possible—software integration. Everything that is needed to do a software build needs to be committed to a version control system. Developers should not have custom build scripts that exist only on their local machines.

Database synchronization

Any database artifacts that are needed to complete a software build should be stored in version control. If you have a relational database, then any database creation scripts, data manipulation scripts, SQL stored procedures, and database triggers should be stored in version control.

If, for example, you have a NoSQL database system, such as MongoDB (https://www.mongodb.com/), and are utilizing a RESTful API, then be sure to document API endpoints in a document. Remember that developers might need database-specific code to actually run a software build.

A missing deployment automation phase

Software deployments should be automated using a deployment tool. Deployment tools that you use can vary depending on different software architectures.

Here is a list of deployment tools:

- Octopus Deploy (https://octopus.com/)
- AWS Elastic Beanstalk (https://aws.amazon.com/elasticbeanstalk/)
- Heroku (https://www.heroku.com/)
- Google App Engine (https://cloud.google.com/appengine/)
- Dokku (http://dokku.viewdocs.io/dokku/)

A deployment tool is valuable because they tend to be cross-platform and can be used in many different software architectures. If, for example, a developer writes a Bash script, then there is an underlying assumption that other developers are working on a Unix-like system, and a developer working in a Windows environment may not be able to run the script depending on the Windows version they are using. Windows 10 is now offering a bash subsystem where Windows developers can run Unix commands and scripts while operating a Windows OS.

Late discovery of defects

A CI build can help prevent the late discovery of software defects. A CI build should have a good enough test suite that covers a large percentage of the codebase. One possible metric for a healthy codebase is having 70% or more code coverage in a code base. We will talk later about code coverage, but any software tests should be in checked into source code and tests should be run on a CI build. Any software tests that you have should be run continuously on a CI system.

Test coverage not known

In general, a high percentage of code coverage indicates a well-tested codebase, but does not necessarily guarantee a codebase has no software bugs—just that the test suite has good test coverage throughout. Try to use a code coverage tool in order to see how much of your tests are actually covering your source code.

Code coverage tools

Here are some popular code coverage tools:

- **Istanbul** (`https://istanbul.js.org/`): Yet another JavaScript code coverage tool that computes statement, line, function, and branch coverage with module loader hooks to transparently add coverage when running tests. Supports all JS coverage use cases including unit tests, server-side functional tests, and browser tests. Built for scale.
- **Goveralls** (`https://github.com/mattn/goveralls`): Go integration for the `https://coveralls.io/` continuous code coverage tracking system.
- **dotCover** (`https://www.jetbrains.com/dotcover/`): JetBrains dotCover is a .NET unit test runner and code coverage tool that integrates with Visual Studio.

Make sure you know to what extent your code is covered with unit tests. dotCover calculates and reports statement-level code coverage in applications targeting .NET Framework, Silverlight, and .NET Core.

Lack of project visibility

A CI system should be configured to send alerts in a multitude of ways:

- Emails
- SMS
- Push notification alerts via smartphone

Some software development offices also use some other creative ways to send issue notifications on a software build, such as some kind of ambient light change or maybe even an intercom system. The main point is that developers need to be notified that the CI build is broken so that they can quickly fix the build. The CI build should not stay broken as this can disrupt other developers work.

Software builds at source code check-in

Software builds should be triggered upon each source code check-in in a version control system. This is an important step in the deployment pipeline, as we will see in the next chapter.

What is a software build again?

A software build can consist of just compiling software components. A build can consist of compiling and running automated tests, but, in general, the more processes you add to the build, the slower the feedback loop becomes on a build.

Scripting tool

Favor using a scripting tool that is designed specifically for building software over personal scripts. Custom Shell scripts or batch scripts tend not to be cross-platform and can hide environment configuration. A scripting tool is the most effective process for developing a consistent, repeatable build solution.

Here is a list of scripting tools:

- Make (`https://www.gnu.org/software/make/`)
- Maven (`https://maven.apache.org/`)
- Leiningen (`https://leiningen.org/`)
- Stack (`https://docs.haskellstack.org/en/stable/README/`)

Performing single command builds

Strive to make single command builds to ease the process of building software, because the easier you make running the build process, the more you will speed up adoption and developer involvement. If doing a software build is a complicated process, then you will end up having only a few developers actually doing a build, which is not what you want.

Building your software in a nutshell

1. Create your build using a scripting tool, such as Ant (`https://ant.apache.org/`), Make (`https://www.gnu.org/software/make/`), Maven (`https://maven.apache.org/`), or Rake (`https://ruby.github.io/rake/`)
2. Start with a simple process in the CI build
3. Add each process to integrate your software within the build script
4. Run your script from the command line or an IDE

Here is an example makefile that runs a Golang API Service from my open source `https://github.com/jbelmont/api-workshop`:

```
BIN_DIR := "bin/apid"
 APID_MAIN := "cmd/apid/main.go"
all: ensure lint test-cover
ensure:
 go get -u github.com/mattn/goveralls
 go get -u github.com/philwinder/gocoverage
 go get -u github.com/alecthomas/gometalinter
 go get -u github.com/golang/dep/cmd/dep
 go get -u golang.org/x/tools/cmd/cover
 dep ensure
lint:
 gometalinter --install
 gometalinter ./cmd/... ./internal/...
compile: cmd/apid/main.go
 CGO_ENABLED=0 go build -i -o ${BIN_DIR} ${APID_MAIN}
```

```
test:
 go test ./... -v
test-cover:
 go test ./... -cover
## Travis automation scripts
travis-install:
 go get -u github.com/mattn/goveralls
 go get -u github.com/philwinder/gocoverage
 go get -u github.com/alecthomas/gometalinter
 go get -u github.com/golang/dep/cmd/dep
 go get -u golang.org/x/tools/cmd/cover
 dep ensure
travis-script:
 set -e
 CGO_ENABLED=0 go build -i -o ${BIN_DIR} ${APID_MAIN}
 gometalinter --install
 gometalinter ./cmd/... ./internal/...
 go test ./... -cover
 gocoverage
 goveralls -coverprofile=profile.cov -repotoken=${COVERALLS_TOKEN}
```

Here is an example build script using `gulp.js` that generates a CSS build from `sass`
source files and runs a linter. The first block sh initialization of variables and getting of
configuration objects ready for use:

```
'use strict';

const gulp = require('gulp');
const webpack = require('webpack');
const sourcemaps = require('gulp-sourcemaps');
const sass = require('gulp-sass');
const autoprefixer = require('gulp-autoprefixer');
const uglify = require('gulp-uglify');
const concat = require('gulp-concat');
const runSequence = require('run-sequence');
const gutil = require('gulp-util');
const merge = require('merge-stream');
const nodemon = require('gulp-nodemon');
const livereload = require('gulp-livereload');
const eslint = require('gulp-eslint');

// Load Environment constiables
require('dotenv').config();
const webpackConfig = process.env.NODE_ENV === 'development'
  ? require('./webpack.config.js')
  : require('./webpack.config.prod.js');

const jsPaths = [
```

```
  'src/js/components/*.js'
];
const sassPaths = [
  'static/scss/*.scss',
  './node_modules/bootstrap/dist/css/bootstrap.min.css'
];

const filesToCopy = [
  {
    src: './node_modules/react/dist/react.min.js',
    dest: './static/build'
  },
  {
    src: './node_modules/react-dom/dist/react-dom.min.js',
    dest: './static/build'
  },
  {
    src: './node_modules/react-bootstrap/dist/react-bootstrap.min.js',
    dest: './static/build'
  },
  {
    src: './images/favicon.ico',
    dest: './static/build'
  },

  {
    src: './icomoon/symbol-defs.svg',
    dest: './static/build'
  }
];
```

This second block of code is where we set up gulp tasks: copying React.js files, doing uglification of JavaScript files, creating a build JavaScript file, and creating CSS files from Sass files.

```
gulp.task('copy:react:files', () => {
  const streams = [];
  filesToCopy.forEach((file) => {
    streams.push(gulp.src(file.src).pipe(gulp.dest(file.dest)));
  });
  return merge.apply(this, streams);
});

gulp.task('uglify:js', () => gulp.src(jsPaths)
    .pipe(uglify())
    .pipe(gulp.dest('static/build')));

gulp.task('build:js', (callback) => {
```

```
  webpack(Object.create(webpackConfig), (err, stats) => {
    if (err) {
      throw new gutil.PluginError('build:js', err);
    }
    gutil.log('[build:js]', stats.toString({ colors: true, chunks: false
}));
    callback();
  });
});

gulp.task('build:sass', () => gulp.src(sassPaths[0])
    .pipe(sourcemaps.init())
    .pipe(sass({
      outputStyle: 'compressed',
      includePaths: ['node_modules']
    }))
    .pipe(autoprefixer({ cascade: false }))
    .pipe(concat('advanced-tech.css'))
    .pipe(sourcemaps.write('.'))
    .pipe(gulp.dest('./static/build'))
    .pipe(livereload()));

gulp.task('build:vendor:sass', () => gulp.src([...sassPaths.slice(1)])
    .pipe(sourcemaps.init())
    .pipe(sass({
      outputStyle: 'compressed',
      includePaths: ['node_modules']
    }))
    .pipe(autoprefixer({ cascade: false }))
    .pipe(concat('vendor.css'))
    .pipe(sourcemaps.write('.'))
    .pipe(gulp.dest('./static/build')));
```

In this final block of code, we run some watcher tasks that will watch any changes in the JavaScript files and Sass files, do linting, and create a nodemon process that will restart the Node server on any file changes:

```
gulp.task('watch:js', () => {
  const config = Object.create(webpackConfig);
  config.watch = true;
  webpack(config, (err, stats) => {
    if (err) {
      throw new gutil.PluginError('watch:js', err);
    }
    gutil.log('[watch:js]', stats.toString({ colors: true, chunks: false
}));
  });
  gulp.watch('static/js/components/*.js', ['uglify:js', 'build:js']);
```

```
});

gulp.task('watch:sass', () => {
  gulp.watch('static/scss/*.scss', ['build:sass']);
});

gulp.task('watch-lint', () => {
  // Lint only files that change after this watch starts
  const lintAndPrint = eslint();
  // format results with each file, since this stream won't end.
  lintAndPrint.pipe(eslint.formatEach());

  return gulp.watch(['*.js', 'routes/*.js', 'models/*.js', 'db/*.js',
'config/*.js', 'bin/www', 'static/js/components/*.jsx',
'static/js/actions/index.js', 'static/js/constants/constants.js',
'static/js/data/data.js', 'static/js/reducers/*.js',
'static/js/store/*.js', 'static/js/utils/ajax.js', '__tests__/*.js'], event
=> {
    if (event.type !== 'deleted') {
      gulp.src(event.path).pipe(lintAndPrint, {end: false});
    }
  });
});

gulp.task('start', () => {
  nodemon({
    script: './bin/www',
    exec: 'node --harmony',
    ignore: ['static/*'],
    env: {
      PORT: '3000'
    }
  });
});

gulp.task('dev:debug', () => {
  nodemon({
    script: './bin/www',
    exec: 'node --inspect --harmony',
    ignore: ['static/*'],
    env: {
      PORT: '3000'
    }
  });
});

gulp.task('build', (cb) => {
  runSequence('copy:react:files', 'uglify:js', 'build:js', 'build:sass',
```

```
'build:vendor:sass', cb);
});

gulp.task('dev', (cb) => {
  livereload.listen();
  runSequence('copy:react:files', 'uglify:js', 'build:sass',
'build:vendor:sass', ['watch:js', 'watch:sass', 'watch-lint'], 'start',
cb);
});

gulp.task('debug', (cb) => {
  livereload.listen();
  runSequence('copy:react:files', 'uglify:js', 'build:sass',
'build:vendor:sass', ['watch:js', 'watch:sass', 'watch-lint'], 'dev:debug',
cb);
});
```

Separating build scripts from your IDE

Try to avoid coupling your build scripts to any particular **Integrated Development Environment (IDE)**. A build script shouldn't be dependent on any IDE.

This is important for two reasons:

- Each developer may be using a different IDE/editor and may have different configurations
- A CI server must execute an automated build without any human intervention

Software assets should be centralized

The following software assets should be available on a centralized version control repository:

- Components, such as source files or library files
- Third-party components, such as DLLs and JAR files
- Configuration files
- Data files that are needed to initialize an application
- Build scripts and build environment settings
- Installation scripts that are needed for some components

You must decide what should go into version control.

Creating a consistent directory structure

You must choose a consistent directory structure for your software assets, as it can help you perform scripted retrievals from a CI server.

Here is a sample folder structure that I have done for a skeleton React/Redux application:

- ca (certificate authority)
- config (configuration files)
- db (database-related stuff)
- docs (documentation)
- images
- models (data files)
- test (all my test files)
    - unit
    - integration
    - e2e
    - helpers
- static
    - build
    - js
        - actions
        - components
        - constants
        - data
        - reducers
        - store
        - utils
    - scss
- utils (utility files)

Here is another directory structure that I have followed, which is package oriented and recommended by **Bill Kennedy from the Golang Community** (`https://www.ardanlabs.com/blog/2017/02/package-oriented-design.html`):

- `kit`:
  - Packages that provide foundational support for the different application projects that exist
  - Logging, configuration, or web functionality
- `cmd/`:
  - Packages that provide support for a specific program that is being built for startup, shutdown, and configuration
- `internal/`:
  - Packages that provide support for the different programs the project owns
  - CRUD, services, or business logic
- `internal/platform/`:
  - Packages that provide internal foundational support for the project
  - Database, authentication, or marshaling

The main point is that you should follow a standard naming convention for your codebase that all developers follow. This will help the developer team work as they will be familiar with particular things laid out in the code. Not everyone will agree with a particular directory layout, but having a standard is the most important part. Anyone working on a newer service, for example, should be able to set up the project structure based on a codified naming convention for folders, where source files go, and where test files are placed:

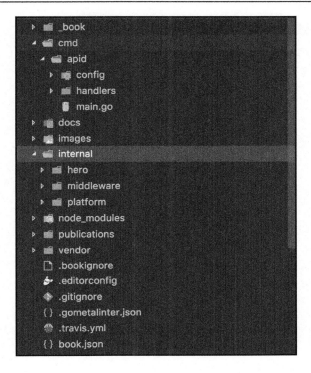

Here is a sample directory structure that I am using for an API Workshop (`https://github.com/jbelmont/api-workshop`) that I created in GitHub.

Software builds should fail fast

This can be achieved by doing the following:

1. Integrating software components.
2. Running true unit tests—unit tests that don't rely on a database but run in isolation.
3. Ensuring that unit tests are able to run quickly. If a unit test takes an order of minutes, then this could be an indication of a problem.
4. Running other automated processes (rebuild database, inspect, and deploy).

 It is up to each company what other steps are necessary for their builds.

Building for any environment

Configuration files and environment variables should be set for different environments, such as dev/prod/test. Logging verbosity should be able to be set as per the environment. Developers might need increased logging for debugging. Application server configuration information can be set in a build file as well as database connection information and framework configuration.

Here is an example text file that can be used. One thing to note is that such files should not be committed to source control as they may contain client secrets and API secrets:

```
API_URL=http://localhost:8080
PORT=8080
AUTH_ZERO_CLIENT_ID=fakeClientId
AUTH_ZERO_JWT_TOKEN=someFaketToken.FakedToken.Faked
AUTH_ZERO_URL=https://fake-api.com
REDIS_PORT=redis:6379
SEND_EMAILS=true
SMTP_SERVER=fakeamazoninstance.us-east-1.amazonaws.com
SMTP_USERNAME=fakeUsername
SMTP_PASSWORD=FakePassword
SMTP_PORT=587
TOKEN_SECRET="A fake Token Secret"
```

Configuration text files such as these can help other developers connect to third-party services and will help organize where client secret information is stored.

Small build and large build breakdown

A small build is usually a build that can be run quickly by the CI server and will usually consist of a compilation step as well as running all the unit tests. A small build can be optimized by running staged builds, which will be discussed in the *CI build practices* section.

A large build is a build that essentially runs all of the build tasks in one large build. The disadvantage of doing a large build is that they discourage developers from running them. If a software build takes a long time to run, then many developers will avoid running the build at all. Smaller builds that run quickly encourage developers to continuously check-in their changes on a version control system and will help keep a codebase healthy.

CI build practices

CI build practices are like stepping stones; they build up on top of each other. As we will see in the next chapter, each step in the CI build process is important and provides assurance that your codebase is in a healthy condition.

Private build

Developers should run private builds prior to committing code to the repository.

Here is a sample developer session using Git:

1. Check out the code you will alter from the repository:
    1. Go into the version controlled folder.
    2. `git checkout -b new_branch`.
2. Make changes to the code:
    1. Edit `myFile.go`.
3. Get the latest system changes from the repository:
    1. `git pull`.
4. Run a build that executes of all your unit tests and possibly integration tests in your local machine.
5. Commit your code changes to the repository.
6. The CI build should automatically trigger a build and run any tests in the repository.
7. The CI build should also do other tasks, such as reporting and calling other services if need be.

Usage of CI server

The CI server should either be polling for changes in version control repository systems, such as GitHub, at a specified time interval, or be configured via WebHook to trigger a software build. A CI build should perform certain actions on a scheduled basis—hourly or daily, if needs be. You should identify a *quiet period* during which no integration builds are performed for the project. A CI server should support different build scripting tools, such as Rake, Make, NPM, or Ant. A CI server should send emails to concerned parties, as well as display a history of previous builds.

A CI server should display a dashboard that is web accessible so that all concerned parties can review integration build information when necessary. Jenkins, Travis, and Circle CI all have dashboards that are web accessible. A CI server should support multiple version control systems for your different projects, such as svn, Git, and mercurial.

Manual integration builds

Running an integration build manually is an approach to reducing integration build errors if there is a long-running feature that will be difficult to run on a CI server—but use such techniques sparingly. For example, you could designate a machine that is not being used to do a manual integration task; although, with the cloud, it is now easier than ever to just spin up a server instance on demand.

Running fast builds

Strive to run software builds as quickly as possible by increasing computing resources. Offload slower running tests, such as system-level tests, onto a secondary build or a nightly build. Offload code inspection to a third-party service. For example, for code coverage analysis, you can use the following third-party services:

- Codecov (`https://codecov.io/#features`)
- Coveralls (`https://coveralls.io/features`)
- Code climate (`https://codeclimate.com/quality/`)
- Codacy (`https://www.codacy.com/product`

Run staged builds to promote fast builds as well. The first build can compile and run all the unit tests. The second build can run all the integration tests and system-level tests. You can have as many stages as necessary to have fast builds. Arguably, the first build should be the fastest, as this will be the primary build that developers use when checking in code to a codebase.

Summary

This chapter provided a foundation on CI concepts and introduced techniques for employing a successful CI server in a developer team. We looked at scripting tools and build tools. We discussed what a software build is, good practices to follow when creating a build script, and also some testing concepts, such as code coverage. The next chapter is on **continuous delivery (CD)**, which is a natural extension to CI, and we will go into detail about the deployment pipeline, configuration management, deployment scripting, and the deployment ecosystem.

Questions

1. What is a software build?
2. What is meant by a staged build?
3. Can you name some scripting tools?
4. Why should you follow a naming convention and folder structure?
5. What is the value of CI?

Further reading

A great book to read that goes into more about CI is *Learning Continuous Integration with Jenkins – Second Edition: A beginner's guide to implementing Continuous Integration and Continuous Delivery using Jenkins 2* (`https://www.amazon.com/dp/1788479351/`), by Packt Publishing.

Basics of Continuous Delivery 3

Arguably the most important part of software is actually getting it delivered and ready to use for the end users. **Continuous Delivery (CD)** is the point at which you deliver a software product to your end users and is the basis of this chapter. A product is only useful if your intended users can actually use it. Throughout this chapter, we will discuss the deployment pipeline and tie in the concept of automation and CD.

The following topics will be covered in this chapter:

- Problems delivering software
- Configuration management
- Deployment pipeline
- Deployment scripting
- Deployment ecosystem

Technical requirements

This chapter assumes that you understand the concept of automation and continuous integration. If you feel unsure about either of these topics, read Chapter 1, *CI/CD with Automated Testing*, and Chapter 2, *Basics of Continuous Integration*, before reading this chapter.

The code files for this chapter can be found at `https://github.com/jbelmont/api-workshop/blob/master/Gopkg.toml`.

Problems delivering software

There are a number of things that can go wrong when trying to deliver a software product to your end users, and we will look at several scenarios that affect delivering software. One possible scenario is that developers are working on a new feature but the new feature may not actually pass CI build stages or may not behave in the intended way initially proposed by product owners. Another possible scenario is that the intended audience was not properly understood, which would affect the usage of the end product by users. Another possible scenario is that the software product was not properly decoupled and was put together with bubblegum and tape, with many regressions occurring with new feature requests.

What do we mean by delivering software?

There can be much argument about what delivering software actually means. For the purposes of this chapter, what is meant is that the actual software product has been delivered to the intended user—not just that the software product was approved by the **quality assurance (QA)** department as working.

Common release anti-patterns

There exists some common release anti-patterns that you should avoid, such as deploying software manually, manual configuration management, and different environment configurations for each environment.

Deploying software manually

This type of anti-pattern is common and can lead to bottlenecks in the delivery of software. The day of software delivery is stressful and error prone. Tom from operations starts his day by copying software artifacts from the version control system into a production environment. Tom copies files through the **File Transmission Protocol (FTP)** but forgets to add a new configuration file and the login page does not work anymore. Tom has to talk to the developer team and ask whether there are new configuration files that have been added, and waits for several hours to get a response.

Once Tom gets the new configuration file, he uploads it to the production environment. The Login page works now, but some pages are loading with weird image placement and irregularities. Tom pings the UI/UX team and finds out that a CSS file is missing in the production environment. Tom uploads the CSS file and now the page loads correctly. Tom asks the customer success team whether they can further test the new changes in the production environment and finally calls it a day around 7 PM.

If there exists a long document detailing the delivery of a software product, this can indicate a manual process. This further complicates delivering a product because mistakes anywhere in the process can lead to more issues. If a delivery tends to be unpredictable, this can point to this anti-pattern as well.

Deployment automation to the rescue

As we discussed in `Chapter 1`, *CI/CD with Automated Testing*, automation is the process in which an action is done in a repeatable and automated fashion. Software delivery should be an automated process as this will help ensure the consistent practice and behavior of software delivery. We will look at tools later on in this chapter that will help you automate the software delivery processes.

Manual configuration management

This type of anti-pattern can be frustrating to operations personnel, as they will be the last to know about new behaviors in a product. If the day of software delivery is the first time the operations team has seen the new feature, then they may be in for a surprise in software behavior. Cindy, an operations team member, has been tasked with delivering software and notices that the install script is completely broken because it cannot communicate with the **Identification** (ID) server. Cindy sends log messages to the development team and finds out that one of the client secrets for the ID server has changed and that the install script needs to use this new value in order to properly connect.

This type of problem could have been mitigated had Cindy been aware of this new change in the ID server, but the developers were working with another environment and the QA department was given this information to test the new feature, but no one thought to pass this information to operations until they encountered the issue on the day of delivery.

Configuration management automation

We will discuss tools that can help with configuration management issues, such as those encountered previously. Using the proper tooling, operations/DevOps personnel can quickly get the right environment configuration for each environment, including the production environment.

How a production environment differs from other environments

This type of anti-pattern can be especially challenging because of all the changes that have been tested in development, and a staging environment may behave erratically in production. For example, Travis works as a tester in the QA department and has been testing the staging environment since the inception of the new feature. Billy, an operations person, has not been able to see the new feature as the staging environment is completely different to the production environment. Billy also notices that the production environment data is missing critical information shown in the staging environment. Billy contacts the development team and finds out that a database migration script must be run for the new feature to work in production.

The production environment should be the same as the staging environment

All the environments, including testing, staging, and production, should all have the necessary migration scripts and any other software assets to prevent production breakages, and the development team should make sure to point operations to any changes in script files or clearly mark such changes in a shared document.

How to conduct a software release

There are some important steps to consider when doing a software release, such as doing frequent releases to avoid introducing too many changes at once and making sure that releases are automated.

Frequent releases

A software release must be frequent. Big software releases tend to be riddled with issues, so it is best to make the deltas (changes) between releases small. By increasing the frequency of software releases, you also get the benefit of faster feedback. Large software releases tend to take longer, and critical feedback may not get delivered as fast.

Automated releases

Manual releases are problematic because they are not repeatable. Each time a manual release is done, it will be different because of configuration changes, changes in the software, and changes in the environment. Manual release steps are riddled with mistakes as each step is manual and can lead to cascading mistakes. A good example of the hazards of manual changes is when **Amazon Web Services (AWS)**, the most popular cloud provider, suffered a major outage in the eastern US region because an operations person entered the wrong command in a series of steps in a manual process. Automation is the key to software releases because they ensure repeatability and control over the software delivery process. We will look at deployment scripting tools further in this chapter to help with automating software deliveries.

The benefits of automation in delivering software

As we illustrated previously, automation is important in software delivery as it ensures the repeatability, reliability, and predictability of a software release. Catastrophic events can be avoided or mitigated by having an automated software delivery process instead of a long manual process.

Team empowerment

The QA department can safely select older versions of software releases to test regressions if automation is in place. Operations personnel can run the scripts used in staging and not encounter issues because of environment-level differences. With an automated software process, operations personnel can safely roll back a release in case of disaster in the delivery process. Also, as we talked about in the Chapter 2, *Basics of Continuous Integration*, automation can help bring push button releases.

Error reduction

Automation can help reduce errors that manual processes can create. As we saw earlier, configuration management issues can lead to poor software delivery. Manual software releases cannot effectively ensure repeatability and therefore are error prone.

Stress reduction

Another benefit is reduced stress by all personnel during software delivery days. Manual processes tend to create undue stress as whoever is doing the manual process must be diligent and not make any mistakes in the delivery process. An automated delivery process is great in that it ensures that each run will be executed in the same manner. A mistake in an manual process might require support from senior personnel in fixing issues.

Configuration management

Configuration files that hold important information, such as client secrets and passwords, must be managed properly and must be kept with sync in other environments. Each environment may have different environment variables that must be used and passed into the application.

What does configuration management mean anyway?

Configuration management can be briefly described as the process by which all software artifacts that are pertinent to each given project—as well as any relationships between the software artifacts—are retrieved, stored, identified, and modified.

Version control

Version control is the means of keeping revisions between all software artifacts. Version control is very important to configuration management as any changes to files that contain environment files should be under version control.

Tony, a member of the development team, has been using a properties file that has not been put under source control and has been making changes to the **single sign-on** (**SSO**) flow in the product. Tony accidentally deletes the file and loses all the client IDs and secrets that are necessary during the SSO flow. Tony must now go to different API portals and regenerate the client secret for some of the properties, as they are only shown once during creation, and now he must notify other members of the team to update their properties files.

Example properties file

I have added a sample properties file that has client secret information and authentication secret information. This is necessary for the given environment to run properly but should not be checked into source control, it is here for demonstration purposes only:

```
API_URL=http://localhost:8080
PORT=8080
AUTH_ZERO_CLIENT_ID=fakeClientId
AUTH_ZERO_JWT_TOKEN=someFakeToken.FakedToken.Faked
AUTH_ZERO_URL=https://fake-api.com
REDIS_PORT=redis:6379
SEND_EMAILS=true
SMTP_SERVER=fakeamazoninstance.us-east-1.amazonaws.com
SMTP_USERNAME=fakeUsername
SMTP_PASSWORD=fakePassword
SMTP_PORT=587
TOKEN_SECRET="A fake token secret"
```

 The TOKEN_SECRET environment variable is only seen once, so if it is lost, then you must regenerate it in the API portal.

Version control management tools

Here is a list of version control management tools:

- **Git** (https://git-scm.com/): Git is a distributed version control system
- **Mercurial** (https://www.mercurial-scm.org/): Mercurial is also a distributed version control system
- **Subversion** (https://subversion.apache.org/): Subversion is considered a centralized version control system
- **Fossil** (https://www.fossil-scm.org/): Fossil is a distributed version control system like Git although lesser known

Version control practices

An important practice is to keep everything that you possibly can under version control to avoid losing important work in a software product. Network files, configuration files, deployments scripts, database scripts, build scripts, and any other artifact that is important for your application to properly run should be under version control, or else you risk losing critical data.

Conducting software check-ins often

It is important to do check-ins into your main branch often, or else you risk introducing breaking changes into your codebase. Additionally, frequent check-ins help developers stay mindful of bringing in small changes at any given time. Large sweeping changes to a codebase should be avoided as they are harder to test and can bring regressions. Frequent check-ins are also beneficial because breaking changes will be noticed much faster.

Writing descriptive and meaningful commit messages

Use descriptive commit messages that include issue tracking information, such as a Jira issue, for example, that clearly describe the intent of the commit. Avoid writing commit messages that are vague, such as `Fixed bug` or `Wrapped up`, as these types of commit messages are not useful and are not helpful to developers later on.

 Here is a sample descriptive commit message [DEV-1003] added a new navigation link to the Parts Supply list. A test case for the new navigation was also added. This is clearly more descriptive. Additionally, in Jira, when you provide an issue such as DEV-1003, it will create a link in the Jira issue that references the work on this issue. Also, if you create a pull request and put `git commit` with the Jira issue, it will link your pull requests with the issue.

Dependency management

It is common for applications to have third-party dependencies that are critical to the software product. Dependency management is an important part of any application and different programming languages handle dependency management differently.

Example Node.js dependency file and Gopkg.toml dependency file

Here is a `Gopkg.toml` file that has version and package information for each dependency in the repository:

```
# Gopkg.toml example
#
# Refer to https://github.com/golang/dep/blob/master/docs/Gopkg.toml.md
# for detailed Gopkg.toml documentation.
#
# required = ["github.com/user/thing/cmd/thing"]
# ignored = ["github.com/user/project/pkgX",
"bitbucket.org/user/project/pkgA/pkgY"]
#
# [[constraint]]
#    name = "github.com/user/project"
#    version = "1.0.0"
#
# [[constraint]]
#    name = "github.com/user/project2"
#    branch = "dev"
#    source = "github.com/myfork/project2"
#
# [[override]]
#    name = "github.com/x/y"
#    version = "2.4.0"
#
# [prune]
#    non-go = false
#    go-tests = true
#    unused-packages = true


[prune]
  go-tests = true
  unused-packages = true

[[constraint]]
  branch = "v2"
  name = "gopkg.in/mgo.v2"

[[constraint]]
  name = "github.com/dgrijalva/jwt-go"
  version = "3.1.0"

[[constraint]]
```

```
      name = "github.com/go-playground/locales"
      version = "0.11.2"

  [[constraint]]
    name = "github.com/pkg/errors"
    version = "0.8.0"

  [[constraint]]
    name = "github.com/pborman/uuid"
    version = "1.1.0"

  [[constraint]]
    name = "gopkg.in/go-playground/validator.v9"
    version = "9.9.3"
```

 Dependency management like this is important because third-party dependencies can easily bring breaking changes to an application, and API changes in a third-party dependency can break critical behavior in any running application.

Managing software components

Usually, software projects will start with a monolithic build that has all the working components in one layer. As an application grows in size and maturity, the layers of an application will break into services or different layers and this is where having separate build pipelines becomes necessary. Perhaps an ID service is used for authentication in an application and perhaps an admin service is run in a separate build pipeline for an administrative portal. Microservices architecture is a continuation of this service level componentization of an application, where each microservice has a clear and focused purpose in an application.

Software configuration management

Configuration is an important part of any application and should be treated with the same level of care as your business-level logic that you use in your code. Configuration therefore needs to be properly managed and tested just like your source code.

Configurability and flexibility concepts

At first thought, it may seem appropriate to make configuration as flexible as you can. *Why not make a system as flexible as possible, and allow it to adapt to any type of environment?* This is commonly known as an anti-pattern of *ultimate configurability*, meaning that a configuration can behave like a programming language and can be made to behave in any manner. Configuration management done in this way can bring a software project to its knees as its users will come to expect such flexibility as necessary. It is more useful to set some constraints in place for your configuration management. Constraints can help rein in the effects of too much flexibility in a configured environment.

Specific types of configuration

Here is a list of possible types of configuration that an application can utilize:

- Configuration can be pulled and incorporated into application binaries at **build time**:
    - Languages such as C/C++ and Rust can do such build-time configuration
- Configuration can be injected at **package time** when creating assemblies or gems:
    - Languages such as C#, Java, and Ruby can use such configuration options
- Configuration can be done at **deployment time** meaning a deployment script or installer can fetch any necessary information as needed, or the deployment script can ask a user to pass such information:
    - We will look at this later in the book with the Jenkins, Travis, and CircleCI tools
- Configuration can be done at **startup time or runtime**, meaning when an application is launching:
    - Languages like Node.js often inject environment variables when a Node.js server is running

Configuration management across applications

Configuration management becomes more complicated when you take configuration across different applications. There are tools that can help with configuration across application boundaries, and here is a list of such tools:

- CFEngine (https://cfengine.com/)
- Puppet (https://puppet.com/)
- Chef (https://www.chef.io/chef/)
- Ansible (https://www.ansible.com/)
- Docker with Kubernetes (https://www.docker.com/)

Environment management

The hardware, software, infrastructure, and any external systems that an application depends on can be thought of as the environment of the application. The creation of any environment should be done in a fully automated manner because the ability to reproduce an environment is important, as we will illustrate.

Manual environment setup

The manual setup of infrastructure can be problematic for several reasons:

- A manually set up server instance may be configured to suit a single operations person. This operations person may be gone from an organization, leaving core infrastructure broken.
- Fixing a manually set up environment may take a long time, and fixing issues in such an environment is not reproducible and repeatable, for that matter.
- Manually setup environments may not be capable of being copied for testing purposes.

Important configuration information for environments

Here is a list of important configuration information that all environments need:

- Third-party dependency and software packages that need to be installed on each environment
- Networking topology information

- External services necessary for an application to run, such as a database service
- Application data or seed data to get a fresh environment set up and running

Containerized environments

Tools such as Docker and Kubernetes have risen in popularity because of their ability to isolate environment-level information and to create reproducible/repeatable environments. Using Docker, you can declare all of your external services, such as Redis and MongoDB.

Here is an example of `docker-compose` YML script for the API workshop repo (`https://github.com/jbelmont/api-workshop`):

```
version: '3'
services:
  mongo:
    image: mongo:3.4.5
    command: --smallfiles --quiet --logpath=/dev/null --dbpath=/data/db
    ports:
      - "27017:27017"
    volumes:
      - data:/data/db
  redis:
    image: redis:3.2-alpine
    ports:
      - "6379:6379"
 apid:
    build:
      context: .
      dockerfile: Dockerfile-go
    depends_on:
      - mongo
      - redis
    env_file:
      - ./common.env
    links:
      - mongo
      - redis
    ports:
      - "8080:8080"
volumes:
    data:
```

We have declared a database as well as a caching service (Redis) and an API that all run as an isolated container, all of which can have environment-level information such as environment variables, that can be configured separately.

Deployment pipeline

We spoke about the importance of CI in `Chapter 2`, *Basics of Continuous Integration*, and while CI is an important productivity enhancer, it is mainly useful for development teams. It is common to see bottlenecks in software life cycles with QA and operations teams when waiting for fixes or updated documentation. QA can be left waiting for a good build by the development team. Development teams may also receive bug reports many weeks after they have completed a new feature. All of these situations lead to non-deployable software, which ultimately leads to software that you cannot deliver to your end users. Creating push button deployment builds that can be deployed to testing, staging, and production environments can help alleviate such issues, as we noted previously.

What is a deployment pipeline?

A deployment pipeline can be thought of as end-to-end automation of build, deploy, test, and release processes. A deployment pipeline can also be thought of as the process for getting software that is written by developers into the hands of your users.

Deployment pipeline practices

In this section, we will discuss some deployment pipeline practices to follow, such as building binaries once, handling deployments the same way in each environment, and making a commit stage in a deployment pipeline.

Building binaries once

Binaries that are compiled multiple times can be problematic for several reasons:

- Binaries can have different contexts at each run, which will introduce unpredictability to your system
- Statically compiled languages, such as C/C++, can have different compiler versions on each run

- Third-party software may have different version specified on different compilation execution contexts
- Compiling binaries multiple times also leads to an inefficient deployment pipeline
- Recompiling binaries can also be time consuming

It is better to compile binaries once during compile time if you can do so.

Deployment should be done the same way in every environment

Developers commonly deploy their software all the time when you consider a CI build that runs on each source code check-in. QA/testers will not deploy as often, and operations even less so. Deploying to a production environment will be done much less frequently than for a development environment, and for good reason.

A deployment script should be created that can be run for development, staging, and production environments. Any changes that are necessary in each environment can be managed with a properties files that is managed in version control. You can use, for example, an environment variable in the deployment script to differentiate the different environments.

Commit stage – first step of the deployment pipeline

The first stage of a deployment pipeline is the commit stage or whenever developers check in code to version control. As soon as code is checked in to a CI build pipeline, the build pipeline should compile any code if necessary, run a suite of unit tests (hopefully some exist) and integration tests, create any binaries if needed for the deployment pipeline later on, run static analysis tooling to check the health of the codebase, and prepare any build artifacts needed later for the deployment pipeline.

There are some other metrics that are important for the commit stage build to look at, such as code coverage, duplication in the code base, cyclomatic complexity (measures the complexity in codebase), monitoring a large number of warning messages, and code style (usually reported by a linting tool).

If the commit build stage passes, then we can think of it as the first gate to pass through, albeit an important one.

Test gates

In extreme programming, developers create acceptance tests that serve as functional-level tests that test a certain aspect of a software system. An example would be a user logging in to a system and a user logging out of a system. Another example would be a user going to their profile and updating information. Such tests are much broader than unit and integration tests and so they uncover system-level issues if they exist.

Acceptance tests build stage

Running a suite of acceptance tests should be the second gate of a deployment pipeline. The acceptance tests also serve as a regression test suite to verify that new features have not been introduced into the system. During this stage, any test failures that occur in the acceptance test suite need to be evaluated on a case-by-case basis. The failure may be due to intentional behavior changes in the system, and so the acceptance test suite needs to be updated or the failure may represent a regression that needs to be addressed. Either way, the acceptance test suite must be fixed as soon as possible. The acceptance tests act as another gate in order for the deployment pipeline to progress down the line.

Manual testing

Acceptance tests do provide a level of assurance that a system behaves as it should, but only a human can detect anomalies in a system. QA/testers can perform user-level testing of a system to ensure the proper usability of a system. The testers can also perform exploratory testing of a system. The automated acceptance test suite helps free up time for the testers to perform this higher-value testing.

Nonfunctional testing

Nonfunctional testing is aptly named because these types of tests are not functional requirements of a system. Instead, nonfunctional tests test things such as capacity and security in a system. Failures in this step of the deployment pipeline may not need to mark a build as a failure but can simply serve as decision-making metrics on a build.

Release preparation

There is always an associated risk when conducting a release, and so it is best to have processes in place when conducting a software release. Problems that occur during a release will be prevented but they can be mitigated by having processes set up during a release.

Here are some possible steps to follow during a release:

- Create a release plan that both involves and is created by everyone involved in delivering a product
- Automate as much of the release process as possible to prevent mistakes
- Releases should be rehearsed often in production like environments to help debug possible issues that may occur
- Set up processes to migrate any production data that is being used and to migrate configuration information in case of a rollback (reverting a release back a version) or upgrading a system

Automating release processes

Try to automate as much of a release process as you can, as the more automation in place, the more control you have over the release process. Manual steps tend to be error prone and can lead to unexpected outcomes. Any changes that occur in a production environment need to be locked down properly, meaning changes are done via automated processes.

Conducting rollbacks

Release days tend to be stressful because mistakes that occur during the release process can create hard-to-detect issues, or the new system that is being released may have defects. Rehearsing releases can help mitigate such issues and can help people quickly solve issues that they may encounter.

The best strategy is to have a previous version of a software system ready before the release and after the release in case you have to roll back the system to a previous version; this excludes any necessary data migration or configuration. As another viable alternative, you can redeploy a known good version of an application. The rollback should be able to be done at a click of a button.

Deployment scripting

Deployment scripting is necessary because the software written by development teams is not just run on their IDE or local environment but instead needs to be run during the deployment pipeline. Deployment scripting refers to the particular build tooling you use to write scripts for the deployment pipeline.

Overview of build tools

There are already many build tools, and each come with their own pros and cons. Here is a small list of build tools:

- **Make** (`https://www.gnu.org/software/make/`): Make is a language-agnostic build tool that has been used for a long time
- **Maven** (`https://maven.apache.org/`): Maven is a build tool primarily used for Java projects
- **MSBuild** (`https://docs.microsoft.com/en-us/visualstudio/msbuild/msbuild`): MSBuild is a build tool primarily used for the .NET family of programming languages
- **Rake** (`https://ruby.github.io/rake/`): Rake is a Make-like build tool that was originally intended for Ruby
- **Gulp.js** (`https://gulpjs.com/`): A build tool that is used for frontend web development
- **Stack** (`https://docs.haskellstack.org/en/stable/README/`): A build tool that is used for Haskell environments

Deployment scripting concepts

Regardless of whatever build tool you use, you need to follow certain practices when conducting deployment scripting.

Writing a script for each stage in the deployment pipeline

During the commit stage of a deployment pipeline, you will have actions that the deployment script will need to do. For example, you might need to compile any source files, run a suite of unit and integration tests, and run a linting tool that checks code style and perhaps a static analysis tool. All of these steps might require using different tools, so writing a script that does all of this is best. Depending on the particular actions of the script, you might want to further break down a script into subscripts that perform focused actions. During the acceptance test stage, your script might run the entire acceptance test suite and additionally generate some reports and metrics about the tests.

Every environment should use the same scripts

You should use the same exact script in all the environments, as this will ensure that the build and deployment process is being done the same way in each environment. If you have a different script for each environment, then you cannot ensure that the particular script being run is behaving the same way in a different environment. The deployment scripts that developers run in their local environments should be the same as those run in other environments, or else you risk environment leakage. What we mean here is that the developers environment might have specific environment variables set than the deployment script or each environment, such as development, staging, and production, might have different environment variables set, which will make debugging harder when issues arise.

The deployment process should not change on each run

The deployment process should remain the same on each run that is done. In mathematics, there is a term called **idempotent**, which basically states a certain operation can be done multiple times with the same outcome. If your deployment process changes on any given run then you cannot guarantee the behavior of each run, which in turn will make troubleshooting much more difficult.

Deployment scripting best practices

This section discusses deployment scripting best practices, such as making sure to test only known good foundations, testing environment configuration, using relative paths, and removing manual processes.

Testing only known good foundations

You should not be testing source code that cannot even compile and you should not bother to run any acceptance tests when the unit and integration tests are failing. Basically, there must exist a known good baseline for any of the additional stages of the deployment process to be run and to continue.

Testing the environment configuration

As the deployment pipeline is going through each stage and subsequently passes through each stage, it is good to check that the respective stage is functioning correctly. The tests you do for the associated stage can be thought of as **smoke** tests. For example, checking that a website is up and running by accessing the URL, and checking that a record in a database can still be fetched.

Using relative paths

It is best to use relative paths over absolute paths. A developer might have a certain filesystem or folder structure that does not exist in the environment where the deployment pipeline is running, so it is best to use relative paths so as not to create unintended breakages. It may be difficult at times to do this, but it is best to follow it as much as you can. Docker containers can map folder structures for each container; for example, if a Docker container is spawned on a particular part of the deployment pipeline, it can be mapped to a certain relative folder structure as well.

Removing manual processes

Avoid making build scripts that contain a list of steps you must do to finish a particular part of a deployment.

Here is a list of possible steps in a manual process:

- Copy all of the images from the root of the project into the `static/build` folder
- Run a manual migration of data on a new production release
- If someone has to SSH into a box and run a script, this could be problematic

Any steps that must be done manually can quickly become out of date in a document, so the easiest instruction to follow is, if you have to do an action a second time, to make an automated process.

Deployment ecosystem

In this section, we will briefly go over some tools that can help you in your deployment pipeline and that serve different purposes.

Infrastructure tooling

We briefly mentioned Chef earlier in the chapter; Chef is a great tool to use to automate standing up infrastructure in a reliable manner. It is difficult without the proper tools to make sure that each new environment that you set up is done in the same manner. Potentially, you could create new environments that have different configurations, which can be very problematic when troubleshooting.

Cloud providers and tooling

The three main cloud providers all have their own associated tooling:

- **AWS** (`https://aws.amazon.com/`): AWS has a suite of tools for CI/CD:
  - **AWS CodeCommit** is a fully managed source control service. For more information, refer to `https://aws.amazon.com/codecommit/`.
  - **AWS CodeDeploy** is a service that automates software deployments to a variety of compute services, including Amazon EC2, AWS Lambda, and instances running on-premises. For more information, refer to `https://aws.amazon.com/codedeploy/`.
- **Microsoft Azure** (`https://azure.microsoft.com/en-us/`): Visual Studio Team Services is an end-to-end CI/CD service. For more information, refer to `https://visualstudio.microsoft.com/team-services/`.

- **Google App Engine** (`https://visualstudio.microsoft.com/team-services/`): Google App Engine is more agnostic than the other cloud providers.

You can use Jenkins, Travis, and CircleCI/CD tooling with all of the major cloud providers, although Microsoft Azure and AWS have created their own CI/CD tooling that you can use as well.

Summary

CD, as we have seen, centers around the concept of automation. Throughout this chapter, we have learned about what delivering software means. We first examined the common issues that arise when delivering software. We also discussed configuration management in detail and the roles that version control and dependency management play in any configuration. We also looked at the deployment pipeline and took an in-depth look at the different build stages. In the deployment scripting section, we looked at some build tools that exist and set some best practices to follow. Lastly, we briefly looked at the deployment ecosystem and some of the cloud providers. In the next chapter, we will discuss the problems of communication among different teams, how to communicate pain points to other team members, sharing responsibility among different teams, demonstrating to stakeholders why CI/CD is important, and how to get approval for CI/CD with business stakeholders.

Questions

1. What do we mean by delivering software?
2. Name some common release anti-patterns.
3. Name some benefits of automation when delivering software.
4. What does configuration management even mean?
5. Why should you write descriptive and meaningful commit messages?
6. What is a deployment pipeline?
7. Why should deployment be done the same way in each environment?

Further reading

Consider reading the book *DevOps: Continuous Delivery, Integration, and Deployment with DevOps*, by *Packt Publishing*, to get a more in-depth understanding of CD.

The Business Value of CI/CD

4

Now that we have a clear understanding of what automation, **continuous integration (CI)**, and **continuous delivery (CD)** are, we need to communicate the business value of these practices to business stakeholders, or else we risk building features without action items that incorporate these practices. This chapter is about convincing the stakeholders of these values, and we will discuss problems with communication, how to communicate pain points to team members, sharing responsibilities among different teams, knowing your key stakeholders, how to demonstrate why CI/CD is important, and how to get approval for CI/CD from your stakeholders.

The following topics will be covered in this chapter:

- Problems with communication
- Communicating pain points to team members
- Sharing responsibilities among different teams
- Knowing your stakeholders
- Demonstrating why CI/CD is important
- Getting approval for CI/CD from your stakeholders

Technical requirements

This chapter assumes that you are already familiar with the concepts of automation and CI/CD; read Chapter 1, *CI/CD with Automated Testing*, and Chapter 2, *Basics of Continuous Integration*, before reading this chapter if you are unsure about these topics. This chapter will mainly be about how to communicate the values of these practices to stakeholders, so there won't be any code samples or installations to do.

Problems with communication

In any working environment, there are bound to be issues with communication, but in particular there are issues in Agile working environments. Some problems with communication are miscommunications of requirements, a lack of proper documentation, timezone differences, a lack of trust and mutual respect, cultural differences, language barriers, and long feedback loop cycles.

Miscommunication of requirements

Here is a depiction of a requirements checklist. The purpose of a requirements checklist is to get all the necessary facts laid out for a particular feature:

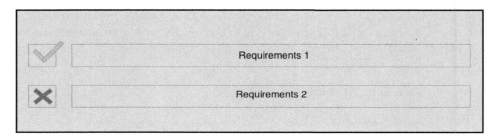

The miscommunication of requirements is a common issue that occurs in sprint cycles in an Agile working environment. It is impossible to truly eliminate the miscommunication of requirements completely, but it is important to minimize the risk of this by making sure that you communicate with the end user or customer from the inception of the feature request.

It is important that the feature request that you are implementing is clearly stated and that each piece of functionality has a clear business intent. This is important because it helps developers, DevOps personnel, and QA/testers be better prepared during the implementation phase.

Understanding the critical business requirements up front will help reduce the miscommunication of requirements between teams, as missing requirements can easily create bottlenecks for development when certain actions are not anticipated. Any critical requirements information needs to be properly documented.

Lack of proper documentation

The documentation needs to be written at the very moment that any requirements are defined and must be updated with additional information continuously while the feature is being worked on. It is only when everything is defined and stated as clearly as possible that you can start writing a plan to implement a specific feature. If a developer encounters an issue and requires clarification from a customer, then the answer needs to be put directly in the requirements for future reference.

Avoid having multiple documents with requirements information, but instead have one document with the requirements information, or else you risk having out-of-date information; or worse, having different requirements scattered in different places that contradict each other.

There should be a single source of truth with the business requirements and they should be understood by all parties.

Timezone differences

As more and more teams are becoming distributed and global, differences in time zones can create communication bottlenecks. Developers working in drastic time zone differences need to ensure that good CI/CD practices are in play. Broken CI builds and configuration management issues can quickly become exacerbated with time zone differences as a team in one time zone will be left flapping in the wind with effective work able to be done. Communication is especially more important with distributed teams as the lack of face-to-face interaction can lead to communication failures, and at worst can create animosity between teams if not properly managed.

I once worked at a startup where there was a 3-hour time zone difference, which in itself is not an issue, but the standup was done at the end of the business day while the other team started the day at noon our time. Naturally, this led to days where changes done by the other team would block us until midday our time, when the other team was available.

Lack of trust and mutual respect

The following is a diagram depicting the fact that trust and mutual respect go hand in hand, and teams need this in order to operate efficiently:

```
┌─────────────────────────┐
│          Trust          │
│                         │
│      Mutual Respect     │
└─────────────────────────┘
```

Trust among teams is critical and is easily *lost* but *won* with difficulty. It is best if there is a good project manager who can facilitate communication between teams and help clarify issues that are bound to occur. Healthy teams will communicate openly when problems arise during feature work, and it is good to have retrospectives in place to help air out frustrations among team members and to build trust.

If possible, it is good to have team outing events where multiple teams can interact with each other and help build cooperation with each other. Some companies institute a quarterly meeting where teams can do fun events together, such as sports or games. Team-building exercises can also be scheduled often to keep people engaged and build a spirit of cooperation.

Cultural differences and language barriers

As Agile working environments have become more global, global teams have become more common. Cultural differences among teams makes communication an even more important ingredient to the success of a project. Humor can be a double-edged sword as many teams can create division and enmity if the intended humor is taken out of context, so it is best if teams can be taught about cultural norms and customs to avoid miscommunication issues.

Language barriers can also create issues, as the requirements of a feature request can become misunderstood. It is best if a project manager can work as a liaison between teams to ensure that all the requirements are clearly understood between teams and to help clarify any communication bottlenecks.

Long feedback loop cycles

The following is a depiction of a feedback loop cycle. The greater the feedback loop is, the longer it takes to make changes. It is important to have a short feedback loop on the deployment pipeline to be effective, and so that you can make timely changes when necessary:

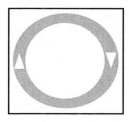

We spoke about long feedback loops in Chapter 1, *CI/CD with Automated Testing*, and in particular we spoke about the dangers of long feedback loops and how it is vital to shorten feedback loop cycles so that the right information is given to the right person at the right time. Likewise, long feedback loop cycles between teams can create issues and natural bottlenecks.

Ideally, teams would get the information they needed as quickly as possible, but this is not always a reality. A proper liaison or project manager can help shorten the feedback loop among teams, and teams need to properly document any processes and make sure that this documentation is visible and known to other teams, or else processes among teams can differ.

 Remember that short feedback loops lead to faster response times.

Communicating pain points to team members

It is important that team members are able to effectively communicate the particular pain points or blockers that are inhibiting progress. There are several pain points we will discuss in this section, including waiting for requirement information, undocumented steps in the deployment pipeline, too many holders of keys to the kingdom, and too many communication channels.

Waiting for requirements information

It is often the case that developers will start work on a particular story/feature and not have all the necessary requirements in order to complete their assigned work. This is especially problematic for developers because whatever code they work on might need to be scrapped and redone depending on how far off the requirements were from being done correctly. Developers need all the requirements up front before they can start on a story; there must exist processes for each feature to work in grabbing all the requirements, and each story ideally will have acceptance tests as an action item for the feature work to be considered done. In an ideal world, developers would have all the necessary information ready before they started their particular feature work, and the acceptance tests written for the story would pass when the feature was completed as was specified in the requirements document.

In `Chapter 1`, *CI/CD with Automated Testing*, we discussed, as an example, the Billy Bob's Machine Parts company. Now, imagine Tom from the development team has started work on showing a supplier name, and Tom discovers that the scope of this ticket appears massive and he may not be able to finish it in time. This scenario is also complicated by the fact that the requirements documentation is severely lacking and critical details were missing during development. Tom asks the product owner if he can provide feedback on some items but has to wait for several days before he gets this necessary information.

Undocumented steps in a deployment pipeline

Each step in the deployment pipeline process should be appropriately documented and automated. We spoke about the importance of automating as much as you can in the deployment pipeline in `Chapter 5`, *Installation and Basics of Jenkins*. To reiterate, manual processes are problematic because they are repeatable and reliable. Automation is important because it brings repeatability and reliability to the deployment pipeline. Anytime someone has to do a manual step, there is no assurance as to whether the process will be done correctly and in the same manner in each run; only with automation can you guarantee the repeatability of a deployment pipeline stage.

Alvin, who is part of the DevOps team, is working on the latest release for the software product and is running a complicated manual process in the deployment pipeline. Alvin types in the wrong command and ends up wiping out the production database. Luckily for Alvin, there is a backup that is a day old and he can restore the production database to this copy. If there had been automated process in place, this would not have occurred.

Keys to the kingdom to select few

The following diagram represents a key, and the main thing to remember about keys to the kingdom is about a select few having the access/key to the production environment:

It is important to control who can make changes in a production environment, and many software companies will often elect a select few or maybe even one individual who can make changes in production. This can become problematic if this particular individual is not available or leaves the company, but some companies have instituted the practice of development teams owning a particular feature end to end, and the same developer who worked on the feature is responsible for fixing issues that are encountered in the deployment pipeline. At one company I worked for, we affectionately said, *only a select few have the keys to the kingdom.*

Alvin is one of the few DevOps personnel to hold the keys to the kingdom. A customer support representative pings the development team about a production outage and the development team is scrambling to get the production environment back up for customers. Alvin and one other member of DevOps are the only ones that can touch the production environment. This issue is exacerbated by the fact that neither Alvin or the other assigned DevOps person is available.

Too many communication channels

There should be a low signal-to-noise ratio when it comes to communication. If a developer is being alerted by email, SMS, voicemail, and Slack messaging about issues, they may soon tune out and not pay attention to issues. It is important to get the attention of the developer to fix issues as they are encountered, but you probably shouldn't be alerted like a military command center, where you are bombarded with notifications from many different sources.

Imagine that Bruce is a newer developer in the team and Bruce receives an alert about a low-priority ticket that he worked on. Bruce receives an email, text alert, Slack message, and phone call about this ticket. Bruce tends to get a lot of messages like this and soon decides to ignore them. On one particular afternoon, Bruce ignores a high-priority ticket because he figures that it is a senseless alert. Bruce has become desensitized to the alerts.

There is too much noise and not really any true signals in the alerting process with all of these alerts.

Pain-Driven Development (PDD)

If something in the CI/CD pipeline is causing you some degree of pain, then it might be a good idea to automate the process. If you have a 15-step process that is error prone in the deployment pipeline and is causing many issues during releases because of mistakes in execution, then this is a pain probably felt by others at some point or another. The idea is that the pain is what should guide you in the right direction to find a better solution. If you are having issues with a process, then you might need to automate the process. It is not always necessary to automate a task for the sake of automation; you need to evaluate your processes continuously and PDD can be an effective tool for finding processes that need to be improved.

Jimmy has been experiencing issues at every commit stage with linting failures. Jimmy forgets to check the lint task before he pushes code up to the repository. This is especially troublesome because Jimmy makes sure to run all the unit tests to check that they are passing but habitually forgets to check linting errors. Jimmy decides that the pain is enough and a new process needs to be put in place. Jimmy writes a pre-Git push hook script that runs the linter on each Git push to the master. Now every time someone pushes to the master, the script runs the linter to make sure that a linting error is not introduced into the codebase.

Sharing responsibilities among different teams

It is not always apparent where particular pain points or practices are occurring in other teams without some collaboration and transparency. It is good if teams are able to share responsibilities and practices with other teams. If possible, you should rotate team members, try to ask for feedback on development practices, and try to create cross-functional teams.

Rotating team members

The following diagram symbolizes a rotation of team members. If possible, creating a team rotation where different team members can cycle through different job duties can help team members to share responsibilities and to build efficient processes, and has the possibility of sparking innovation:

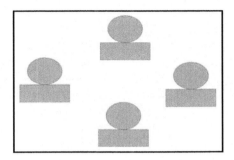

By rotating team members into different teams, you help shape their perspective and provide a broader understanding of development practices and increase their product knowledge. This isn't always possible, especially, with highly specialized teams, such as a security team or a machine learning team, as the level of ramp-up time necessary for any given developer to be effective can vary. If possible, rotating team members into related projects and technologies can help prevent developer burnout and can help developers learn from each other. It is easy to become complacent and become accustomed to how things are done, and it is often the case that a fresh pair of eyes can see things in a new light and help bring necessary changes into a development team.

Bruce works in the API development team and has been rotated into the network engineering team. The rotation period is about 3 to 6 months and Bruce has already learned some practices that will be helpful to the API development team. Some of the advantages of cross-training engineers is that skills they learn in other development teams can transfer back into other teams. Bruce learned some caching optimizations that he can apply in the network layer and in the OSI layer that will help the API development team. The **Open System Interconnection (OSI)** is a conceptual model that breaks down information sent over the wire, so to speak, into distinct layers. There are seven layers in the OSI model—the **Application layer** (seventh), the **Presentation layer** (sixth), the **Session layer** (fifth), the **Transport layer**, (fourth), the **Network layer** (third), the **Data Link layer** (second), and the **Physical layer** (first). Bruce has been utilizing optimization strategies in the Application layer, but with some new-found knowledge of the network layer, Bruce has come up with newer optimization strategies.

Asking for feedback on development practices

Communication among team members is critical for the long-term success of a team. Developers should not be afraid to ask for feedback on why things are done in a particular way and it is important to create a healthy environment where *constructive criticism* is welcomed. Team members can become complacent about team processes and may miss out on opportunities to optimize processes.

Let's go back to our example company, Billy Bob's Machine Parts company. Let's say that Tom has recently joined the team and has noticed that the steps to get set up in the API repo are overly complicated and require many steps to get a particular environment up and running. Tom asks whether anyone has considered automating some of the steps using a build tool, and is told to work on automating any steps he thinks would be helpful. Tom decides to write a Makefile that can encapsulate all of the steps to get started for a particular environment by simply running the `make` command. Tom creates a pull request to the API repo and introduces this new functionality, which helps automate the steps to create a particular environment.

Creating cross-functional teams

If possible, and if you have the resources, try to create cross-functional teams so that teams can share expertise among other team members. For example, a team could have two to three developers, one QA team member, a security team member, a DevOps team member, and a product owner who all work together and are able to develop efficiencies that would not otherwise occur if they were working in isolation.

Back to our example company—imagine the following cross-functional team ensemble. Tom, Steven, and Bob are all the developers, Ricky is the security team member, Susan is the DevOps team member, and Nicky is the product owner. All work together in the same space and meet with each other for a morning standup everyday. Now, the team members are able to own the deployment pipeline stages end to end, as they can work together and help each other automate processes. Tom and Steven help write an automated test suite using a new library, and Ricky is able to add a tertiary build stage that runs security checks for changes that are made to the master branch. Susan has added monitoring and reporting metrics as each item is progressing through the deployment pipeline. Nicky quickly updates the requirements documentation for Bob, as he notices an edge case with his new feature work. The team members are openly communicating about each step in their process and are able to optimize processes because they openly collaborate with each other.

Knowing your stakeholders

It is important for a development team to know all of their stakeholders, as the stakeholders will hold critical information that can help a team succeed or fail. The development team should be able to communicate with project managers when necessary, communicate openly to members of the executive leadership team, and be able to speak with the end users.

Project managers

Although a product owner might take on the role of a project manager and can help facilitate the duties of a scrum master, it is best if the roles are done by separate people. A project manager can be seen as an *agent of change* who adapts to a dynamic work environment. At the end of the day, the project manager wants to be able to get the deliverable shipped to the end users and can help open the channels of communication between different teams. It is important that developers are able to communicate openly and notify project managers of any issues they encounter during their feature work.

Some companies also employ an Agile program manager who is in charge of the workflow and methodologies in an Agile working environment. The Agile program manager will develop a roadmap for the sprint schedule and make sure that each developer in the development team is properly allocated work to their scheduled capacity. This type of manager will usually be more aware of all the team's work and will make sure that all the interested parties have all the tools and information that they need to accomplish their deliverables.

Executive leadership team

The company culture can largely be affected by the executive leadership teams, such as the **chief executive officer (CEO)**, **chief information officer (CIO)**, **chief technical officer (CTO)**, and **chief operating officer (COO)**. It is not always possible to make broad company impact unless you operate at these executive levels. If development teams feel that decisions come down as edicts and that they have no say in the decisions made, they may not be able to prevent issues that would otherwise be preventable. Many companies state they have an open-door policy and welcome constructive feedback, but often a development team will not empowered to speak up when they fight with broken processes.

Let's say that Tom read a blog post over the weekend and has discovered a way to reduce the feedback loop in the automated acceptance test suite. This change that Tom wants to introduce requires a spike in work. Tom tries to mention this at the Monday morning standup but gets stonewalled by the team because there is higher value work to be done. Tom decides that this is important enough for upper management to become aware of. Tom proceeds to talk to the CTO about this using the open-door policy but gets verbally reprimanded the next day for not going through the proper leadership channels. In this way, Tom is not able to make the decisions that could most benefit the team as none of the team members feel empowered to make changes in their workflow processes.

End users

Here is a depiction of an end user; at the end of the day, they are the most important stakeholder. The feedback that your end users have holds the most weight:

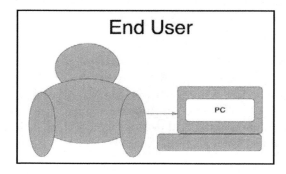

At the end of the day, the end user will be using the new functionality that you are adding to the product. In this sense, they can help clarify the necessary requirements for developers. It is often the case that the end user is not exactly clear on what they are looking for until it is right in front of them. It is important that the product owner gets all the necessary requirements up front from the customer if needs be, and some software organizations go as far as having tests written by product owner/customers that specify the requirements in code that must be implemented. In any case, the product owner and the end user must be in sync with the requested feature before the developer can start his or her work.

The development team is largely removed from the end user and will not interface with any end user. It is important, however, for the development team to be aware of the specific pain points that end users are encountering when working with the software system. Developers in this sense are the most capable of creating the changes in the system that will benefit end users, but if developers are not aware of such pain points, they will not be able to create the necessary changes to benefit the end users. It might be helpful to have developers work with a customer success team when appropriate to see how the end users work with the software system.

Demonstrating why CI/CD is important

The importance of a CI/CD pipeline cannot be understated and developers will need to demonstrate its importance by providing metrics, reporting, and in general educating leadership on the importance of automation.

Metrics and reporting

The following diagram is a depiction of charts and graphs that you can use to demonstrate to your stakeholders why CI/CD is important. It is a good idea to develop graphs and charts as visuals are very convincing:

Typically, at the executive level at companies, the numbers and the PowerPoint slides must demonstrate why something is important. Developers should be able to illustrate with metrics—charts, diagrams and any other visual forms—how CI/CD can improve existing processes. There exist enterprise solutions already that can help generate this information, but a development team can aggregate this information in an Excel spreadsheet.

Let's say that Bob from the development team has decided that enough is enough and the manual processes currently in place during release day are in desperate need of automation. Bob aggregates all the time spent in the last 6 months working on emergency fixes and the man hours wasted per developer on issues that creep up during a release day. Bob creates a nice visual diagram that helps convince management to create an Agile epic that deals with creating an automated deployment pipeline.

Educating leadership on automation

A development team cannot assume that leadership understands what automation means and what areas are ripe for automation. It is best if a technology representative such as a CTO can help by being a proponent of automation and help to explain it to the executive leadership team. Someone such as a CTO can help be the agent of change to speak on behalf of developers, but regardless of who relays this information, the executive team must understand what automation is and what things are capable of being automated.

The leadership team tends to be far removed from what developers are doing on a daily basis. The leadership team has more global concerns for the company and will tend to work with other members, such as sales, marketing, operations, and project managers. It is still important for the executive leadership team to be educated on automation so that developers are given the necessary time to develop an automated deployment pipeline, and so they are given the time during each sprint to conduct testing and to continually add automation processes to a CI/CD build pipeline and to the deployment pipeline. There needs to be clear understanding about automation at the highest levels of an organization so that developers, system admins, and DevOps personnel can incorporate automation practices to the key deliverables in the company roadmap.

Getting approval for CI/CD from your stakeholders

Even when stressing the importance of automation and educating your stakeholders on its importance, you might need to take action without official approval. Many software projects have started as a skunkworks project that a sole developer worked on without official approval. A developer can also work on a deployment pipeline automation task on his local machine or an unused machine if need be.

Starting a skunkworks project

The origins of the term skunkworks project is open for debate, but the general idea is that it is a project that is worked on in secret by a select individual or select individuals that is intended to bring innovation and change to an organization. It is not always possible for developers to get approval for a given task and they may need to resort to alternative tactics to get their point across.

Imagine Bob from the development team has an idea to write a CLI application that will help on-board third-party developers to utilize the company dashboard. Bob has tried communicating the idea to upper management but with no luck. Bob decides to write a CLI application over the next couple of weeks and has decided to write the CLI project using a newer programming language called **Rust**. Bob creates an intuitive CLI application that is easy to use and pluggable. Bob is able to showcase this new application to the team and in turn convince upper management to commit resources to work on the CLI project.

Starting CI/CD on your local machine

It may not be possible for a development team to get the financial approval to get started with a CI/CD pipeline. For the purposes of discovery and to convince others of the importance an automated CI/CD pipeline, a developer can replicate the deployment pipeline on his or her machine and demonstrate the benefits of building automated pipeline stages to the team and upper management.

It is possible with big cloud providers today, such as Azure, AWS, and Google App Engine, to get free account plans to provision cloud services. In this way, a developer could easily set up a more realistic deployment pipeline, by showcasing a small project and showing all the stages in a CI/CD pipeline such as the commit stage, an automated acceptance test stage, and an optional security and capacity build stage.

Company presentation

A company-wide presentation might be the most effective way to get approval for CI/CD in your organization. Some companies sponsor hackathons, and you could create a new automation process for the company on a sponsored hackathon. The advantage of doing this is that you can drive the message automation to the highest levels of an organization during a company presentation.

Imagine that Tommy from the development team is experimenting with Docker and has the idea to create a Docker image for each deployment pipeline. Tommy shows that the Docker container can be used as an isolated versioning system that QA can use to test versions of a software product, which also has the advantage of environment isolation. Tommy builds this automated process, and shows in the company presentation that this can save the QA department 25 hours of regression testing man hours. The CEO was not aware that QA spent many hours during deployment trying to get an environment set up to conduct regression testing. Tommy has shown the leadership via a convincing presentation why automation is important.

Lunch and learn

The following diagram is just a depiction of a fork and knife, but the main point is that breaking bread with others is a good way to open channels of communication and to bring people together. You can incorporate an automation presentation into a company meeting over lunch:

You can invite upper management and use diagrams and PowerPoint slides with metrics that help explain what automation is, and also show the money spent on manual processes. Usually, upper management are more interested in the monetary impact of an activity, and if you can show the cost of manual processes to them, they will be more inclined to listen.

Summary

Communicating the business value of CI/CD is very important, as this chapter has illustrated. We started this chapter by discussing the problems with communicating and talked about some strategies to communicate pain points to team members. We discussed sharing responsibilities among different team members, knowing your stakeholders, demonstrating why CI/CD is important to your stakeholders, and finally getting approval for CI/CD from your stakeholders.

The next chapter will be about getting Jenkins CI set up in your local environment. This chapter will introduce the first CI/CD tool of the book.

Questions

1. Why should you have all the requirements information in the beginning?
2. Why is meant by pain-driven development?
3. Why is having many communication channels problematic?
4. What are some of the benefits of rotating team members?
5. What is a benefit of asking for feedback on existing development practices?
6. How is using metrics and reporting useful in demonstrating the value of CI/CD to stakeholders?
7. Why do you need to educate leadership on automation?

Further reading

Consider reading *Continuous Integration, Delivery, and Deployment*, by *Packt Publishing*, as this book discusses the value of CI/CD for software organizations:

- https://www.packtpub.com/application-development/continuous-integration-delivery-and-deployment

Installation and Basics of Jenkins **5**

This chapter will help you get Jenkins installed in Windows, Linux, and macOS. We will also look at the basics of the Jenkins UI.

The following topics will be covered in this chapter:

- Windows installation have our first build
- Linux installation
- macOS installation
- Running Jenkins locally
- Managing Jenkins

Technical requirements

This chapter is about using Jenkins for CI/CD processes. We will not be talking about CI/CD concepts in this chapter, as we are getting our environment set up to use Jenkins.

Windows installation

There are some preliminary steps to getting Jenkins installed.

Prerequisites to installing Jenkins

You need to make sure that Java is installed and starting with Jenkins 2.54. Jenkins now requires Java 8.

Finding your version of Windows

Click the Start Windows icon, type `system` in the search box, and then click **System** in the **Programs** list.

With the **System** applet now open, titled **View basic information about your computer**, find the **System** area, located under the large Windows logo.

The system type will say either 64-bit operating system or 32-bit operating system.

Installing Java

To install Java, please go to the Java downloads page (`http://www.oracle.com/technetwork/java/javase/downloads/index.html`):

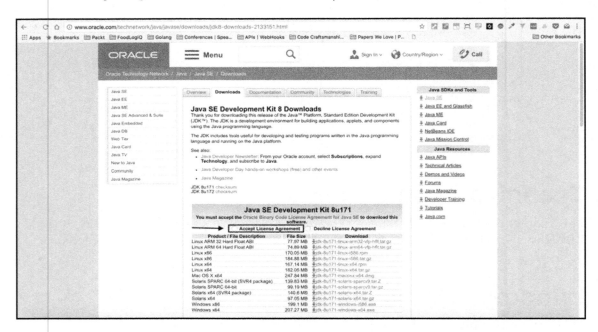

Make sure to click the **Accept License Agreement** radio button and then click **Windows Download** and make sure to pick the right architecture you have; namely, 32-bit or 64-bit OS.

Then use the installer to install Java in Windows.

Windows installer

Installing Jenkins in the Windows OS is relatively easy; just go to the Jenkins download page (`https://jenkins.io/download/`):

If you scroll to the end of the page, you will see a list of operating systems that you can install Jenkins on according to the current version:

Installing Jenkins in Windows

I have downloaded and unzipped the Jenkins file from the Jenkins download page, as shown in the following screenshot:

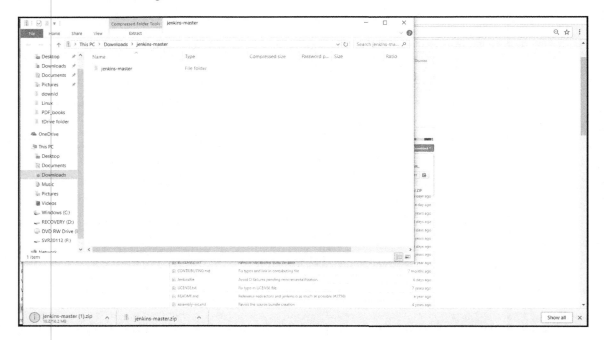

Running the Jenkins Installer in Windows

The following screenshot shows the Jenkins Installer in Windows:

Once you have gone through all the steps in the installer, you will see the following screen:

After you click **Finish**, you can go to `http://localhost:8080` in your web browser and you will see the following screenshot:

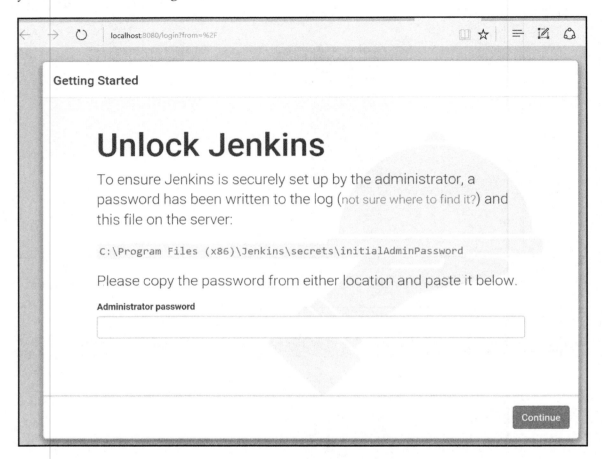

Installing Jenkins with the Chocolatey Package Manager

Chocolatey installation instructions can be found at `chocolatey.org/install`.

You can install Chocolatey with `cmd.exe` with the help of the following command:

```
@"%SystemRoot%\System32\WindowsPowerShell\v1.0\powershell.exe" -NoProfile -
InputFormat None -ExecutionPolicy Bypass -Command "iex ((New-Object
```

```
System.Net.WebClient).DownloadString('https://chocolatey.org/install.ps1'))
" && SET "PATH=%PATH%;%ALLUSERSPROFILE%\chocolatey\bin"
```

Once Chocolatey is installed, you can simply run `choco install jenkins` to install Jenkins via Chocolatey.

Starting and stopping Jenkins in Windows in Command Prompt

Click the **Start** button and type in `cmd` and hit *Enter*. This will open a Command Prompt session.

Next, you can enter the following command into Command Prompt:

```
cd 'C:\Program Files (x86)\Jenkins'
```

You can then utilize the following commands:

```
$ C:\Program Files (x86)\Jenkins>jenkins.exe start
$ C:\Program Files (x86)\Jenkins>jenkins.exe stop
$ C:\Program Files (x86)\Jenkins>jenkins.exe restart
```

You can also utilize `curl` and use the following commands:

```
$ curl -X POST -u <user>:<password> http://<jenkins.server>/restart
$ curl -X POST -u <user>:<password> http://<jenkins.server>/safeRestart
$ curl -X POST -u <user>:<password> http://<jenkins.server>/exit
$ curl -X POST -u <user>:<password> http://<jenkins.server>/safeExit
$ curl -X POST -u <user>:<password> http://<jenkins.server>/quietDown
$ curl -X POST -u <user>:<password> http://<jenkins.server>/cancelQuietDown
```

Linux installation

We will install Jenkins on a Ubuntu 16.04 Digital Ocean Droplet; please follow the instructions to install Jenkins on your specific Linux distribution on the button link on the Jenkins download page (`https://jenkins.io/download/`). You can click on one of the Linux distributions that Jenkins is officially supported on, but, for the purposes of this section, we will be looking at installing Jenkins on the Ubuntu operating system on a Digital Ocean Droplet.

Installing Jenkins on Ubuntu

Run the following command to add the repository key to your system:

```
wget -q -O - https://pkg.jenkins.io/debian/jenkins-ci.org.key | sudo apt-key add -
```

When the key is added, the system will return OK.

Next, we will append the Debian package repository address to the server's sources.list by running this command:

```
echo deb https://pkg.jenkins.io/debian-stable binary/ | sudo tee /etc/apt/sources.list.d/jenkins.list
```

Next, we need to update the repositories in the system by running the following command:

```
sudo apt-get update
```

Make sure to install Java as it is a dependency for Jenkins to run, so run the following command:

```
sudo apt install openjdk-9-jre
```

Next, we install Jenkins onto Ubuntu:

```
sudo apt-get install jenkins
```

Starting the Jenkins service in Ubuntu

Finally, we need to get the Jenkins service started by the following command:

```
sudo systemctl start jenkins
```

Now we need to confirm that Jenkins has started without issues:

```
sudo systemctl status jenkins
```

You should get output like this:

```
root@ubuntu-s-2vcpu-4gb-nyc1-01:~# sudo systemctl status jenkins
                  - LSB: Start Jenkins at boot time
   Loaded: loaded (/etc/init.d/jenkins; bad; vendor preset: enabled)
   Active: active (exited) since Fri 2018-06-08 02:29:52 UTC; 23s ago
     Docs: man:systemd-sysv-generator(8)
  Process: 9756 ExecStart=/etc/init.d/jenkins start (code=exited, status=0/SUCCESS)

Jun 08 02:29:50 ubuntu-s-2vcpu-4gb-nyc1-01 systemd[1]: Starting LSB: Start Jenkins at boot time...
Jun 08 02:29:50 ubuntu-s-2vcpu-4gb-nyc1-01 jenkins[9756]: Correct java version found
Jun 08 02:29:50 ubuntu-s-2vcpu-4gb-nyc1-01 jenkins[9756]:  * Starting Jenkins Automation Server jenkins
Jun 08 02:29:51 ubuntu-s-2vcpu-4gb-nyc1-01 su[9791]: Successful su for jenkins by root
Jun 08 02:29:51 ubuntu-s-2vcpu-4gb-nyc1-01 su[9791]: + ??? root:jenkins
Jun 08 02:29:51 ubuntu-s-2vcpu-4gb-nyc1-01 su[9791]: pam_unix(su:session): session opened for user jenkins by (uid=0)
Jun 08 02:29:52 ubuntu-s-2vcpu-4gb-nyc1-01 jenkins[9756]:    ...done.
Jun 08 02:29:52 ubuntu-s-2vcpu-4gb-nyc1-01 systemd[1]: Started LSB: Start Jenkins at boot time.
root@ubuntu-s-2vcpu-4gb-nyc1-01:~#
```

Opening network traffic firewalls

By default, Jenkins runs on HTTP port 8080, so we need to make sure that this port allows traffic:

```
sudo ufw allow 8080
```

You will get the following output:

```
Rules updated
 Rules updated (v6)
```

Next, we need to see the status of the rules:

```
sudo ufw status
```

You will see output like this:

```
Status: inactive
```

Unlocking Jenkins for the first login

The first time you are running Jenkins in Digital Ocean Droplet, you will see a screen like the following one:

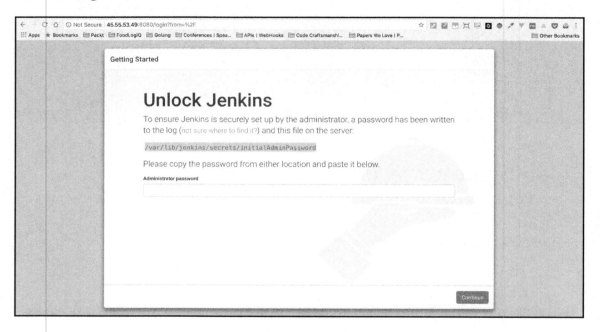

Run the following command in a Ubuntu Terminal session:

```
cat /var/lib/jenkins/secrets/initialAdminPassword
```

Copy the password that gets printed into standard output into your system clipboard, then paste this password into the initial login screen, and then click the **Continue** button.

Next you will see a screen like this where you can install suggested plugins or select plugins that you want to install:

This screen is not 100% necessary to run at first, so you can click the **X** on the top right of the screen:

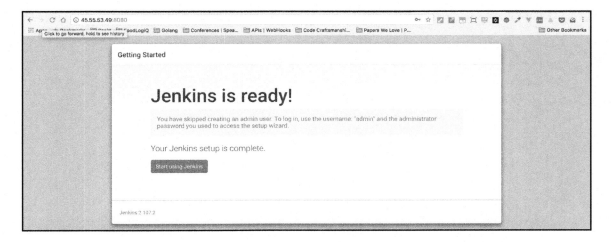

After you click the **X** and decide to launch Jenkins, you will see this screen:

macOS installation

Installing Jenkins in macOS is relatively easy and you can do it in a couple of ways.

Jenkins downloads package

In this section, we will cover how to install Jenkins using the Mac Package Installer (.pkg) files:

1. Go to the Jenkins download URL (https://jenkins.io/download/).
2. Scroll to the bottom of the page and you should see a list of operating systems that you can install Jenkins on.
3. Click the **Mac OS X** button link, and you should be taken to a page like this:

4. Either click on the `.pkg` file that you can see at the bottom of your browser window or double-click the Jenkins `.pkg` file in your downloads file:

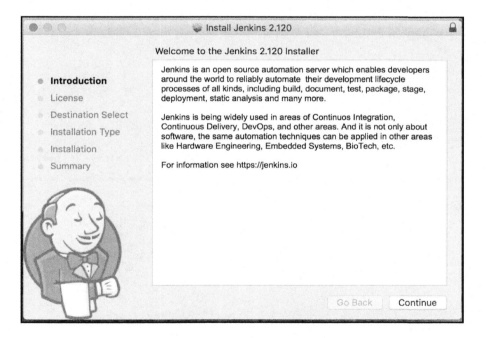

5. Notice that there are two buttons in the bottom-right corner aptly named **Go Back** and **Continue**. Just click on **Continue** and you will go the next window, which is the license agreement.

6. Click **Continue** and make sure to click on the **Agree** button:

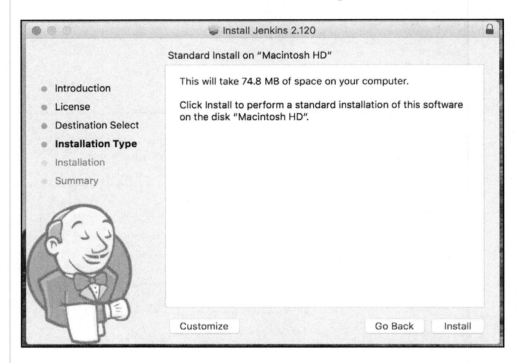

7. Ordinarily, you can just click the **Install** button, but if you want to customize, you can choose to not install documentation, among other things:

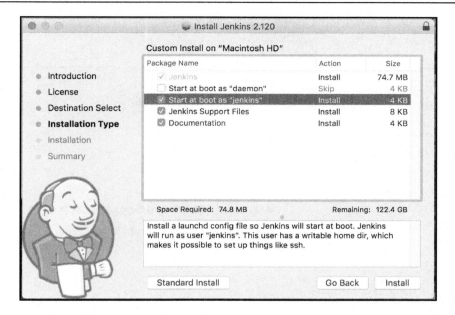

8. Unless you are concerned about disk space, it is typically easier to just click **Standard Install** and then click on **Install**:

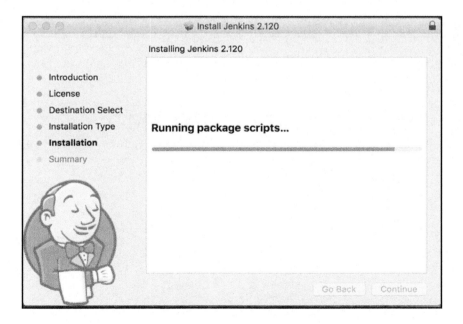

9. Once the installation scripts have finished running, you will see the following screen:

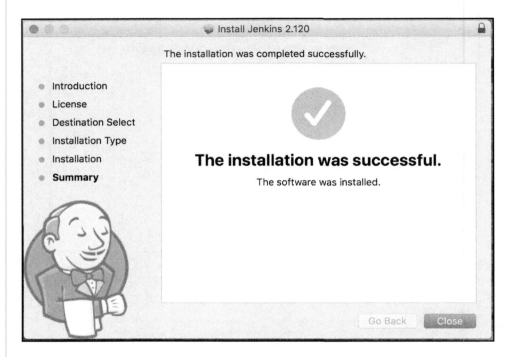

10. Click on **Close** and Jenkins should be running in your local machine.

Unlocking Jenkins for the first login

The first time you are running Jenkins locally in your host machine, you will see a screen like the following one:

Run the following command in a Mac Terminal if Jenkins is running in the main user account:

```
pbcopy < /Users/jean-marcelbelmont/.jenkins/secrets/initialAdminPassword
```

This will copy the initial admin password onto your system clipboard. It is also possible that your initial password is running in the Users/Shared/Jenkins if this is the case then, please try the following command:

```
pbcopy < /Users/Shared/Jenkins/Home/secrets/initialAdminPassword
```

Next, paste this password into the initial login screen and then click **Continue**:

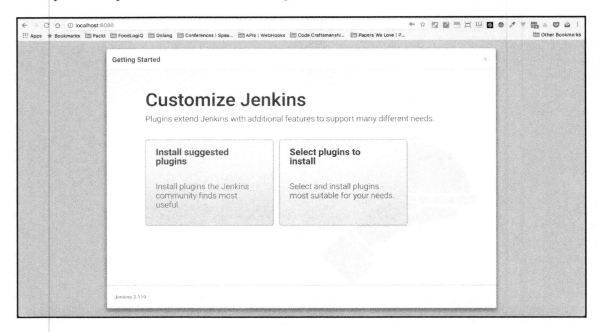

This screen is not 100% necessary to run at first, so you can click the **X** on the top right of the screen. After you click the **X** and decide to launch Jenkins, you will see this screen:

Installing Jenkins via Homebrew

You can also install Jenkins via the Homebrew package manager in macOS.

If you don't have Homebrew installed, then first go to the Homebrew page (`https://brew.sh/`).

Installing Homebrew is relatively easy. Open the Terminal application by clicking the Mac **Finder** button, press *Ctrl + Shift + G*, then enter `/applications`, and hit the **Go** button. Make sure to double-click the `Utilities` folder and then double-click the Terminal app icon.

Just paste the Homebrew install script into the Terminal application prompt:

```
/usr/bin/ruby -e "$(curl -fsSL
https://raw.githubusercontent.com/Homebrew/install/master/install)"
```

Once Homebrew is successfully installed, just run the following command into the Terminal application:

```
1. jean-marcelbelmont@Admins-MacBook-Pro-6: ~ (zsh)
~ brew install jenkins
==> Downloading http://mirrors.jenkins.io/war/2.119/jenkins.war
Already downloaded: /Users/jean-marcelbelmont/Library/Caches/Homebrew/jenkins-2.119.war
==> jar xvf jenkins.war
==> Caveats
Note: When using launchctl the port will be 8080.

To have launchd start jenkins now and restart at login:
  brew services start jenkins
Or, if you don't want/need a background service you can just run:
  jenkins
==> Summary
/usr/local/Cellar/jenkins/2.119: 7 files, 74.4MB, built in 6 seconds
```

Once Jenkins is installed, you can start the Jenkins service by issuing the command into the Terminal application:

```
brew services start jenkins
```

After you run this command, you just simply visit the `localhost:8080`, and you can then follow the same steps that we ran in the *Unlocking Jenkins for the first login* section.

Running Jenkins locally

The following is a screenshot of the main dashboard page of Jenkins. We will go over each item in detail:

Creating a new item

In the following steps, we will create a **Freestyle project** as a new item, but there could potentially be many more items to add depending on the plugins that are installed:

1. If you click the **New Item** link, you will go to the following page:

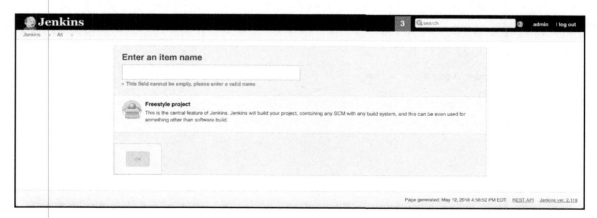

2. We have not installed any plugins, so the only type of item we can use is a **Freestyle project**.

3. Let's enter a name for the **Freestyle project** and click **OK**:

4. You will be presented with the following screen to configure your **Freestyle project**:

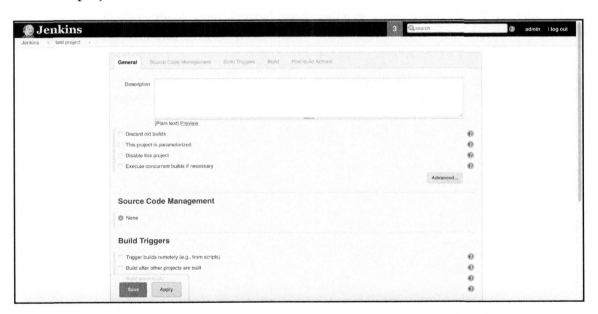

5. Let's create a simple build for Jenkins that prints out `Hello World`:

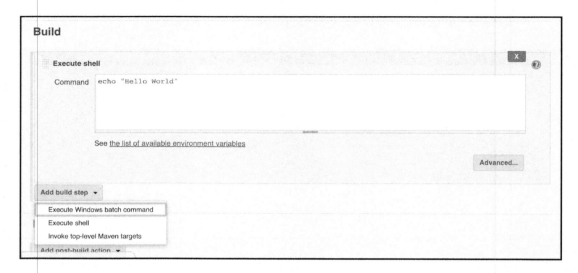

6. Make sure to click the **Add build step** button and then choose **Execute shell**.
7. Lastly, click **Save** and you will go back to the project dashboard screen.
8. Next make sure to click the **Build Now** button to get a build triggered, and you will see a text popup that says **Build Scheduled**:

9. Notice that in the following screenshot we have our first build labeled **#1** in the **Build History** section:

10. Notice that we now have a **Build History** section, and you will typically want to go the **Console Output** to see the log information for the build.

Console Output

The following is a typical **Console Output** screen in Jenkins:

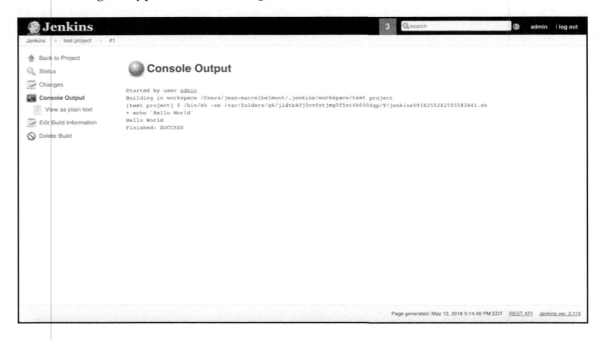

This is an extremely simple screen where we only printed out `Hello World` to the screen.

Managing Jenkins

Once you are logged into Jenkins, you can simply click the **Manage Jenkins** link:

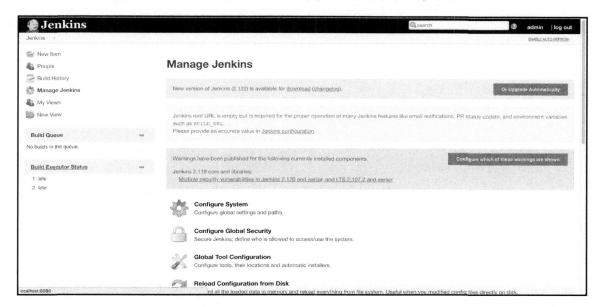

Then make sure to click the **Manage Plugins** link:

Manage Plugins

Add, remove, disable or enable plugins that can extend the functionality of Jenkins.

You will then be taken to the plugins page, which looks like this:

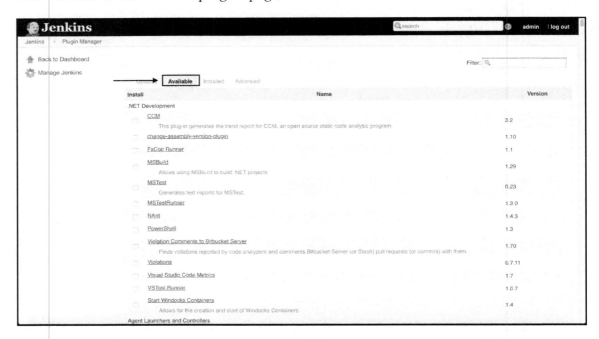

Make sure to click the **Available** tab, and you will see a list of available plugins that you can install.

We will install the **Go** plugin (you can quickly find plugins by using the **Filter** input box):

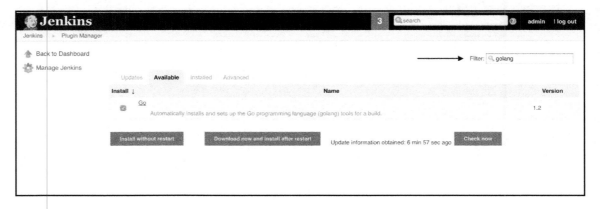

Notice that we typed in `golang` in the filter input. You can then either click the **Install without restart** button or the **Download now and install after restart** button. We will use the **Install without restart** button.

Once you click the button, you will see the following screen:

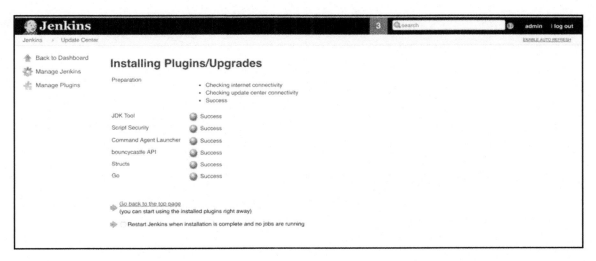

We will click the **Go back to the top page button.**

Let's go back to the Jenkins dashboard, click **Manage Jenkins**, and then click **Manage Plugins**.

Make sure to type `git` in the **Filter** input box:

Now we will click the **Download now and install after restart** button.

Now if you click the **Restart Jenkins flag,** Jenkins will restart and then you will be prompted to log in.

Next, make sure to click the **Back to Dashboard** link:

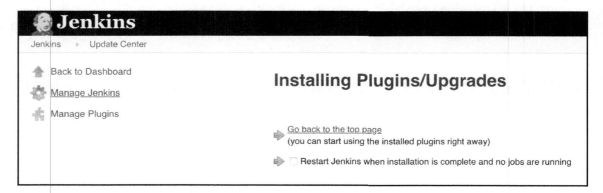

Configuring environment variables and tools

Now we will look at how to add environment variables in the Jenkins dashboard. Make sure to click **Manage Jenkins**, and then click **Configure System**:

Then you need to scroll down into the **Global properties**:

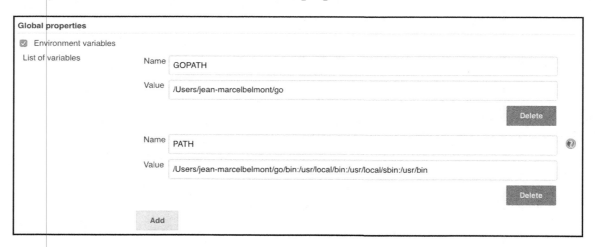

Then make sure to configure all the tools, such as adding paths to GitHub and golang.

Configuring a job to poll the GitHub version control repository

Make sure to click the **New Item** button, and now notice that we have an additional item that has been added.

Now we will create another Jenkins build job called **Golang Project**:

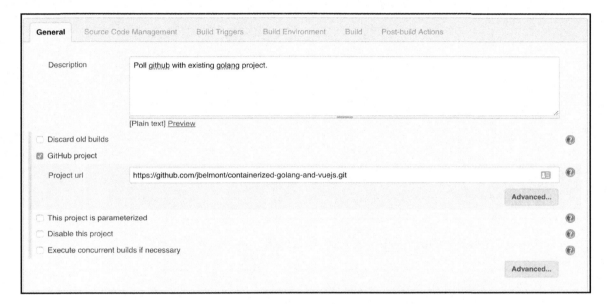

You can scroll down further or click the **Source Code Management** tab:

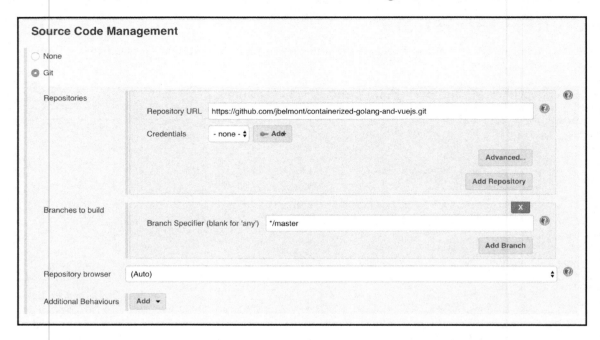

Now if you scroll down, you will go to the **Build Triggers** section:

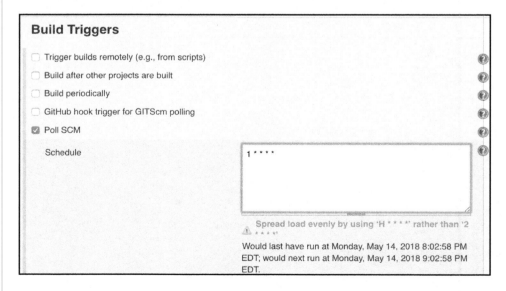

Here we configure polling with Jenkins and specify a cron schedule. The cron job is displayed as follows: minutes, hour, day, month, and weekday.

You can read more about the Crontab under the Linux manual pages (`http://man7.org/linux/man-pages/man5/crontab.5.html`).

We then add the following configuration:

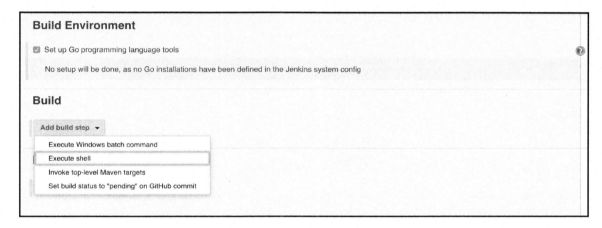

We will create another shell script where we execute tests.

Make sure to click the **Build Now** button:

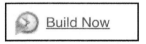

Then make sure to click on the **Build number** and then click the **Console Output** link:

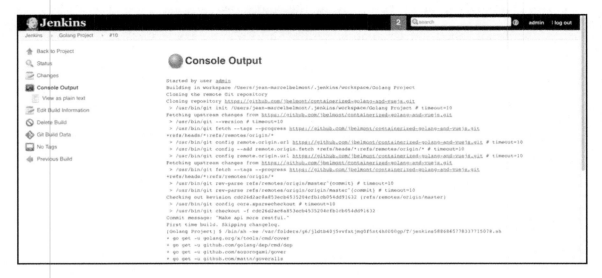

Notice here that the **Console Output** prints out each step that Jenkins is doing.

Summary

This chapter dealt with the installation of Jenkins and the basics of navigating the Jenkins UI. The next chapter will go over more of the Jenkins dashboard and UI.

Questions

1. What is the package manager that we use in Windows to install Jenkins called?
2. What prerequisites need to be installed for Jenkins to be installed?
3. Name one way to restart Jenkins in the Windows operating system.
4. What was the command we used to open network traffic firewalls in Linux?
5. What is the package manager that we use in macOS to install Jenkins called?
6. Where do you go to install plugins in Jenkins?
7. Where do you go to configure environment variables in Jenkins?

Further reading

Please check out *Learning Continuous Integration with Jenkins - Second Edition* (`https://www.amazon.com/dp/1788479351`), by Packt Publishing.

Writing Freestyle Scripts

This chapter will go into detail about adding a new build item, configuring a build job, adding environment variables globally, and project-level environment variables. You will also learn about debugging issues with a freestyle job.

The following topics will be covered in this chapter:

- Creating a simple freestyle script
- Configuring a freestyle job
- Adding environment variables
- Debugging issues with a freestyle job

Technical requirements

This chapter is about using Jenkins to create simple freestyle scripts. You should have a basic understanding of Unix, Bash, and what is meant by an environment variable.

Creating a simple freestyle script

We created a simple freestyle script in Jenkins in the chapter, but we will quickly review what you need to do to set up a freestyle script project.

Jenkins dashboard navigation

If you followed along with the instructions in `Chapter 5`, *Installation and Basics of Jenkins*, then you should have the Jenkins service installed and/or running on your local computer. If Jenkins is not running locally, then please revisit `Chapter 5`, *Installation and Basics of Jenkins*, and read the section corresponding to your operating system.

Jenkins login screen

If Jenkins is running locally, you should see a login screen.

Enter your user and password information and then click the log in button.

Jenkins dashboard

Once you are logged in, you should be routed to the Jenkins dashboard, which looks like this:

Adding a new build job item

In the Jenkins dashboard, there is a link called **New Item**; make sure to click it to add a new item:

Once you click **New Item**, you will be taken to the following screen:

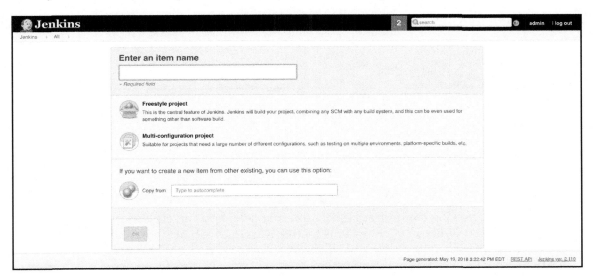

Now, depending on the number of Jenkins plugins that you have installed, you will see more or less on this screen in terms of build items. We will enter a name of `Freestyle Scripting` for the purposes of this chapter, but you can choose any name you like for the build job. Once you enter a name, make sure to click the **Freestyle Project** button and then click the **OK** button.

Build configuration options

Whenever you create a new item under Jenkins, you will see the following screen:

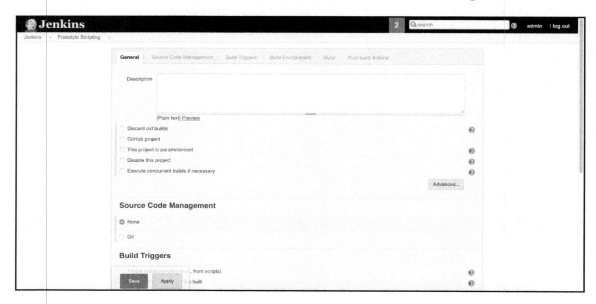

Depending on what Jenkins plugins you have already installed, you may see more tabs or items in the build configuration.

Configuring a freestyle job

Notice that the build job configuration has multiple tabs. You can either scroll to each section in the tab or you can click the tabs themselves. Each tab has different functionality that you can configure in your Jenkins build job.

General

The **General** tab has basic information about the Jenkins build you are creating, such as a description and other general build information. Look at the **General** tab information:

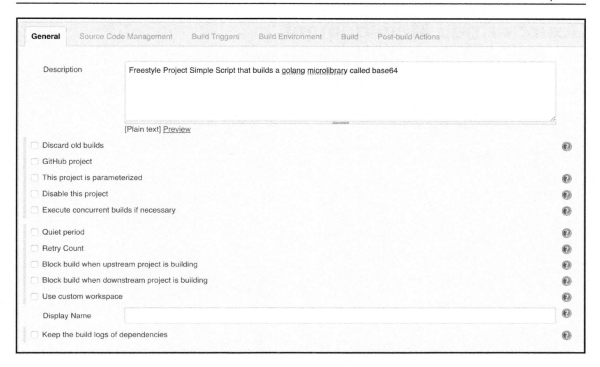

It is generally up to you which options you want to toggle on; you can click on the question mark symbol to get information. Let's look at what is meant by the **Quiet period** option:

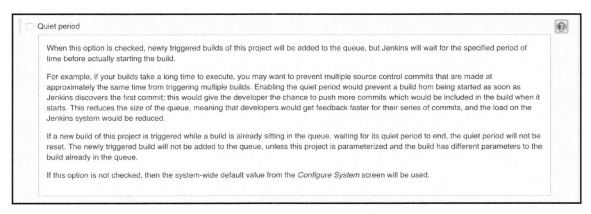

To remove the detailed information, just click the question mark symbol again.

Source Code Management

The **Source Code Management** tab is where you specify the type of version control management system you are using, such as Git, SVN, and Mercurial. For the purposes of a build job, we will click on the **Git** radio button and specify a GitHub repository URL:

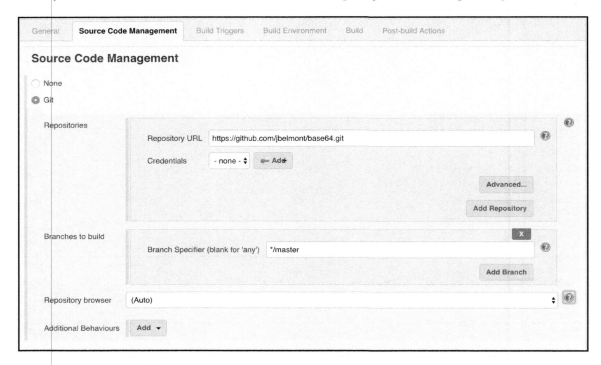

Notice that the **Branch Specifier** defaults to the ***/master** branch, but you can specify any number of branches that you want by just clicking the **Add Branch** button. We will not add credentials as we are working locally here, but if you click the **Add** button that has a key, you will see the following overlay screen:

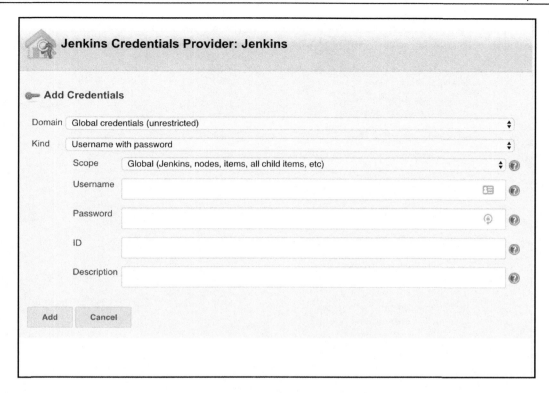

You can choose different types of credentials by clicking the **Kind** input box:

You can also click the **Add** button in the bottom section of the **Source Code Management** tab and you will see the additional behaviors you can add:

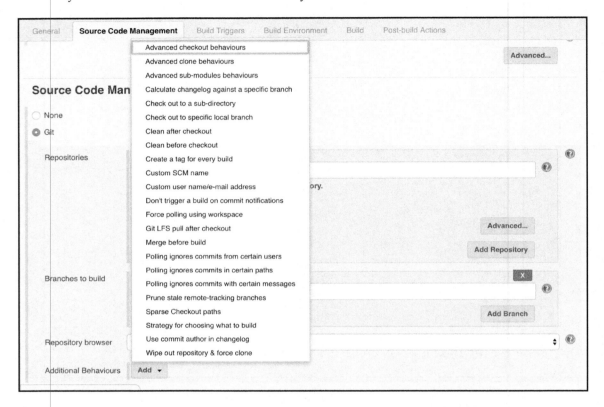

There are a number of advanced configuration options, such as sub-modules, that you can configure.

Build Triggers

The **Build Triggers** tab configuration section deals with configuring when your build job triggers. This could include configuring a GitHub hook trigger that fires whenever you push a commit to the master branch in GitHub, triggering a build whenever another project is built, when you build periodically, or when you poll your version control system for changes:

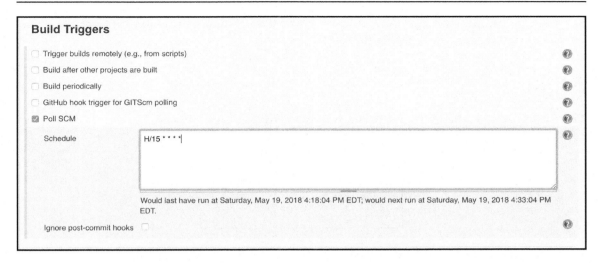

We checked the **Poll SCM** option, which is GitHub in our case, and utilizes a cron syntax that runs the Jenkins job at a particular time and date. In our case, we will trigger the polling job to run every 15 minutes. You can read more about the syntax by clicking the question mark symbol.

 Later on, we will discuss how to use GitHub and Bitbucket to trigger jobs in Jenkins whenever you push code up to your remote repository, which is better than polling for changes.

Build environment

This section will have more or less environment options to use depending on the Jenkins plugins that you have installed. In my case, I have Golang and Node.js plugins installed, but you could have any number of environments, such as Clojure and Ruby:

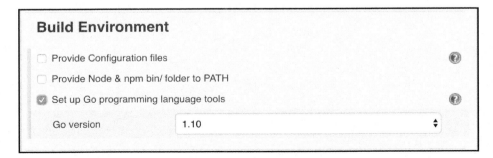

Since we are building a Golang microlibrary, we checked the **Set up Go programming language tools** checkbox in this configuration section.

Build

The **Build** section is where you specify how you want to build your project:

If you click the **Add build step** button, you will see the following options:

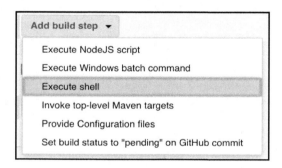

We will click on the **Execute shell** option, which will give us a Unix shell scripting environment to utilize.

Notice that we now have a text area available, where we can add Unix script commands:

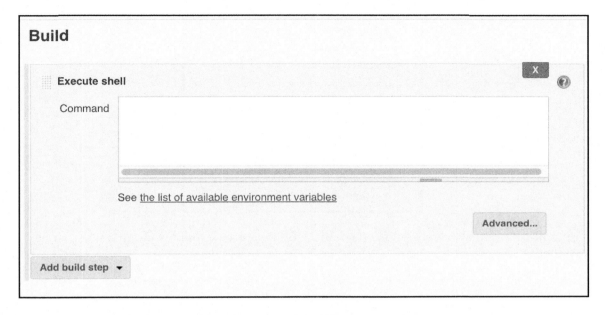

We will add the following commands to this shell script: `go test`.

Post-build actions

In this build section, you can specify any actions to run after a successful build, such as, running code coverage and generating a JUnit report:

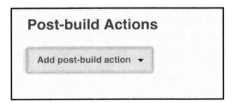

If you click the **Add post-build action** button, you will the following options:

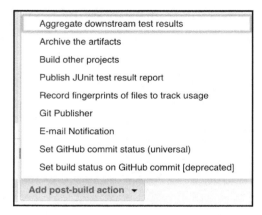

You will see more or fewer options depending on the specific Jenkins plugins that you have installed.

Once you are satisfied with the build configuration, click either the **Apply** button, which will save your current configuration options, or click the **Save** button, which will both save your options and then navigate you to a newly configured build item:

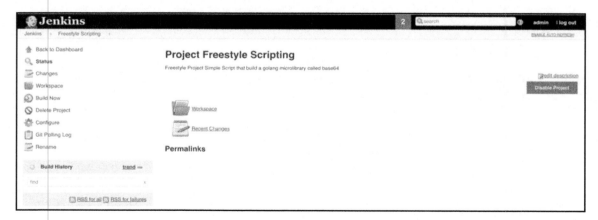

The **Post-build Actions** section is valuable because you can call other services, such as reporting and gathering metrics on a successful build.

Adding environment variables

You can add environment variables in Jenkins in a number of different ways.

Global environment variable configuration

From the Jenkins dashboard, click the **Manage Jenkins** button:

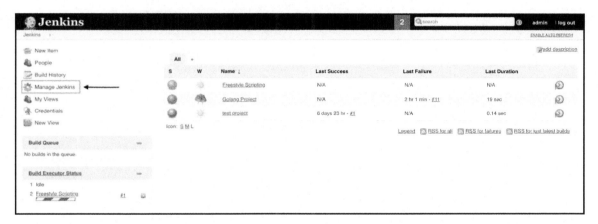

Once you click the **Manage Jenkins** button, you will need to click the **Configure System** button:

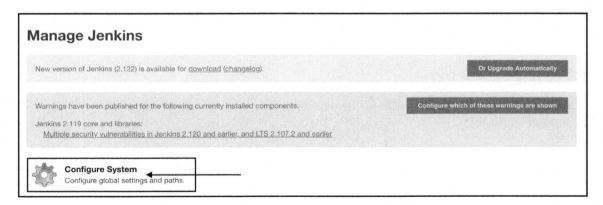

You will then be navigated to the **Configure System** section and will then be able to add environment variables using the **Global properties** section:

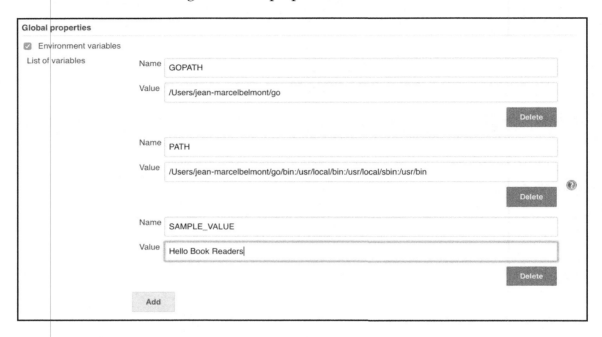

Notice here that I added a **Name**, SAMPLE_VALUE, with the **Value** as Hello Book Readers. Now, this global property is available as an environment variable in the shell environment variable. You can add as many environment variables as you need in this section. Note that this global property will be available for every single job now.

EnvInject Plugin

You can also choose a more granular level of setting environment variables for each particular build item.

Install the EnvInject Plugin (https://wiki.jenkins.io/display/JENKINS/ EnvInject+Plugin) by performing the following steps. Click the Jenkins main dashboard link:

Make sure to click the Jenkins link, and you will be routed to the Jenkins dashboard. Then click the **Manage Jenkins** button, like you did to add the **Global properties**.

Next click the **Manage Plugins** button, which looks like this:

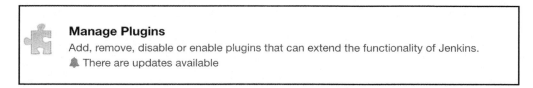

Manage Plugins

Add, remove, disable or enable plugins that can extend the functionality of Jenkins.

There are updates available

You will now be taken to the following screen:

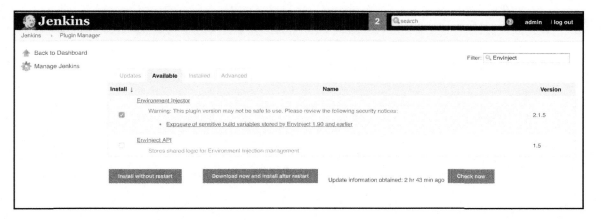

Notice that we clicked the **Available** tab and then put `EnvInject` into the **Filter** box. Make sure to click the Jenkins plugin that you want and then click the **Install without restart** or **Download now and install after restart** button.

Notice that we now have a couple of new build options in the **Build Environment** section in the build configuration area:

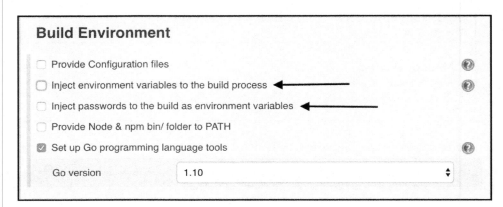

If you click **Inject environment variables to the build process**, you can then add your new environment variable, like this:

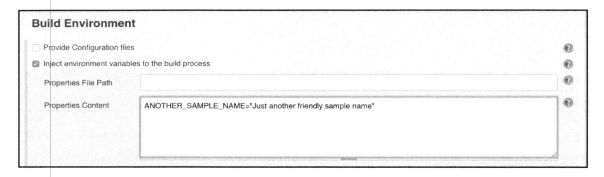

Make sure to save your changes. One thing to note is that this environment variable is only for this particular build item; it is not a global property like we set before.

Debugging issues with a freestyle job

Whenever you run a build in Jenkins for a build item, you can see all the details of the build by clicking on the specific build job that you want to see.

Build Project View

Here is the **Build History** that you need to focus on:

Now if you click on an actual build, you will go to the following screen:

If you click the **Console Output** link, then you will see a detailed CI Build log that shows all the steps the CI server did. Remember that we wrote a freestyle shell script. I'm adding the contents of the shell script for you to see:

```
echo "$SAMPLE_VALUE"
echo "$ANOTHER_SAMPLE_NAME"
go test
```

Notice here that I added the two different environment variables that we defined earlier and I'm simply sending them to the standard output.

Now if you look at the output of the build job, you will see the following output:

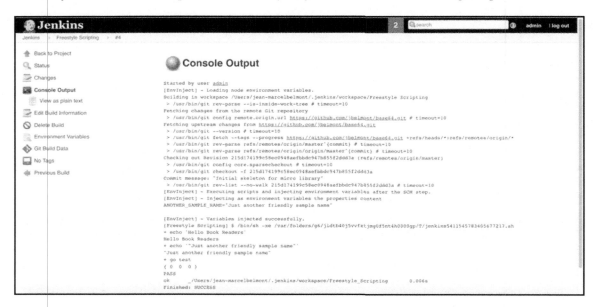

Notice here that Jenkins starts the job by running as the currently logged in user. Next, the EnvInject Plugin runs and injects any environment variables that we specified in our project. Then Jenkins fetches the latest changes from the GitHub repository. Then the EnvInject Plugin runs again and injects any necessary environment variables.

The last operation is the actual execution of the shell script. One thing to notice in the preceding screenshot is that each command in the shell script is printed to standard output because execution tracing is enabled in Jenkins. Remember that execution tracing simply means that each command that you run in a shell script will be shown as well as the output of the command itself. For example, the `echo "$ANOTHER_SAMPLE_NAME"` command, which has the value `echo "Hello Book Readers"`, is printed to standard output and then the message `Hello Book Readers` is printed. The last thing to note is the build that has the text **PASS** and the text finished with **SUCCESS**.

Debugging issues with freestyle script

Notice how we logged out environment variables that had simple information. There will be times where values are not being set in a CI environment, as you would expect, and this is where logging values out to standard output can be very helpful. One good aspect of using the EnvInject Plugin is that it will mask passwords that you inject to a build job so that you don't accidentally log secrets or confidential information:

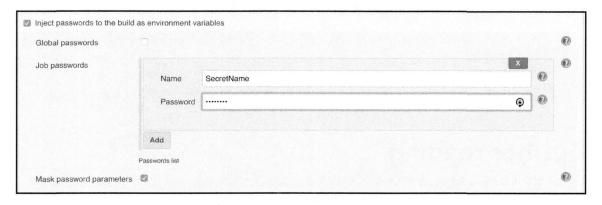

Notice that in the preceding screenshot we have checked the inject passwords to the build as environment variables and given a name and password to the environment variable. If you accidentally do `echo $SecretName` in the build job, it will mask the value of `$SecretName` so that you don't leak confidential information in the build.

Summary

In this chapter, you learned more about the Jenkins dashboard. You learned about adding build job items and all the parts of configuring a freestyle build job, how to add environment variables into a Jenkins job, and how to debug issues in a freestyle job.

The next chapter will cover how to build a Jenkins plugin and will specifically go over the build process, which involves writing Java code and using the Maven Build tool.

Questions

1. Why is clicking the question mark symbol in the build configuration useful?
2. What type of syntax do you write if you want to poll your version control system in the Build Trigger section?
3. Can you use more than one programming language in the build environment?
4. What type of environment does the freestyle script operate in—is it a Unix environment?
5. What is the difference between a global property and a project-level environment variable?
6. Why do you think Jenkins uses execution tracing for the console output?
7. What is the value of the post-build action section in the build configuration?

Further reading

Please check out *Learning Continuous Integration with Jenkins - Second Edition* (https://www.amazon.com/dp/1788479351), from Packt Publishing.

Developing Plugins 7

This chapter will go into detail about plugins in Jenkins, and we will first look at how to get Maven set up in Windows, Linux, and macOS. We will then look at plugin development by creating a `Hello World` plugin for Jenkins, and then we will briefly look at the Jenkins plugin site and how to navigate and use it to find a wide array of plugins.

The following topics will be covered in this chapter:

- Jenkins plugins explained
- Building a simple Jenkins plugin
- Jenkins plugin development
- Jenkins plugin ecosystem

Technical requirements

This chapter is about building plugins in Jenkins and you will need to have a basic understanding of the Java programming language and understand what a build tool such as Maven is intended for.

Jenkins plugins explained

Jenkins CI already provides certain functionality, including building, deploying, and automating software projects. Any additional behavior that you want out of Jenkins is generally provided by the large plugin ecosystem in Jenkins.

Why are plugins useful?

The purpose of plugins/extensions in software is to add specific functionality to a software component. Web browsers such as Chrome have extensions that extend the functionality of the browser and Firefox has add-ons that serve the same purpose as extensions in Chrome. There also exist plugins in other software systems, but we will specifically focus on plugins in Jenkins.

Jenkins plugin documentation

Go to the **Plugin Index** to find any plugins that you need, and we will look at this in a later section of this chapter. If you visit the plugin tutorial in the Jenkins wiki, you will get complete instructions on creating Jenkins plugins. There are also tutorials outside of the Jenkins wiki that you can use. You can go to Jenkins archetypes repo for the `Hello World` plugin example.

Installing plugins in Jenkins

You will need to navigate to the **Manage Jenkins** link in the Jenkins dashboard:

Once you click the **Manage Jenkins** link, you will be routed to a URL path that ends with `manage`, such as `http://localhost:8080/manage`, or some other domain depending on whether you are running Jenkins locally or not. You will need to click the **Manage Plugins** link, and then make sure to click the **Installed** tab and/or filter for any plugins that you wish to install. We have already covered this before, but we will be installing our own Jenkins plugin by installing it just as any other Jenkins plugin.

Building a simple Jenkins plugin

There are a couple of prerequisites to creating a Jenkins plugin. You will need to have Java installed, which should already be installed if you have been following along. You will also need to install the Maven software project management tool (`https://maven.apache.org/`) as well.

Java installation

You will need to make sure that you have Java 1.6 or higher installed, and I would recommend installing Java 1.9 if you can. To install Java, please go to the Java downloads page (`http://www.oracle.com/technetwork/java/javase/downloads/index.html`):

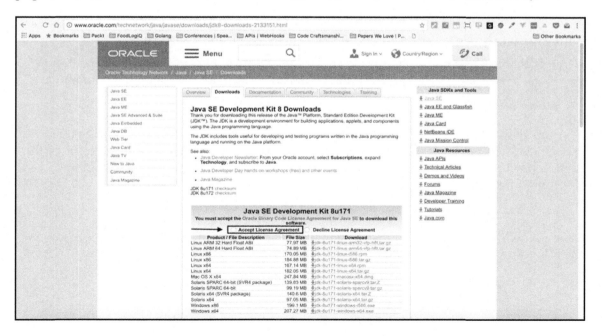

Make sure to click the **Accept License Agreement** radio button and then click **Windows**. Download and make sure to pick the right architecture; namely, a 32-bit or 64-bit operating system.

Once Java is installed, just verify the installation with the following command:

```
java -version
```

This should return the current version of Java that has been installed.

Maven installation instructions

To install Maven, please go to the Maven install page (https://maven.apache.org/install.html) and make sure to follow the instructions for your given operating system.

Windows installation

You can install Maven in a couple of different ways on Windows, but make sure that you have at least the Windows 7 operating system and the Java **Software Development Kit** (**SDK**) 1.7 or higher installed. If you followed along in Chapter 5, *Installation and Basics of Jenkins*, then you should have Java already installed.

Maven installation through the Chocolatey package manager

If you have the Chocolatey package manager already installed at Chocolatey installation (https://chocolatey.org/install), then you can simply run the following command:

```
choco install maven
```

You can also download the Maven binary executable from the Maven install page (https://maven.apache.org/install.html) and you will need to additionally find the value of the Java environment variable. You can find this by running the following command in Command Prompt:

```
echo %JAVA_HOME%
```

Then you will need to run add this Maven binary executable to the Windows path by doing the following:

1. Right-click on **My Computer**
2. Click on **Properties**
3. Click on **Advanced System Setting**

4. Click on **Environment Variable**
5. Click on **New user variable** and add **Maven_Home** with value `C:\apache-maven-3.5.3`
6. Add it to the path variable with `%Maven_Home%\bin`
7. Open Command Prompt and ask for `mvn -version` on your desktop

Maven installation through the Maven source code

First make sure that you have the Java SDK installed, which you can confirm in Command Prompt:

```
echo %JAVA_HOME%
```

This should print out the current version of Java that you have installed. Next, download the Maven source code from the Maven source repository (`https://gitbox.apache.org/repos/asf?p=maven-sources.git`) and then unpack the Maven source code in a suitable location in your Windows operating system.

> `C:\Program Files\Apache\maven` is a possible location that you could use.

Environment variables setup for the Windows operating system

You will need to add both the `M2_HOME` and `MAVEN_HOME` variables to your Windows environment using system properties, and you will need to point the environment variables to your Maven folder.

Update the PATH variable by appending the Maven `bin` folder, `%M2_HOME%\bin`, so that you can run the Maven executable anywhere in your system.

To verify that Maven is running correctly, run the following command in Command Prompt:

```
mvn --version
```

This command should display the current Maven version, Java version, and the operating system information.

macOS installation

You will need to make sure that the Java SDK is installed in the macOS operating system. If you followed along in Chapter 5, *Installation and Basics of Jenkins*, then you should have Java already installed.

Maven installation through the Homebrew package manager

First make sure that Java is installed by running the following command in the Mac Terminal application:

```
java -version
java version "1.8.0_162"
Java(TM) SE Runtime Environment (build 1.8.0_162-b12)
Java HotSpot(TM) 64-Bit Server VM (build 25.162-b12, mixed mode)
```

You will need to have Java 1.7 or higher installed on your system.

Next, if you have the Homebrew package manager installed (https://brew.sh/), then you can easily install Maven by issuing the following command in your Mac Terminal application:

```
brew install maven
```

Make sure that you set the following environment variable in your .bashrc, or .zshrc file:

```
export JAVA_HOME=`/usr/libexec/java_home -v 1.8`
```

Ensure that Maven has been properly installed by running the following command in your Mac Terminal:

```
mvn --version
Apache Maven 3.5.3 (3383c37e1f9e9b3bc3df5050c29c8aff9f295297;
2018-02-24T14:49:05-05:00)
Maven home: /usr/local/Cellar/maven/3.5.3/libexec
Java version: 1.8.0_162, vendor: Oracle Corporation
Java home:
/Library/Java/JavaVirtualMachines/jdk1.8.0_162.jdk/Contents/Home/jre
Default locale: en_US, platform encoding: UTF-8
OS name: "mac os x", version: "10.13.4", arch: "x86_64", family: "mac"
```

Notice here that the mvn binary executable printed out the installed Maven version, the Java version, and OS-specific information.

Unix installation

We will install Maven on a Ubuntu 16.04 Digital Ocean Droplet, but you should be able to run similar commands on other Linux distributions. Please follow the instructions to install Maven on your specific Linux distribution.

Maven installation through the apt-get package manager

Make sure that Java is installed in your Linux distribution, which you can check by running the following command in a Terminal shell:

```
java -version
openjdk version "9-internal"
OpenJDK Runtime Environment (build 9-
internal+0-2016-04-14-195246.buildd.src)
OpenJDK 64-Bit Server VM (build 9-internal+0-2016-04-14-195246.buildd.src,
mixed mode)
```

If Java has not been installed, then run the following command:

```
sudo apt-get update && sudo apt install openjdk-9-jre
```

Next, install Maven by running the following command in your Terminal application:

```
sudo apt-get install maven
```

Next, you will need to make sure that your JAVA_HOME environment variable has been set. Since we installed Java 1.9 in a Ubuntu Linux operating system, we will run the following command:

```
export JAVA_HOME=/usr/lib/jvm/java-1.9.0-openjdk-amd64/
```

 The directory that you use could be different, but if you do not set this environment variable, then Maven will report this as a warning.

Check that Maven has been installed correctly by running the following command in your Terminal application:

```
mvn --version
Apache Maven 3.3.9
Maven home: /usr/share/maven
Java version: 9-internal, vendor: Oracle Corporation
```

```
Java home: /usr/lib/jvm/java-9-openjdk-amd64
Default locale: en_US, platform encoding: UTF-8
OS name: "linux", version: "4.4.0-127-generic", arch: "amd64", family:
"unix"
```

Notice here that the Maven binary executable printed out the current Maven version installed, the current Java version installed, and OS-specific information, just like the Windows and Mac operating systems.

Jenkins plugin development

There are several steps necessary to get a Jenkins plugin set up, running, and installed.

Maven settings file

Depending on your current operating system, you will need to create/edit the .m2/settings.xml file.

Windows users will find the settings.xml file by issuing the following command in Command Prompt:

```
echo %USERPROFILE%\.m2\settings.xml
```

Mac operating system users can edit/create the settings.xml file in ~/.m2/settings.xml.

The settings element in the settings.xml file contains elements used to define values that configure Maven execution in various ways, such as pom.xml, but should not be bundled to any specific project, or distributed to an audience. These include values such as the local repository location, alternate remote repository servers, and authentication information.

Place the following content into the `settings.xml` file:

```xml
<settings>
  <pluginGroups>
    <pluginGroup>org.jenkins-ci.tools</pluginGroup>
  </pluginGroups>

  <profiles>
    <!-- Give access to Jenkins plugins -->
    <profile>
      <id>jenkins</id>
      <activation>
        <activeByDefault>true</activeByDefault> <!-- change this to false, if you don't like to have it on per default -->
      </activation>
      <repositories>
        <repository>
          <id>repo.jenkins-ci.org</id>
          <url>https://repo.jenkins-ci.org/public/</url>
        </repository>
      </repositories>
      <pluginRepositories>
        <pluginRepository>
          <id>repo.jenkins-ci.org</id>
          <url>https://repo.jenkins-ci.org/public/</url>
        </pluginRepository>
      </pluginRepositories>
    </profile>
  </profiles>
  <mirrors>
    <mirror>
      <id>repo.jenkins-ci.org</id>
      <url>https://repo.jenkins-ci.org/public/</url>
      <mirrorOf>m.g.o-public</mirrorOf>
    </mirror>
  </mirrors>
</settings>
```

Notice here that we entered specific information related to Jenkins plugins.

It is highly encouraged that you set your `settings.xml` file to get your Jenkins plugins working correctly!

HelloWorld Jenkins plugin

In order to create a Jenkins plugin, you will need to use Maven archetypes, which you can read about here (https://maven.apache.org/guides/introduction/introduction-to-archetypes.html).

We will issue the following command in order to generate a Jenkins Hello World plugin:

```
mvn archetype:generate -Dfilter=io.jenkins.archetypes:hello-world
```

Here is a sample running session that I did to create the plugin:

```
[INFO]
[INFO] --------------------< org.apache.maven:standalone-pom >--------------------
[INFO] Building Maven Stub Project (No POM) 1
[INFO] --------------------------------[ pom ]---------------------------------
[INFO]
[INFO] >>> maven-archetype-plugin:3.0.1:generate (default-cli) > generate-sources @ standalone-pom >>>
[INFO]
[INFO] <<< maven-archetype-plugin:3.0.1:generate (default-cli) < generate-sources @ standalone-pom <<<
[INFO]
[INFO]
[INFO] --- maven-archetype-plugin:3.0.1:generate (default-cli) @ standalone-pom ---
[INFO] Generating project in Interactive mode
[INFO] No archetype defined. Using maven-archetype-quickstart (org.apache.maven.archetypes:maven-archetype-quickstart:1.0)
Choose archetype:
1: remote -> io.jenkins.archetypes:hello-world-plugin (Skeleton of a Jenkins plugin with a POM and an example build step.)
Choose a number or apply filter (format: [groupId:]artifactId, case sensitive contains): : 1
Choose io.jenkins.archetypes:hello-world-plugin version:
1: 1.1
2: 1.2
3: 1.3
4: 1.4
Choose a number: 4: 4
[INFO] Using property: groupId = unused
Define value for property 'artifactId': jenkins-helloworld-example-plugin
Define value for property 'version' 1.0-SNAPSHOT: :
[INFO] Using property: package = io.jenkins.plugins.sample
Confirm properties configuration:
groupId: unused
artifactId: jenkins-helloworld-example-plugin
version: 1.0-SNAPSHOT
package: io.jenkins.plugins.sample
 Y: : Y
[INFO] ----------------------------------------------------------------------------
[INFO] Using following parameters for creating project from Archetype: hello-world-plugin:1.4
[INFO] ----------------------------------------------------------------------------
[INFO] Parameter: groupId, Value: unused
[INFO] Parameter: artifactId, Value: jenkins-helloworld-example-plugin
[INFO] Parameter: version, Value: 1.0-SNAPSHOT
[INFO] Parameter: package, Value: io.jenkins.plugins.sample
[INFO] Parameter: packageInPathFormat, Value: io/jenkins/plugins/sample
[INFO] Parameter: version, Value: 1.0-SNAPSHOT
[INFO] Parameter: package, Value: io.jenkins.plugins.sample
[INFO] Parameter: groupId, Value: unused
```

Notice here that I entered `1` for the archetype, then I chose a plugin version of `4`, and defined a value of `jenkins-helloworld-example-plugin`, and then hit *Enter* for the default values:

```
[INFO] Project created from Archetype in dir: /Users/jean-marcelbelmont/dev-temp/jenkins-helloworld-example-plugin
[INFO] ----------------------------------------------------------------------------
[INFO] BUILD SUCCESS
[INFO] ----------------------------------------------------------------------------
[INFO] Total time: 01:47 min
[INFO] Finished at: 2018-06-02T17:27:43-04:00
[INFO] ----------------------------------------------------------------------------
```

If all goes successfully, you should get the output of `BUILD SUCCESS` in Command Prompt.

You need to make sure that you can build your Jenkins plugin, so make sure to run the following command in Command Prompt:

```
// First go into the newly created directory
cd jenkins-helloworld-example-plugin
// Then run the maven build command
mvn package
```

The `mvn package` command will create a `target` directory and will run any tests that you have created in the directory:

```
[INFO] --- maven-surefire-plugin:2.20:test (default-test) @ jenkins-helloworld-example-plugin ---
[INFO]
[INFO]
[INFO]  T E S T S
[INFO] -------------------------------------------------------
[INFO] Running InjectedTest
[INFO] Tests run: 19, Failures: 0, Errors: 0, Skipped: 0, Time elapsed: 10.184 s - in InjectedTest
[INFO] Running io.jenkins.plugins.sample.HelloWorldBuilderTest
[INFO] Tests run: 5, Failures: 0, Errors: 0, Skipped: 0, Time elapsed: 37.713 s - in io.jenkins.plugins.sample.HelloWorldBuilderTest
[INFO]
[INFO] Results:
[INFO]
[INFO] Tests run: 24, Failures: 0, Errors: 0, Skipped: 0
[INFO]
[INFO]
[INFO] --- maven-license-plugin:1.7:process (default) @ jenkins-helloworld-example-plugin ---
[INFO] Generated /Users/jean-marcelbelmont/dev-temp/jenkins-helloworld-example-plugin/target/jenkins-helloworld-example-plugin/WEB-INF/licenses.xml
[INFO]
[INFO] --- maven-hpi-plugin:2.2:hpi (default-hpi) @ jenkins-helloworld-example-plugin ---
[INFO] Generating /Users/jean-marcelbelmont/dev-temp/jenkins-helloworld-example-plugin/target/jenkins-helloworld-example-plugin/META-INF/MANIFEST.MF
[INFO] Checking for attached .jar artifact ...
[INFO] Generating jar /Users/jean-marcelbelmont/dev-temp/jenkins-helloworld-example-plugin/target/jenkins-helloworld-example-plugin.jar
[INFO] Building jar: /Users/jean-marcelbelmont/dev-temp/jenkins-helloworld-example-plugin/target/jenkins-helloworld-example-plugin.jar
[INFO] Exploding webapp...
[INFO] Copy webapp webResources to /Users/jean-marcelbelmont/dev-temp/jenkins-helloworld-example-plugin/target/jenkins-helloworld-example-plugin
[INFO] Assembling webapp jenkins-helloworld-example-plugin in /Users/jean-marcelbelmont/dev-temp/jenkins-helloworld-example-plugin/target/jenkins-helloworld-example-plugin
[INFO] Generating hpi /Users/jean-marcelbelmont/dev-temp/jenkins-helloworld-example-plugin/target/jenkins-helloworld-example-plugin.hpi
[INFO] Building jar: /Users/jean-marcelbelmont/dev-temp/jenkins-helloworld-example-plugin/target/jenkins-helloworld-example-plugin.hpi
[INFO]
[INFO] --- maven-jar-plugin:3.0.2:test-jar (maybe-test-jar) @ jenkins-helloworld-example-plugin ---
[INFO] Skipping packaging of the test-jar
[INFO] -------------------------------------------------------
[INFO] BUILD SUCCESS
[INFO] -------------------------------------------------------
[INFO] Total time: 01:04 min
[INFO] Finished at: 2018-06-02T17:44:42-04:00
[INFO] -------------------------------------------------------
```

Notice here that the Jenkins archetype actually created some tests for our `Hello World` Jenkins plugin example.

Folder layout explanation

The following is a screenshot of the newly created `jenkins-helloworld-example-plugin` directory:

```
↦ jenkins-helloworld-example-plugin git:(master) tree -d -L 3
├── src
│   ├── main
│   │   ├── java
│   │   └── resources
│   └── test
│       └── java
└── target
    ├── classes
    │   ├── META-INF
    │   └── io
    ├── generated-sources
    │   ├── annotations
    │   └── localizer
    ├── generated-test-sources
    │   ├── injected
    │   └── test-annotations
    ├── javadoc-bundle-options
    ├── jenkins-for-test
    │   ├── META-INF
    │   ├── WEB-INF
    │   ├── css
    │   ├── executable
    │   ├── help
    │   ├── images
    │   ├── jsbundles
    │   └── scripts
    ├── jenkins-helloworld-example-plugin
    │   ├── META-INF
    │   └── WEB-INF
    ├── maven-status
    │   └── maven-compiler-plugin
    ├── site
    │   └── apidocs
    ├── surefire-reports
    └── test-classes
        ├── io
        └── test-dependencies

37 directories
```

The `src` directory contains the source files for the Jenkins plugin as well as tests for the plugins.

The target directory is generated with the `mvn` package. There is also a `pom.xml` file, which Maven created when we ran the archetype sub-command.

A **Project Object Model (POM)** is the fundamental unit of work in Maven. It is an XML file that contains information about the project and configuration details used by Maven to build the project. It contains default values for most projects. Examples for this include the build directory, which is `target`, the source directory, which is `src/main/java`, and the test source directory, which is `src/test/java`.

Jenkins plugin source code explanation

As we mentioned earlier, the `src` directory contains the source files for the Jenkins plugin. In order to build plugins in Jenkins, you will need to write in the Java programming language. Teaching the Java programming language is out of the scope of this book but we will briefly discuss some of the files that Maven created for us.

Notice that Maven created a rather long directory structure, which is common, and, as such, the directory structure for the `helloworld` plugin is `./src/main/java/io/jenkins/plugins/sample/HelloWorldBuilder.java`. The test file itself is in `./src/test/java/io/jenkins/plugins/sample/HelloWorldBuilderTest.java`.

I have included the source code for the `HelloWorldBuild.java` class here:

```
package io.jenkins.plugins.sample;

import hudson.Launcher;
/* More Import Statements Here */

public class HelloWorldBuilder extends Builder implements SimpleBuildStep {

    /* Rest of methods in Github Source */

    @Override
    public void perform(Run<?, ?> run, FilePath workspace, Launcher
launcher, TaskListener listener) throws InterruptedException, IOException {
        if (useFrench) {
            listener.getLogger().println("Bonjour, " + name + "!");
        } else {
            listener.getLogger().println("Hello, " + name + "!");
        }
    }

    @Symbol("greet")
    @Extension
```

```
    public static final class DescriptorImpl extends
BuildStepDescriptor<Builder> {

        /* Rest of the source in Github */

}
```

Notice that the `HelloWorldBuilder` class extends the `Builder` class, which is a Jenkins core class; and also notice that we are using a class called `BuildStepDescriptor`, which is also a Jenkins class. The source code for this file can be seen in my GitHub repository called `jenkins-plugin-example` in the `HelloWorldBuilder.java` (https://github.com/jbelmont/jenkins-plugin-example/blob/master/src/main/java/io/jenkins/plugins/sample/HelloWorldBuilder.java) file.

For the test cases in `HelloWorldBuilderTest.java`, we use JUnit, which is a popular unit testing library for the Java programming language.

```
package io.jenkins.plugins.sample;

import hudson.model.FreeStyleBuild;
/* More Import Statements Here */

public class HelloWorldBuilderTest {

    @Rule
    public JenkinsRule jenkins = new JenkinsRule();

    final String name = "Bobby";

    @Test
    public void testConfigRoundtrip() throws Exception {
        FreeStyleProject project = jenkins.createFreeStyleProject();
        project.getBuildersList().add(new HelloWorldBuilder(name));
        project = jenkins.configRoundtrip(project);
        jenkins.assertEqualDataBoundBeans(new HelloWorldBuilder(name),
project.getBuildersList().get(0));
    }

    /* More test Cases in this file. */

}
```

The preceding Java test file has annotations such as `@Rule`, `@Override`, `@Test`, and `@DataBoundSetter`, which are a form of metadata that provide data about a program that is not part of the program itself. Annotations have no direct effect on the operation of the code they annotate. The source code for this file can be seen in my GitHub repository called `jenkins-plugin-example` in the `HelloWorldBuilderTest.java` file (`https://github.com/jbelmont/jenkins-plugin-example/blob/master/src/test/java/io/jenkins/plugins/sample/HelloWorldBuilderTest.java`).

Building a Jenkins plugin

In order to build a Jenkins plugin, you need to run the `mvn install` command in the plugin directory.

The `mvn install` command will both build and test the Jenkins plugin and, more importantly, create a file called `pluginname.hpi`; or, in our case, it will create a file called `jenkins-helloworld-example-plugin.hpi` in the `target` directory that we can use to deploy to Jenkins.

I have attached a sample install run in the following screenshot:

Notice that this run finished by installing our Jenkins plugin into several
locations, which we will use to install our Jenkins plugin.

Installing a Jenkins plugin

Now, in order to install a newly built and installed `HelloWorld` example plugin, we will
need to go to the Jenkins **Dashboard** | **Manage Jenkins** | **Manage Plugins** view and then
click the **Advanced** tab. Please refer to `Chapter 6`, *Writing Freestyle Scripts*, in the *EnvInject
Plugin* section, for more details if necessary. You can also directly go to the plugin section
by going to `scheme://domain/pluginManager`; or, if you are running Jenkins locally, just
go to `http://localhost:8080/pluginManager/`.

Then make sure to click the **Advanced** tab or go
to `http://localhost:8080/pluginManager/advanced`:

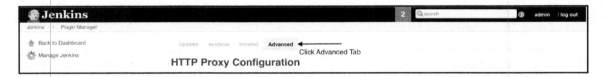

You will then need to go to the *Upload Plugin* section:

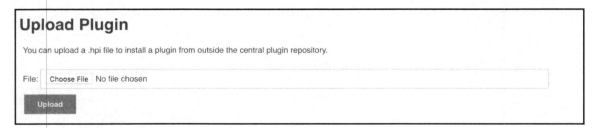

Click **Choose File** and then find our newly created `Helloworld` Jenkins plugin, which
should be in the directory:

```
jenkins-helloworld-example-plugin/target/jenkins-helloworld-example-
plugin.hpi
```

Then make sure to click the **Upload** button.

The following is a screenshot of the newly installed `Helloworld` example plugin:

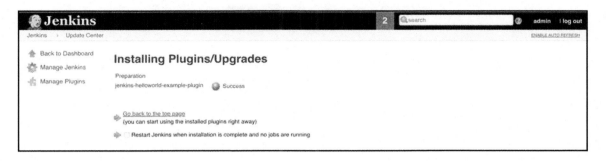

Jenkins plugin ecosystem

There is a wide array of plugins available for Jenkins, and you can find the full list at the Jenkins plugins site (https://plugins.jenkins.io/).

List of available plugins

The following screenshot shows a plugins search related to JSON in Jenkins:

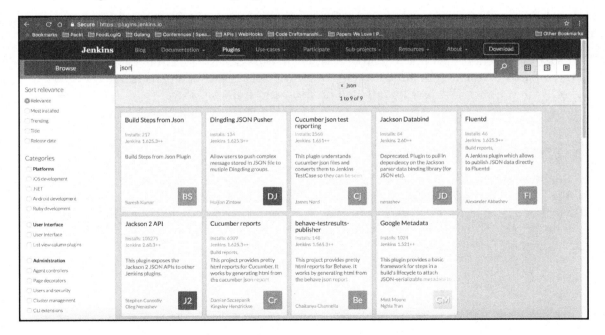

Notice that the Jenkins plugin site has multiple views that you can utilize besides this default view:

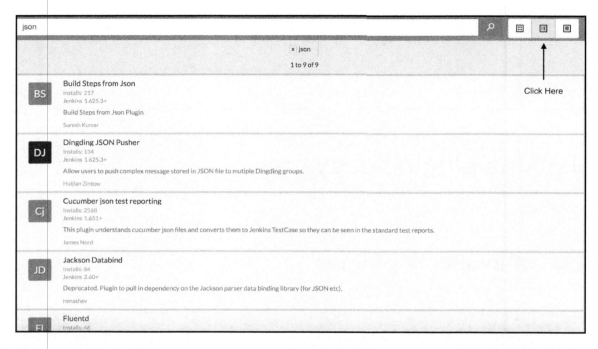

Notice that I clicked the middle icon, but you can also click the rightmost icon to get a small outline view. The search defaults to relevant search items, but you can choose different search criteria, such as **Most Installed**, **Trending** and **Release Date**.

Summary

In this chapter, you learned about the Maven build tool for Java and how to install it for Windows, Linux, and macOS. You also learned about how to create a Jenkins plugin by using the Maven build tool, and we briefly discussed some Java syntax and how to install a Jenkins plugin by using the **Advanced Options** in the manage plugins UI in the Jenkins dashboard. We also looked at the Jenkins plugin ecosystem.

Questions

1. What is the build tool that we used to create a Jenkins plugin?
2. Which package manager did we use to install Maven in the Windows operating system?
3. Which package manager did we use to install Maven in the macOS operating system?
4. What was the name of the configuration file that we briefly discussed in our `HelloWorld` plugin?
5. What is the URL we can directly navigate to in order to manage plugins in Jenkins?
6. What was the command we used to build and install a Jenkins plugin in Maven?
7. What type of file does Maven create for us so that we can install a Jenkins plugin?

Further reading

Please check out the book *Extending Jenkins* (`https://www.amazon.com/dp/B015CYBP2A/ref=dp-kindle-redirect?_encoding=UTF8btkr=1`), by Packt Publishing, to learn more about Jenkins plugins.

Building Pipelines with Jenkins

8

This chapter will go into detail about how to set up Jenkins Blue Ocean using an existing Jenkins instance and how to set it up using Docker. We will look in detail at the Blue Ocean **User Interface** (**UI**) and discuss the differences between the Jenkins Classic view and the Blue Ocean view. We will also look at the Pipeline Syntax and briefly discuss its uses and explain the two different types of Pipeline Syntax.

The following topics will be covered in this chapter:

- Jenkins 2.0
- The Jenkins Pipeline
- Navigating in Jenkins Blue Ocean
- Pipeline Syntax

Technical requirements

This chapter requires a basic understanding of how to interact with a Unix Shell environment. We will also briefly discuss the Pipeline Syntax so it would help if you have some basic programming skills to understand what a keyword is used for in a programming language.

Jenkins 2.0

Jenkins 2.0 has a different design methodology and flow compared to Jenkins 1.0. Instead of using freestyle jobs, there is a new **Domain Specific Language** (**DSL**) that is an abbreviated form of the Groovy programming language.

The Pipeline views also function differently to how they do in Jenkins 1.0. The Pipeline stage views also help us visualize the various stages in a pipeline.

Why move to Jenkins 2.0?

So, to begin with, why move to Jenkins 2.0 at all and not stay with Jenkins 1.0? The Jenkins Classic views are considered to be cluttered and did not take ease of use into account. Jenkins 2.0 made a big push on using Docker Images in a more intuitive manner. Also, the new UI includes a Jenkins pipeline editor and changes the way you find your builds by introducing a pipeline view. The goal for the new UI is to reduce clutter and increase clarity for every member of a team that uses Jenkins. The new UI also has GitHub and Bitbucket integration as well as Git integration. The Jenkins 2.0 UI is essentially a collection of plugins that you install called Blue Ocean.

Installing the Blue Ocean plugin on an existing instance

If you install Jenkins on most platforms, you will not have the Blue Ocean plugin installed with all of its dependent plugins by default. You will need to make sure that you are running on Jenkins version 2.7.x or greater to install the Blue Ocean plugin.

In order to install plugins on a Jenkins instance, you must have administrator permission that is set through matrix-based security, and any Jenkins administrators can also configure the permissions of other users in the system.

The steps to install the Blue Ocean plugin are as follows:

1. Make sure that you are logged in as a user with administrator permission
2. From the Jenkins home page, or the dashboard in Jenkins Classic, click **Manage Jenkins** on the left side of the dashboard
3. Next click **Manage Plugins** in the center of the **Manage Jenkins** page
4. Click the **Available** tab and type `Blue Ocean` into the **Filter** textbox, that filters the list of plugins to those whose name and/or description contains the words blue and ocean

Please read `Chapter 7`, *Developing Plugins*, specifically the *Installing Jenkins plugins* section for more information.

Installing the Blue Ocean plugin through a Jenkins Docker Image

You will need to make sure that you have Docker installed in order to get the Jenkins CI Docker Image.

Docker prerequisites

Since Docker leverages the operating system's virtualization technologies, the installation requirements for Docker are specific.

The OS X requirements are:

- 2010 or newer model Mac with Intel's MMU virtualization
- OS X El Capitan 10.11 or newer

The Windows requirements are:

- 64-bit Windows
- Windows 10 Pro, Enterprise, or Education (not Home, not Windows 7 or 8) to install Hyper-V
- Windows 10 Anniversary Update or better
- Access to your machine's BIOS to turn on virtualization

To install Docker on your operating system, visit the Docker store (`https://store.docker.com/search?type=editionoffering=community`) website and click the Docker Community Edition box that is suitable for your operating system or cloud service. Follow the installation instructions on their website.

Make sure that Docker is installed by checking the Docker version using either a Windows Command Prompt or an OS X/Linux Terminal application. Run the following in your command-line:

```
~ docker --version
Docker version 18.03.1-ce, build 9ee9f40
~
```

Notice here that I have Docker version 18 installed.

Installing Docker images

In order to get Docker images, you need to make sure that you have an account in Docker Hub (https://hub.docker.com/). Once you have an account in Docker Hub and Docker is installed, grabbing the latest Jenkins CI Docker image is straightforward.

Run the following command in a Windows Command Prompt or a Terminal:

```
↦  ~ docker pull jenkinsci/blueocean
Using default tag: latest
latest: Pulling from jenkinsci/blueocean
Digest: sha256:c8a7442658b96028c736ef727fa802c7e38e996d7c57831c32affa540c37e8d0
Status: Image is up to date for jenkinsci/blueocean:latest
↦  ~
```

Notice here that I have already pulled the `jenkinsci/blueocean` Docker image and so the command did not get pulled from Docker Hub but instead printed out a SHA hash checksum. This shows that I already have the latest Docker image for `jenkinsci/blueocean`.

Next, you will need to get the Jenkins Docker container up and running, and you will need to run the following command in a Terminal or Command Prompt shell:

```
↦  ~ docker run \
-u root \
--rm \
-d \
-p 8080:8080 \
-p 50000:50000 \
-v jenkins-data:/var/jenkins_home \
-v /var/run/docker.sock:/var/run/docker.sock \
jenkinsci/blueocean
e821061d527056894a00a8fa1fc461a54539961e06ce257a7bc9354479174b47
↦  ~
```

You can make this easier by simply creating a shell script that does this for you or by creating an alias.

Here is a shell script that I created in a text editor:

```
#! /bin/bash

docker run \
  -u root \
  --group-add docker \
  --rm \
  --name jenkins-blueocean \
  -d \
  -p 8080:8080 \
  -p 50000:50000 \
  -v jenkins-data:/var/jenkins_home \
  -v /var/run/docker.sock:/var/run/docker.sock \
  jenkinsci/blueocean
```

I have a personal `bin` directory where I store all of my personal scripts in `~/bin`, and then I make sure to add it to the `PATH` variable. The script filename is called `run-jenkinsci-blueocean`. We need to make sure that the script is executable by issuing the following command:

```
chmod +x run-jenkinsci-blueocean
```

Then all I have to do is run the `~/bin/run-jenkinsci-blueocean` command.

You can also create an alias in Unix similar to this:

```
# inside ~/.zshrc

alias runJenkinsDockerImage='docker run -u root jenkins-blueocean --rm -d -p 8080:8080 -p 50000:50000 -v jenkins-data:/var/jenkins_home -v /var/run/docker.sock:/var/run/docker.sock jenkinsci/blueocean'
```

Notice here that I added this shell alias in my `.zshrc` file, but you can just as easily add this to a `.bashrc` file.

Windows users can create a batch file or find some other way to make running the Docker command easier.

In order to stop the Docker container, you can run the following command:

```
docker ps -a
```

This command will show all the running containers in your system; you will need to look at the Container ID, NAMES column, and copy the ID that corresponds to the Docker image jenkinsci/blueocean. Lastly, to stop the container you need to run the following command:

```
docker stop jenkins-blueocean
```

Notice that because we used the --name jenkins-blueocean options in the docker run command in the shell script, Docker created a container with the name jenkins-blueocean; if we had not done so, then Docker would have created a name for the container for us. We can also use the container ID and name to stop the container, that is shown when you issue the docker ps -a command in a Terminal or Command Prompt.

Once Jenkins is running, you can go here: http://localhost:8080 and you will need to unlock Jenkins by providing the default password generated for the administrator. In Chapter 5, *Installation and Basics of Jenkins*, we skipped the getting started step of installing suggested plugins, but this time I would recommend that you install the suggested plugins on the **Getting Started** screen:

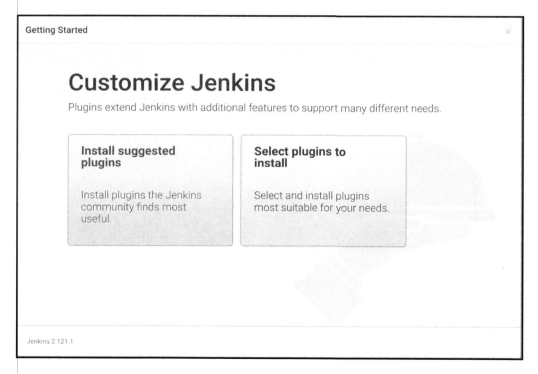

By clicking the **Install suggested plugins** button, you will get all of the suggested plugins and dependent plugins, that will help you work on the new Jenkins 2.0 flow with pipelines and more.

Accessing Blue Ocean Jenkins view

You need to make sure that you click the **Open Blue Ocean** button, that looks similar to this:

Once you click the **Open Blue Ocean** button, you will be redirected to this URL: `http://localhost:8080/blue/organizations/jenkins/pipelines`. The Jenkins UI will look very different and behave differently.

Here is the initial screen you will see, as we have not created any pipelines yet:

 We will explore the Pipeline Syntax and how to navigate the Jenkins 2.0 UI in the following sections.

The Jenkins pipeline

We will create our first pipeline by using the Jenkins 2.0 UI and will also create a Jenkinsfile with the pipeline editor that is built in to the new Jenkins 2.0 UI.

Creating a Jenkins pipeline

The first step we will do is click the **Create a new Pipeline** button. You will be redirected to the following screen:

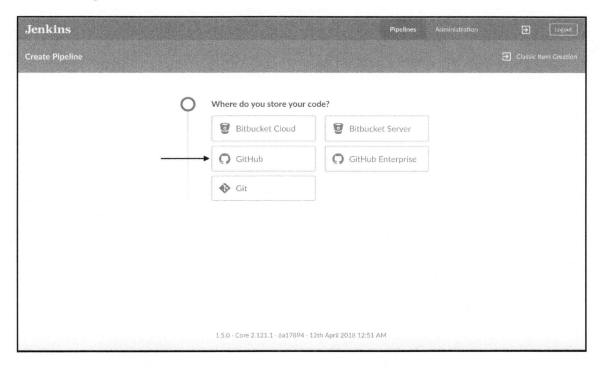

For the purposes of this chapter, we will use an existing GitHub repository that I created, but you can easily use Bitbucket and your own code that is hosted on either GitHub or Bitbucket. In order for this to work, you will need to make sure that you have an account on GitHub, and if you do not, make sure to sign up for GitHub (https://github.com/).

Providing a personal access token for GitHub

You will need to create a personal access token if you don't have one already in GitHub. Notice in the following screenshot that there is a link called **Create an access key here**:

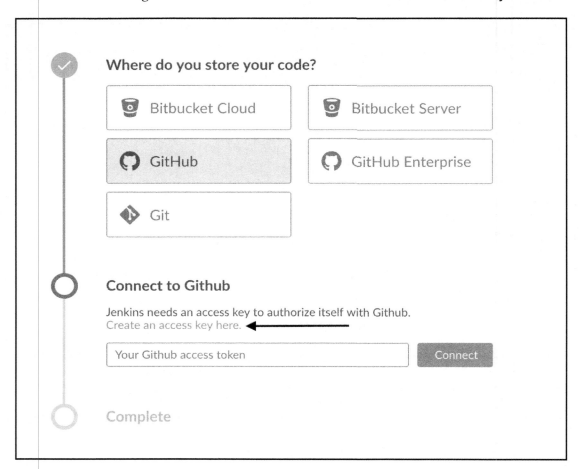

Once you click the **Create an access key here** link, you will be redirected to the following GitHub page:

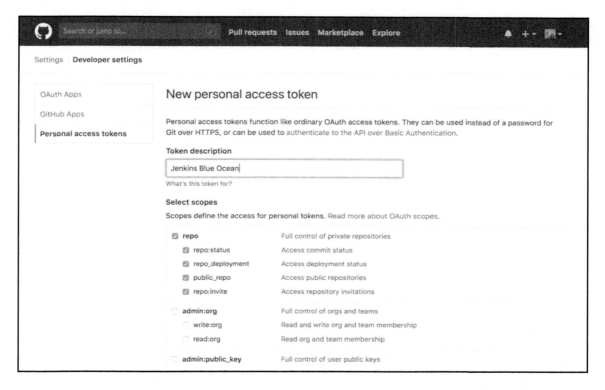

You can just keep the default options checked and then click the green button titled **Generate token**. Make sure to keep this personal access token in a safe place as it will only be shown once; copy it as we will need it. You will need to paste the access token into the **Connect to Github** input box and then click the blue **Connect** button:

Picking your GitHub organization

You will need to pick the GitHub organization that you belong to. In the screenshot that follows, I pick the GitHub username organization of `jbelmont`:

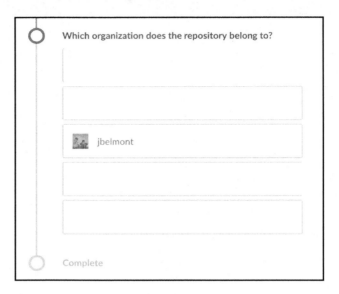

Picking the GitHub repository

The last step that you need to do is to actually pick the GitHub repository where you want to create the Jenkins pipeline. In the screenshot here, I entered `cucumber-examples` and picked the dropdown. Then the blue **Create Pipeline** button was enabled:

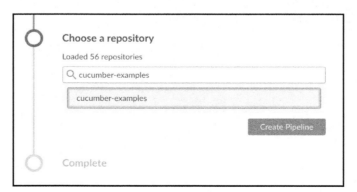

Creating a pipeline with the pipeline editor

In the GitHub repo that we have chosen, there is no existing Jenkinsfile and so we are redirected to the pipeline editor screen, where we can create our first Jenkinsfile:

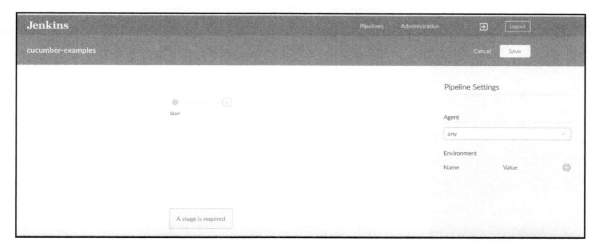

We need to add a Docker image for Node.js and for the agent, that looks similar to this:

Notice that we give an image and argument to mount a data volume using the −v option for Docker.

Next we click the gray plus button and we will see the following change:

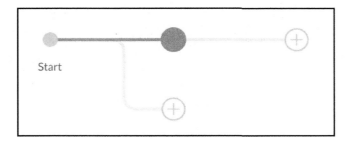

Next we click the blue **Add Step** button after we give the stage a name. For the purposes of this demo, we will chose **Build**:

Next we need to pick an option for the step. We will choose the option titled **Shell Script**, and this will install all of our Node.js dependencies:

Next we enter some commands to run in our **Shell Script**:

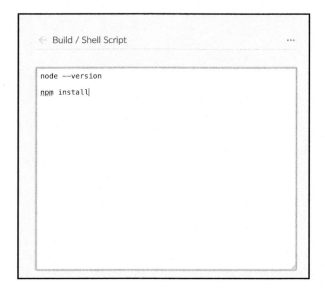

Next we will click the gray plus button again to add one more stage to our pipeline, that now looks similar to this:

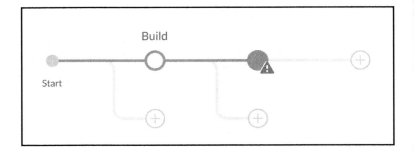

Next we will enter a name for this stage, and for the purposes of this chapter, we will choose Cucumber Tests:

Next we add a step for this stage, and we will once again pick **Shell Script** as an option:

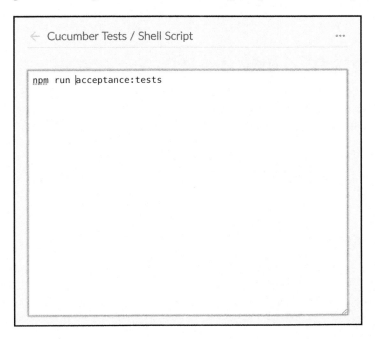

Lastly, we will click the **Save** button and provide a commit message so that this change gets pushed to our GitHub repository:

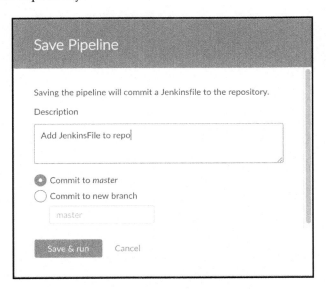

Once you click the blue **Save & run** button, the Jenkinsfile will be merged into the master branch and the pipeline will run.

Navigating in Jenkins Blue Ocean

Some of the views that you are accustomed to using in Jenkins Classic view are not available in Jenkins Blue Ocean. The main concept behind Jenkins Blue Ocean is to make navigation within Jenkins more accessible, and to improve the Jenkins UI in terms of better icons and page navigation. A lot of the inspiration for the new Jenkins UI is based on the book *Blue Ocean Strategy* that emphasizes that the world has moved on from functional developer tooling to developer experience and the new UI has aspired to improve the developer experience of Jenkins.

Pipelines view

The following screenshot depicts a pipeline view for Jenkins Blue Ocean. Note that we have two different pipelines for two different GitHub repositories. The second pipeline was created by clicking the **New Pipeline** button and adding a personal base64 (`https://github.com/jbelmont/decode-jwt`) Golang library that decodes JSON web tokens via a command-line tool:

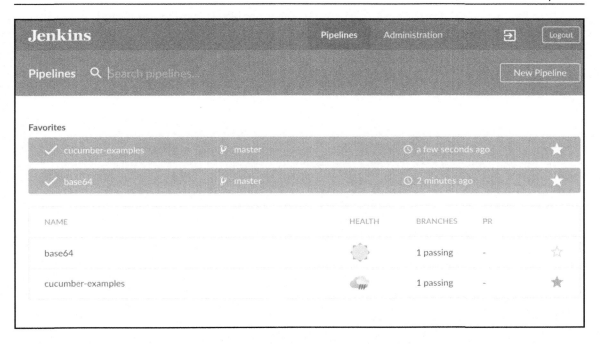

This list will be different depending on the number of pipelines that you have added to your Jenkins instance. Notice that you can star a pipeline and that there are columns labelled **NAME**, **HEALTH**, **BRANCHES**, and **PR**.

Pipeline detail view

If you click on an actual pipeline, then you will go into a pipeline details page that has all the details concerning all the stages run in your particular pipeline. The screenshot that follows is the base64 pipeline:

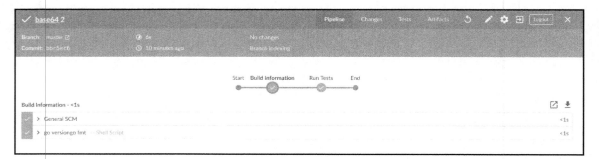

Pipeline build view

You can click on each node in the pipeline view and see the all work done for that stage. In the first screenshot, we clicked on the **Build Information** node to see the commands run in that particular stage, that encompass pulling down a fresh copy of the GitHub repository and running the `go version` and `go fmt` commands:

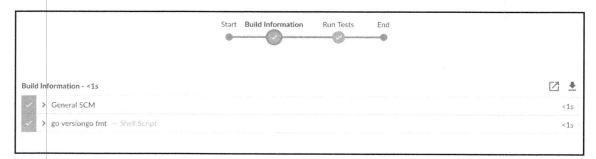

Notice that the second node is labeled **Run Tests**, and when we click that particular node, we only see the `go test` command, that runs our unit test cases in Golang:

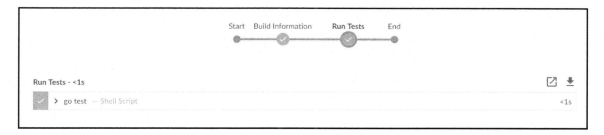

One of the great things about pipeline views is that you get a more crisp and better laid out visualizations for each stage in your continuous integration builds.

Pipeline stage view

If you click on an actual stage in the pipeline, that is depicted by the > symbol, it will show you a drop-down view with the details of that particular stage:

Notice that here we clicked on the **Run Tests** stage to see a report saying that our unit test case written in Golang passed.

Other views in Jenkins pipelines

There are other views that you can use, such as the **Pull Requests** view, that shows you all the open pull requests and a branch view as well:

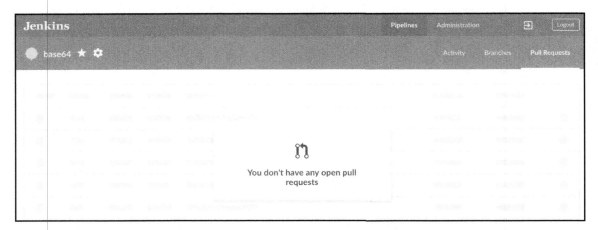

The Jenkins Blue Ocean view is still being worked on, so any administrative task such as adding plugins and adding security information are still done in the Jenkins Classic view.

Pipeline Syntax

The Pipeline Syntax has two forms (`https://jenkins.io/doc/book/pipeline/syntax/#declarative-pipeline`):

- Declarative Pipeline
- Scripted Pipeline

The difference between the two forms is that the Declarative Pipeline syntax is meant to be a simpler syntax than the Scripted Pipeline. The Scripted Pipeline syntax is a DSL, that follows the Groovy programming language semantics.

Pipeline Editor

In the *cucumber-examples* repository, we created a Jenkinsfile by using the Pipeline Editor. You can actually write the Jenkinsfile without using the Pipeline Editor, although I would recommend using it to debug a pipeline script as the editor has some nice features.

Jenkinsfile

Here we have the actual Pipeline Syntax that the pipeline editor created for us. It is using the Declarative Pipeline syntax and there are several items to discuss in this syntax:

```
pipeline {
  agent {
    docker {
      args '-v /Users/jean-marcelbelmont/jenkins_data'
      image 'node:10-alpine'
    }
  }
  stages {
    stage('Build') {
      steps {
        sh '''node --version

npm install'''
      }
    }
    stage('Cucumber Tests') {
      steps {
        sh 'npm run acceptance:tests'
      }
    }
  }
}
```

Pipeline keyword

All valid Declarative Pipelines must be enclosed within a pipeline block, as you can see in the preceding Jenkinsfile.

Agent keyword

The agent section specifies where the entire pipeline, or a specific stage, will execute in the Jenkins environment depending on where the agent section is placed. The section must be defined at the top level inside the pipeline block, but stage-level usage is optional.

Stages keyword

The stages keyword contains a sequence of one or more stage directives; the stages section is where the bulk of the work described by a pipeline will be located.

Pipeline Syntax documentation

If you are keen to read more about the Pipeline Syntax, then check out the documentation (`https://jenkins.io/doc/book/pipeline/syntax/`).

Summary

This chapter discussed how to get set up using the Jenkins Blue Ocean view in an existing Jenkins instance and how to set up the Blue Ocean view by using Docker. We looked at many different Jenkins Blue Ocean views and discussed some of the differences between them and the Jenkins Classic view. We also discussed the Pipeline Syntax and the Jenkinsfile. The next chapter will go over the installation and basic usage of Travis CI.

Questions

1. If you install Jenkins via Docker, can you use the Blue Ocean view?
2. Why is it useful to use the Pipeline Editor in the Blue Ocean view?
3. What are some differences between the Jenkins Classic view and the Blue Ocean view?
4. Can you look at each stage of a pipeline in detail?
5. Can the Blue Ocean view handle administrative tasks in Jenkins?
6. What is the stages syntax for?
7. Does the Declarative Pipeline syntax need to be wrapped in pipeline blocks?

Further reading

Please check out the book *Extending Jenkins* (`https://www.amazon.com/dp/B015CYBP2A`) from *Packt Publishing*, to learn more about Jenkins plugins.

Installation and Basics of Travis CI

9

This chapter will help you get set up with Travis **Continuous Integration (CI)**. We will explain the concept of app-embedded configuration for hosted solutions like Travis CI. We will also explain what a YAML configuration is and how to use it. We will look at the basics of using Travis CI and take some time to explore some of the differences between Travis CI and Jenkins, as well as Travis CI concepts. We will go over the different part of Travis CI including the syntax and the build life cycle, and look at real-world examples.

The following topics will be covered in this chapter:

- Travis CI introduction
- Travis CI prerequisites
- Adding a simple Travis CI YAML configuration script
- Travis CI script breakdown

Technical requirements

This chapter will require some basic programming skills and many of the CI concepts we have discussed in the earlier chapters will be utilized in this chapter. It will be helpful if you try to create a GitHub account and Travis CI account. You can follow the steps in the *Travis CI prerequisites* section. Some of the examples use Docker, which is a container technology, so it would be helpful if you have some understanding about containers and Docker. You will learn about the YAML syntax in this chapter. There are some commands in the chapter that use command-line applications, so it would be helpful to be familiar with command-line applications or CLIs.

Travis CI introduction

Travis CI is a hosted and automated solution for CI builds. Travis CI uses an in-application configuration file that uses YAML (`http://yaml.org/spec/1.2/spec.html`) syntax, which we will go over in more detail later in this chapter. Since Travis CI is hosted in the cloud, it therefore has the advantage that it can quickly be used in other environments and different operating systems without us worrying about setup and installation. This means that Travis CI setup is much faster than Jenkins.

Comparing Travis CI and Jenkins

Jenkins is a self-contained and open source automation server that is customizable and requires setup and configuration at the organization level. Remember, in the Jenkins CI chapters we spent some time installing Jenkins on Windows, Linux, and macOS. We also had the ability to configure Jenkins however we wanted. While this is great for software companies with dedicated teams in operations, DevOps and more, it is not as great for open source projects where often lone developers are setting up environments for their personal projects.

Travis CI was designed around the principle of open source development and for ease of use. Travis CI can be set up within minutes of creating a project in the GitHub. Although Travis CI is not as customizable as Jenkins CI in this respect, it has the distinct advantage of fast setup and use. Travis CI uses an in-application configuration file to accomplish this, however must be used with GitHub (`https://github.com/`) development platform at the moment, though perhaps it may be extended to other platforms such as Bitbucket (`https://bitbucket.org/dashboard/overview`) in the future, but this is still an open discussion.

Travis CI prerequisites

In order to get started with Travis CI, you will need to create a GitHub account, which you can do at GitHub (`https://github.com/`).

Creating a GitHub account

Look at the screenshot—all that you have to do is provide a **Username**, **Email**, and **Password**, then click the **Sign up for GitHub** button:

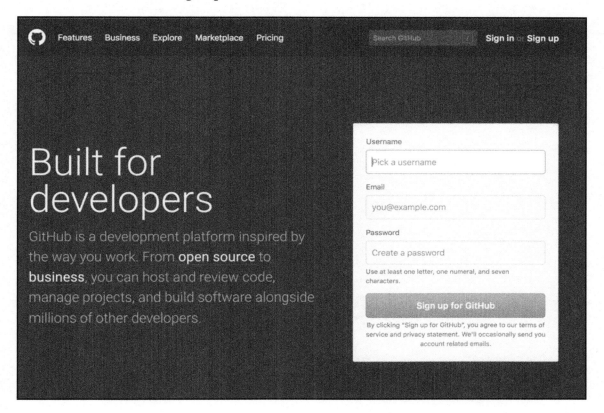

For the purposes of this chapter, we will create a GitHub username called `packtci`. Once you click the **Sign up for GitHub** button, you will be taken to the following page:

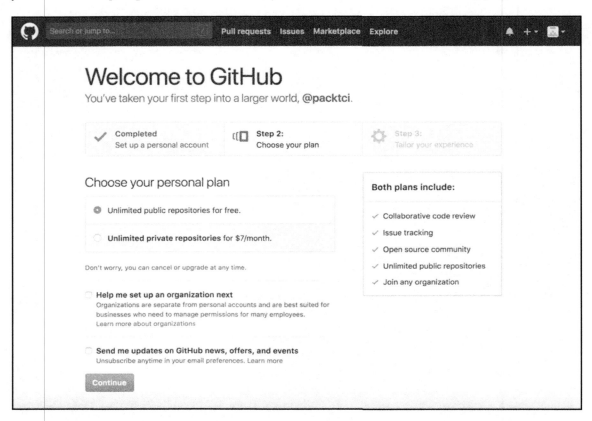

Notice here that you can create an unlimited amount of public repositories in GitHub for free, while private repositories require a monthly subscription fee. Once you click the **Continue** button you will be redirected to the following page:

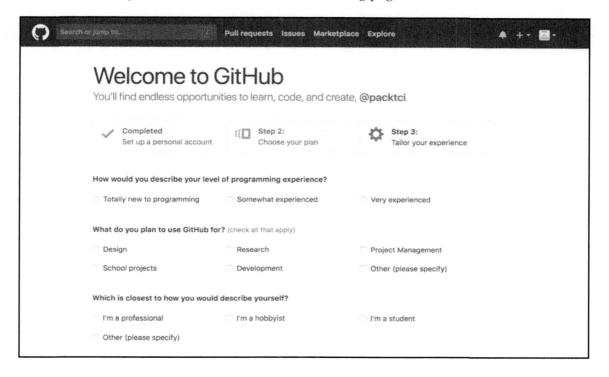

You can skip all of these options if you want by scrolling to the bottom of the page and clicking the **Skip this step** button. Once you click either the **Submit** button or the **Skip this step** button you will be taken to this page:

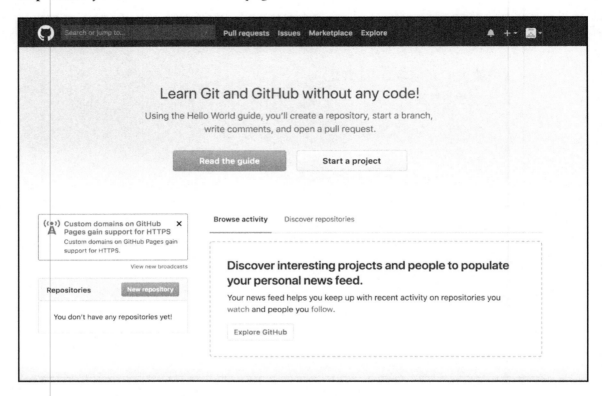

You should a receive an email from GitHub; look at the following screenshot:

You will need to click the link in order to verify your account in GitHub and then you should be all set up with your GitHub account.

Creating a Travis CI account

You will need to create a Travis CI account in order to get started with Travis CI. You will need to login with your GitHub login credentials. In the screenshot here, notice that you can click the **Sign Up** button or the **Sign in with GitHub** button:

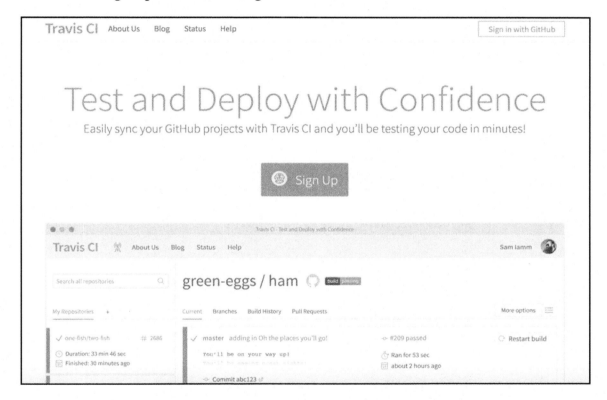

For the purposes of this chapter, I clicked the **Sign in with GitHub** button and then entered my login credentials for the GitHub account that I created with the username `packtci`. Once you enter your GitHub credentials, you will be redirected to the following page:

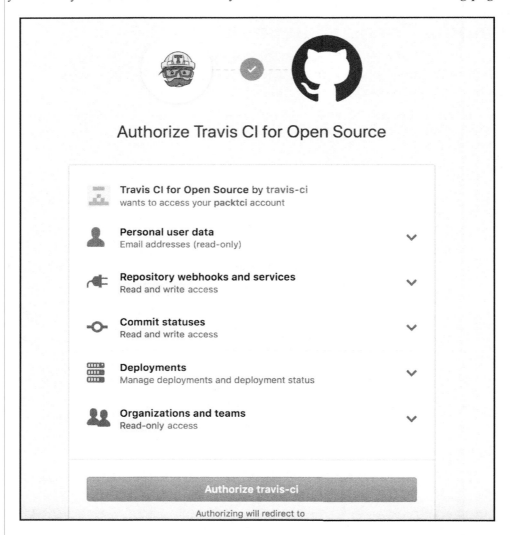

You will need to click the **Authorize travis-ci** button in order to finalize Travis CI setup. Once you click the **Authorize travis-ci** button, you will be redirected to the following page once Travis CI finishes the final setup steps:

Notice here that we have an API token for Travis CI which we will use utilize at a later time. We don't have any GitHub projects in this new account so none are shown. For the purposes of this chapter, I will create a GitHub project that runs some basic tests.

Adding an SSH Key to your new GitHub Account

In order to create a new GitHub repository, you will need add your SSH keys into your user account. If you don't have any SSH keys in your system they can be created with the following command:

```
↦  functional-summer git:(master) ssh-keygen -t rsa -b 4096 -C "example@example.com"
Generating public/private rsa key pair.
Enter file in which to save the key (                    /.ssh/id_rsa): /                    /.ssh/id_rsa_example
Enter passphrase (empty for no passphrase):
Enter same passphrase again:
Your identification has been saved in /                    /.ssh/id_rsa_example.
Your public key has been saved in /Users/jean-marcelbelmont/.ssh/id_rsa_example.pub.
The key fingerprint is:
SHA256:                              example@example.com
The key's randomart image is:
+---[RSA 4096]----+
|     **++..o.    |
|      ..o+0.o.+  |
|       ...+0.o.o. |
|       oo*ooo.o.  |
|      o So* ..ooo |
|      + . = o .Eo |
|     o o     . .*|
|      +        .. |
|      .          |
+----[SHA256]-----+
↦  functional-summer git:(master) █
```

Notice here that I provided an email address and specified a type of RSA which is a type of encryption algorithm. Once you run this command, it will create a public and private key on your system.

Once you have created SSH keys you simply need to upload the public key into GitHub. You need to copy the contents of the file; if you are using macOS you can run the following command to copy it to your system clipboard:

```
ssh-keygen -t rsa -b 4096 -C "myemail@someemailaddress.com"
# This command generates a file in the path that you pick in the
interactive prompt which in this case is ~/.ssh/id_rsa_example.pub

pbcopy < ~/.ssh/id_rsa_example.pub
```

You will need to go into the **Settings** page in GitHub:

Then you will need to click the following button in the **Settings** page:

Next you will need to click the **New SSH key** button and then provide a name and paste in the contents of your SSH key. In the following screenshot, I provided a name of Example SSH Key and then pasted in the contents of my public key:

You just need to click the **Add SSH key** button and then you are ready to commit changes to any of the repositories that you own in GitHub.

Adding a simple Travis CI YAML configuration script

I created a sample GitHub repository that you can see at functional summer at Github (`https://github.com/packtci/functional-summer`). This repository is a Node.js project that has a `package.json` script, a file called `summer.js` and a test file called `summer_test.js`. We will add configuration for Travis CI in a file called `.travis.yml` at the root of the repository. This configuration script will do a couple of things. First, it will notify Travis CI that we are running a Node.js project and then it will install the dependencies for the project, and last it will run the tests specified in the CI build.

Travis CI YML script contents

We will first create a file called `.travis.yml` at the root of the repository and then copy the following contents into this file:

```
language: node_js

node_js:
    - "6.14.1"

install:
    - npm install

script: npm test
```

We will go into much more detail about each entry of this YML script but essentially what we are saying to Travis CI is that this a Node.js project and we want to Travis CI to use node version 6.14.1 in the CI build, then install all the dependencies required for the project using the **npm package manager** and then finally to run all of the tests using the `npm test` script command. I will commit this change into the `functional-summer` repository and then we will see how to toggle on Travis CI for this project.

Adding a Github repository into your Travis CI account

The first step is that you must go to `https://travis-ci.org/` and then provide your login credentials for your GitHub account. Then go to your profile page by clicking your avatar in the upper-right corner of the screen, which looks like this:

Next I have added a screenshot detailing the steps to add a new repository into Travis CI:

Notice that in the screenshot I added a text block saying that the first step is to click the **Sync account** button which is necessary so that Travis CI will see any new repositories that you have added into your GitHub account. Once Travis CI has synced your account then should be able to see your repository in your account. Depending on how many projects you already have, you may need to filter by your repository name to find your project. The next step is to toggle the slider with your repository name, as the screenshot depicts.

In the following screenshot, we have toggled on the `functional-summer` repository on the Travis UI now and now we can simply click the row to go into this newly added Travis CI build job:

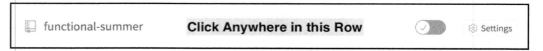

Once you click the row you be redirected to the following page in Travis CI:

We do not have any builds that have been triggered yet but Travis CI has some default settings that are set. If you commit changes onto any pushed branches or you open a pull request in GitHub, Travis CI will kick off a build. Let us commit a minor change to the `functional-summer` repository which will trigger a build in Travis CI. If you click the **Build History** tab you will notice that a build has been created with a Git commit change:

Travis CI job log

You can click the build job item on the left of the Travis CI screen which looks like this:

Alternatively, you can click the **Current** tab to see the currently executing job for the configured repository. In order to see the job log, you need to scroll down to the **Job Log** tab and see the running commands in the Travis CI build, which for the `functional-summer` repository look like this:

Remember that in the `.travis.yml` script that we added to GitHub we specified four things:

1. At the top of the `.yml` script we specified a language of Node.js
2. We specified version 6.14.1 of Node.js
3. We ran `npm install` command to install all the dependencies for a project
4. Finally, we ran `npm test` command

You can confirm that these steps were run in the **Job Log**. Notice that in the previous screenshot, there are right arrow links that expand into further details on each command in the CI build.

Travis CI script breakdown

Now that we have gone over YAML syntax, we can explain in more detail the various parts of the Travis CI script.

Select a programming language

```
language: go
```

In this block of the `.travis.yml` script we add the programming language that we will be using in the continuous integration build. This is usually the first entry in the `.travis.yml` script that you add.

Travis CI supports many programming languages such as:

- C
- C++
- JavaScript with Node.js
- Elixir
- Go
- Haskell
- Ruby

You can look at languages (`https://docs.travis-ci.com/user/languages`) in the Travis CI docs for a complete list of supported programming languages.

Selecting infrastructure

You can set a more customized environment in Travis CI by using the `sudo` and `dist` fields in the YML script.

Virtual image with Ubuntu Precise (12.04) infrastructure

You can use Ubuntu Precise infrastructure by using the following entries in the Travis YML script:

```
sudo: enabled
dist: precise
```

Default infrastructure

You can explicitly set the default infrastructure which is a containerized Ubuntu 14.04 environment by adding this entry:

```
sudo: false
```

This is not necessary to do as you can just set the language and the default infrastructure will be done for you.

Virtual Image with Ubuntu Trusty (14.04) infrastructure

You can use Ubuntu Trusty infrastructure by using the following entries in the Travis YML script:

```
sudo: enabled
dist: trusty
```

Container based infrastructure

You can use container based infrastructure by using the following entries in the Travis YML script:

```
sudo: false
dist: trusty
```

Notice here that we explicitly set sudo privileges to false and use Ubuntu Trusty.

macOS infrastructure

You can use macOS infrastructure by using the following entry in the Travis YML script:

```
os: osx
```

Build customization

In Travis CI, you can customize the build in a variety of ways and we will start by explaining the build life cycle.

The build life cycle

A build in Travis CI is made up of two steps:

- **Install**: Install any dependencies required. We saw this step in the install block of the YML script.
- **Script**: Run the build script. This can be a series of scripts that are run.

before_install step

This step is formally called the **before_install** step and it is where you install any additional dependencies in your CI build and where you get custom services initiated.

install step

We have already seen this step in action; in the **install** step you install any dependencies needed for the CI build to run correctly.

before_script step

In the **before_script** step you specify any commands that need to be executed before your script block can execute correctly. For example, you may have a PostgreSQL (https://www.postgresql.org/) database and need to seed the database before you run any of your tests.

script step

In the **script** step, you execute any commands which are central to a healthy code base. For example, it is common to run any tests you have in your code base, to lint the code base. A linter or lint tool is a tool that analyzes a code base to find any programming related errors, software bugs, style errors, or any code that may have **code smells**.

after_script step

In the **after_script** step you execute any commands that are helpful such as reporting and analytics. You may need to publish a code coverage report or create a report on metrics in the code base.

List of build life cycle

Here is the complete life cycle for Travis CI:

- Optional install: **apt addons**
- Optional install: **cache components**
- **before_install**
- **install**
- **before_script**
- **script**
- Optional: **before_cache**
- **after_success** or **after_failure**
- **before_deploy**
- **deploy**
- **after_deploy**
- **after_script**

Build failure behavior

If an error occurs in the before_install, install, or before_script life cycle events then the CI build will immediately error out and the CI build will stop.

If an error occurs in the script life cycle event then the build will fail but the CI build will continue to run.

If an error occurs in the after_success, after_failure, after_script, and after_deploy life cycle events then the build will not be marked as a failure but if any of these life cycle events results in a timeout then the build will be marked as a failure.

Installing a secondary programming language for a CI build

You can easily install another programming language in the CI build by adding an entry into the **before_install** life cycle event. It is best to specify your primary language and then a secondary language.

Example Travis CI YML script with multiple languages

In the Travis CI YML script here, we specify Go version 1.10 as the primary programming language and then Node.js as the secondary language. We install Node.js dependencies in the before_install life cycle event and then we run a Golang test followed by a Node.js test:

```
language: go

go:
    - "1.10"

env:
    - NODE_VERSION="6"

before_install:
    - nvm install $NODE_VERSION

install:
    - npm install

script:
    - go test
    - npm test
```

If you would like to further explore this example, then check out the `multiple-languages` repository (`https://github.com/packtci/multiple-languages`).

Docker in Travis CI

Docker can be utilized in Travis CI and the only step required to enable Docker is to add the following entry into your Travis CI YML script:

```
sudo: required

services:
    - docker
```

 Notice here that we added an entry into the `services` block and we added a list entry of Docker.

Example Travis CI YML script with a Dockerfile

In the Travis YML script here, we are specifying `sudo` privileges, a programming language of Golang, then we are specifying the Docker service, pulling down a custom Docker image of `jbelmont/print-average:1.0` and then running the Docker container and removing it:

```
sudo: required

language: go

services:
    - docker

before_install:
    - docker pull jbelmont/print-average:1.0

script:
    - docker run --rm jbelmont/print-average:1.0
```

I have added a screenshot of the Travis CI build for your reference:

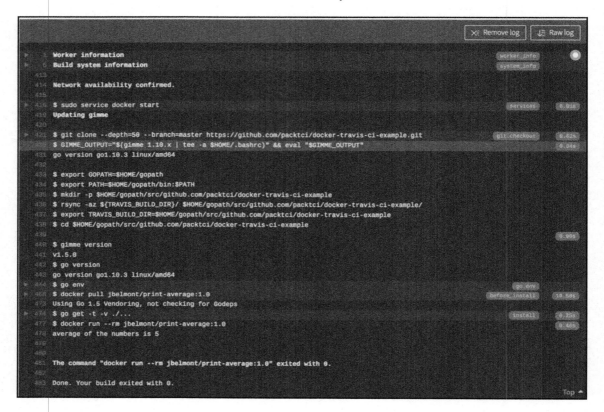

Notice that Docker is running in the CI build because we specified Docker as a service to be run in Travis CI. When we run the Docker container, it prints out the average computed in the `main.go` in the `docker-travis-ci-example` repository (https://github.com/packtci/docker-travis-ci-example). You can check out my Docker image at Docker Hub (https://hub.docker.com/r/jbelmont/print-average/).

GUI and headless browsers in Travis CI

You can run headless browsers in Travis CI in a couple of ways. You can utilize an X Virtual Framebuffer, or XVFB in short form, which you can read more about in the XVFB docs (https://www.x.org/archive/X11R7.6/doc/man/man1/Xvfb.1.xhtml). We will look at using headless chrome with Puppeteer (https://pptr.dev/), which is a library developed by Google that provides a high level API to work with headless Chrome.

Example Travis yml script with headless Chrome, Puppeteer, and the Jest Testing Library

In the Travis YML script here, we have set a number of different actions in the Travis CI build. First, we set the language to node_js, then we set the version of node_js to 8.11, then we set a new property called dist: trusty which set the Travis CI environment to Ubuntu 14.04, which is called **Trusty**. We then use the add-ons block to add the latest stable Chrome version. We then get the stable version of Google Chrome running on the CI build on port 9222, and then we use the cache block so that node_modules is cached on each CI build run. Then we install our Node.js dependencies and finally we run the Node.js tests using the Jest library:

```
language: node_js

node_js:
 - "8.11"

dist: trusty

sudo: false

addons:
 chrome: stable

before_install:
 - google-chrome-stable --headless --disable-gpu --remote-debugging-port=9222 http://localhost &

cache:
 directories:
 - node_modules

install:
 - npm install

script:
 - npm test
```

In this first screenshot, notice the section where we start running `google-chrome` in `headless` mode in the Travis CI build and then install the dependencies:

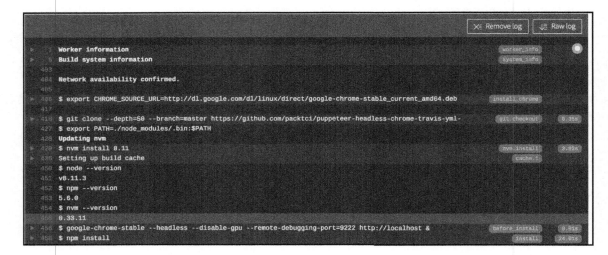

In this second screenshot, we run the tests using the Google Chrome Puppeteer library. Notice that the build runs with an exit status of `0` and finishes successfully:

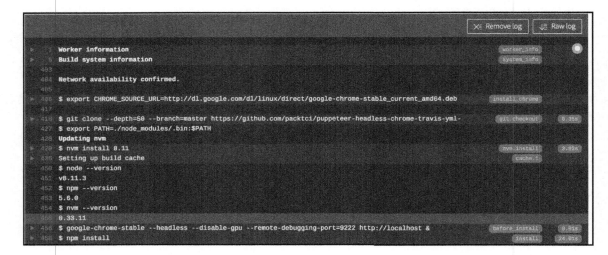

You can find this Travis CI build at `https://travis-ci.org/packtci/puppeteer-headless-chrome-travis-yml-script/jobs/395882388#L70` and you can find the source code for this repository at `https://github.com/packtci/puppeteer-headless-chrome-travis-yml-script` and at GitHub.

Summary

We have gone over many aspects of Travis CI in this chapter, including the differences between Travis CI and Jenkins. We went over some prerequisite actions in order to get Travis CI set up and learned to add an SSH key to your GitHub account. We then explained the Travis CI build job and went over the YAML syntax in detail. We then explored many real-world examples of Travis YML scripts and explained the build life cycle in Travis CI and went over different aspects such as initiating services such as Docker and their uses in Travis CI.

In the next chapter, we will go over all of the Travis CLI commands, explain how to get Travis CLI installed on Linux, macOS, and Windows, and go over automating tasks like encrypting credentials using the Travis CLI commands.

Questions

1. What is the primary difference between Jenkins and Travis CI?
2. Can Travis CI work in Bitbucket?
3. How do you add new repositories to Travis CI?
4. What is a scalar variable in YAML?
5. What is a list in YAML?
6. Why are anchors useful in YAMl?
7. Is it possible to use a secondary programming language in a Travis CI build?
8. How would you use docker in a Travis CI build?

Further reading

You can further explore concepts in Travis CI by looking at the user documentation at the Travis CI website (`https://docs.travis-ci.com/`).

10
Travis CI CLI Commands and Automation

In the previous chapter, we showed you how to configure Travis CI in a software project and explained the basics of how to use Travis CI. This chapter will help you get Travis CLI installed on your operating system and we will go over all the different types of commands in Travis CI, such as the general API commands, repository commands, and more. We will go over the different options that the CLI commands can use and we will also go over the meaning of each command in detail. We will also take a look at working with the Travis API directly by using our access token and the curl REST client. We will briefly look at the Travis Pro and Enterprise versions as well.

The following topics will be covered in this chapter:

- Travis CLI installation
- Travis CLI commands

Technical requirements

This chapter will require some basic Unix programming skills and knowledge about using a command-line terminal application. If you are in a Windows OS then consider using either the Command Prompt or the PowerShell application. If you are on the macOS operating system then use the Terminal application that is installed for you by default. If you are using Linux, then you should already have a Terminal installed or available.

Travis CLI installation

The first prerequisite to install Travis CLI is to have Ruby (https://www.ruby-lang.org/en/documentation/installation/) installed on your OS and make sure that it is version 1.9.3 or greater.

You can check that you have Ruby installed by running the following command in a command shell or Terminal:

```
↦ ~ ruby -v
ruby 2.4.1p111 (2017-03-22 revision 58053) [x86_64-darwin17]
↦ ~
```

Windows installation

The Travis CLI user documentation at https://github.com/travis-ci/travis.rb#windows recommends that you use the RubyInstaller (http://rubyinstaller.org/) to install the latest version of Ruby on the Windows OS.

We need to pick Ruby Devkit version 2.5.1 at the RubyInstaller download site and then make sure to accept the license agreement and then choose the appropriate options for the installation. Make sure to install the development toolchain.

When the installer window closes, a Command Prompt will open and you will need to pick an option; you can just hit enter to install all three options on your system. The installation process could take a while to finish. Mine took about 20 minutes to update GPG keys and to install other dependencies required for the Ruby programming language:

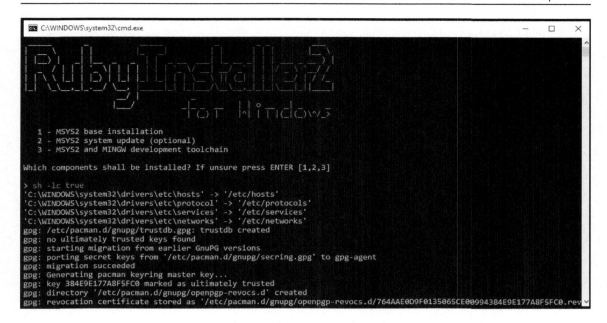

Here that we have Ruby version 2.5.1 installed on our system as we would expect:

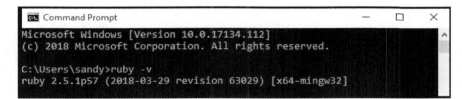

In this step, we install Travis RubyGems in the Windows Command Prompt:

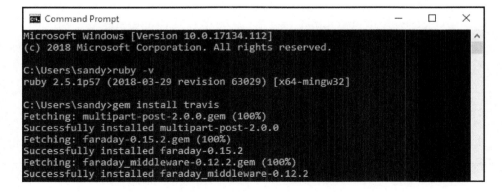

In this last step, we verify that Travis CLI RubyGem is installed on our system; it reports version 1.8.8:

```
C:\Users\sandy>travis version
1.8.8
```

Linux installation

The Linux OS has multiple different package managers, so how you install Ruby on your system is dependent on your particular Linux OS. We will look at installing Ruby and Travis CLI on Ubuntu 14.04 in a DigitalOcean server:

1. To install Ruby on Ubuntu, run the following commands:

   ```
   sudo apt-get install python-software-properties
   sudo apt-add-repository ppa:brightbox/ruby-ng
   sudo apt-get update
   sudo apt-get install ruby2.1 ruby-switch
   sudo ruby-switch --set ruby2.1
   ```

2. Next, confirm that Ruby is installed by running the following command:

   ```
   root@ubuntu-s-2vcpu-4gb-nyc1-01:~# ruby -v
   ruby 2.1.9p495 (2017-12-15 revision 54437) [x86_64-linux-gnu]
   root@ubuntu-s-2vcpu-4gb-nyc1-01:~#
   ```

3. Next we need to install the Travis CLI RubyGem with the following command:

   ```
   gem install travis -v 1.8.8 --no-rdoc --no-ri
   ```

4. The last step is to check that Travis CLI is installed with the following command:

   ```
   travis version
   1.8.8
   ```

macOS installation

You need to install the Xcode Command Line tools, which you can do so with the following command:

```
xcode-select --install
```

If you already have the Xcode Command Line tools installed, you will see the following information displayed in the Terminal:

```
↦ travis-init-command git:(master) xcode-select --install
xcode-select: error: command line tools are already installed, use "Software Update" to install updates
↦ travis-init-command git:(master) ▊
```

Ruby comes preinstalled on current macOS operating system, so you only need to run the following command to install Travis CLI:

```
↦ multiple-languages git:(master) sudo gem install travis
Password:
Successfully installed travis-1.8.8
Parsing documentation for travis-1.8.8
Done installing documentation for travis after 1 seconds
1 gem installed
↦ multiple-languages git:(master) ▊
```

 Here I used `sudo` because I needed elevated administrator privileges to install RubyGem.

You will know that Travis CLI is installed if you see this message in your Terminal:

```
↦ multiple-languages git:(master) travis version
1.8.8
↦ multiple-languages git:(master) ▊
```

 Here that I am using Travis CLI version `1.8.8` but your particular version could be different.

Travis CLI commands

The Travis CLI is fully featured, with the Travis API (https://github.com/travis-ci/travis-api) in GitHub and has CLI commands that come in the following three different forms:

- **Non-API commands**:
    - Non-API commands documentation (https://github.com/travis-ci/travis.rb#non-api-commands)
    - These commands include help and version and do not directly hit the Travis CI API
- **General API commands**:
    - General API commands documentation (https://github.com/travis-ci/travis.rb#general-api-commands)
    - These commands directly hit the Travis API and inherit all options from the non-API commands
- **Repository commands**:
    - Repository commands documentation (https://github.com/travis-ci/travis.rb#repository-commands)
    - These commands have all the options that General API commands have and additionally you can specify the repo owner/name to talk to

The Travis CLI library is written in the Ruby programming language and if you want to directly interface with it, be prepared to read more about in the *Ruby Library* section at GitHub (https://github.com/travis-ci/travis.rb#ruby-library).

We will be using the packtci GitHub (https://github.com/packtci) user that we created in Chapter 9, *Installation and Basics of Travis CI* in *Creating a GitHub account* section and the packtci Travis CI account that we created in Chapter 9, *Installation and Basics of Travis CI* in *Creating a Travis CI account* section.

Non-API commands

The non-API Travis CLI commands include the help and the version commands. These commands do not directly hit the Travis API but instead print out useful information about the Travis CLI.

Printing help information

The `help` command will display the arguments and options that a particular command takes.

In the following screenshot, we run the `travis help` command in a command-line Terminal:

```
↳ multiple-languages git:(master) travis help
Usage: travis COMMAND ...

Available commands:

        accounts       displays accounts and their subscription status
        branches       displays the most recent build for each branch
        cache          lists or deletes repository caches
        cancel         cancels a job or build
        console        interactive shell
        disable        disables a project
        enable         enables a project
        encrypt        encrypts values for the .travis.yml
        encrypt-file   encrypts a file and adds decryption steps to .travis.yml
        endpoint       displays or changes the API endpoint
        env            show or modify build environment variables
        help           helps you out when in dire need of information
        history        displays a projects build history
        init           generates a .travis.yml and enables the project
        lint           display warnings for a .travis.yml
        login          authenticates against the API and stores the token
        logout         deletes the stored API token
        logs           streams test logs
        monitor        live monitor for what's going on
        open           opens a build or job in the browser
        pubkey         prints out a repository's public key
        raw            makes an (authenticated) API call and prints out the result
        report         generates a report useful for filing issues
        repos          lists repositories the user has certain permissions on
        requests       lists recent requests
        restart        restarts a build or job
        settings       access repository settings
        setup          sets up an addon or deploy target
        show           displays a build or job
        sshkey         checks, updates or deletes an SSH key
        status         checks status of the latest build
        sync           triggers a new sync with GitHub
        token          outputs the secret API token
        version        outputs the client version
        whatsup        lists most recent builds
        whoami         outputs the current user

run `/usr/local/bin/travis help COMMAND` for more infos
↳ multiple-languages git:(master) █
```

If you want to get help on a particular command, then you simply need to use `travis help COMMAND`.

The following is a screenshot with more information about the whoami command in Travis:

```
↦ multiple-languages git:(master) travis help whoami
Outputs the current user.
Usage: travis whoami [OPTIONS]
    -h, --help                    Display help
    -i, --[no-]interactive        be interactive and colorful
    -E, --[no-]explode            don't rescue exceptions
        --skip-version-check      don't check if travis client is up to date
        --skip-completion-check   don't check if auto-completion is set up
    -e, --api-endpoint URL        Travis API server to talk to
    -I, --[no-]insecure           do not verify SSL certificate of API endpoint
        --pro                     short-cut for --api-endpoint 'https://api.travis-ci.com/'
        --org                     short-cut for --api-endpoint 'https://api.travis-ci.org/'
        --staging                 talks to staging system
    -t, --token [ACCESS_TOKEN]    access token to use
        --debug                   show API requests
        --debug-http              show HTTP(S) exchange
    -X, --enterprise [NAME]       use enterprise setup (optionally takes name for multiple setups)
        --adapter ADAPTER         Faraday adapter to use for HTTP requests
↦ multiple-languages git:(master) ▊
```

Printing version information

The version command displays the current Travis CLI client that is installed on the system. The following screenshot displays the current client version of 1.8.8 for Travis CLI:

```
↦ multiple-languages git:(master) travis version
1.8.8
↦ multiple-languages git:(master) ▊
```

API commands

The API commands directly hit the Travis API, and some require that you have a proper access token which you can get by using the travis login command.

Logging in to Travis CI

The login command is typically the first command that you will need to use in order to work with the Travis API as it authenticates you with the Travis API.

The `login` command will ask you for your GitHub username and password, but does not send these credentials to Travis CI. Instead it uses your username and password to create a GitHub API token and then shows the token to Travis API and then run a series of checks to make sure that you are who you say you are. It then gives you an access token for the Travis API in return, and finally the Travis Client will delete the GitHub token again. All of these steps occur under the hood once you successfully run the `travis login` command.

The following screenshot shows where we try to run the `travis accounts` commands, and it notifies us that we we need to be logged in:

```
→  multiple-languages git:(master) travis accounts
not logged in, please run travis login
→  multiple-languages git:(master)
```

In the following screenshot, we run the `travis login` command and provide the GitHub username and password:

```
→  multiple-languages git:(master) travis login
We need your GitHub login to identify you.
This information will not be sent to Travis CI, only to api.github.com.
The password will not be displayed.

Try running with --github-token or --auto if you don't want to enter your password anyway.

Username: packtci
Password for packtci: ********************************stty: 'standard input': unable to perform all requested operations

Successfully logged in as packtci!
→  multiple-languages git:(master)
```

Now we have successfully logged in to the Travis CI system and Travis CI has issued us an access token.

Displaying the current access token

The `token` command is useful to display the current access token. The screenshot has an access token that has been greyed out for security purposes:

```
→  multiple-languages git:(master) travis token
Your access token is
→  multiple-languages git:(master)
```

Logging out of Travis CI

The logout command will log you out of Travis CI and remove your access token.

Notice in the following screenshot that after we initiated the travis logout command, the travis token command shows that we need to log back in:

```
↦  multiple-languages git:(master) travis logout
Successfully logged out!
↦  multiple-languages git:(master) travis token
not logged in, please run travis login
↦  multiple-languages git:(master) 
```

We will need to log back in to Travis CI in order to get a token again. In the following screenshot, we log back in to Travis and then get another access token so that we can issue commands to Travis API:

```
↦  multiple-languages git:(master) travis login
We need your GitHub login to identify you.
This information will not be sent to Travis CI, only to api.github.com.
The password will not be displayed.

Try running with --github-token or --auto if you don't want to enter your password anyway.

Username: packtci
Password for packtci: ********************************
Successfully logged in as packtci!
↦  multiple-languages git:(master) travis token
Your access token is ▮▮▮▮▮▮▮▮▮▮▮▮▮▮▮▮▮
↦  multiple-languages git:(master) 
```

Displaying accounts information

The accounts command is used to list all the accounts that you can set up repositories for. Remember that when we ran this command earlier, Travis informed us that we needed to log in to Travis to execute this command. In the following screenshot, Travis informs us that we are subscribed to four different repositories in Travis:

```
↦  multiple-languages git:(master) travis accounts
packtci (Packtci): subscribed, 4 repositories
```

Displaying help information for Travis commands

Remember that we can find all the options for a particular command in Travis by running the following command:

```
travis help
```

In the following screenshot, we run the `help` command for the `accounts` command:

```
↳  multiple-languages git:(master) travis help accounts
Displays accounts and their subscription status.
Usage: travis accounts [OPTIONS]
    -h, --help                        Display help
    -i, --[no-]interactive            be interactive and colorful
    -E, --[no-]explode                don't rescue exceptions
        --skip-version-check          don't check if travis client is up to date
        --skip-completion-check       don't check if auto-completion is set up
    -e, --api-endpoint URL            Travis API server to talk to
    -I, --[no-]insecure               do not verify SSL certificate of API endpoint
        --pro                         short-cut for --api-endpoint 'https://api.travis-ci.com/'
        --org                         short-cut for --api-endpoint 'https://api.travis-ci.org/'
        --staging                     talks to staging system
    -t, --token [ACCESS_TOKEN]        access token to use
        --debug                       show API requests
        --debug-http                  show HTTP(S) exchange
    -X, --enterprise [NAME]           use enterprise setup (optionally takes name for multiple setups)
        --adapter ADAPTER             Faraday adapter to use for HTTP requests
↳  multiple-languages git:(master) 
```

There is an option called `--debug` which we will use to debug the HTTP request made to the Travis API. In the following screenshot we get additional information about the request made to Travis, such as the endpoint hit which is GET "accounts/" {:all=>true} as well as other information:

```
↳  multiple-languages git:(master) travis accounts --debug
** Loading "/Users/jean-marcelbelmont/.travis/config.yml"
** GET "accounts/" {:all=>true}
**     took 0.13 seconds
packtci (Packtci): subscribed, 4 repositories
** Storing "/Users/jean-marcelbelmont/.travis/config.yml"
↳  multiple-languages git:(master) 
```

Interactive console session

The console command drops you into an interactive Ruby session with all the entities imported into global namespaces, as well as making sure that you are authenticated with Travis and if you are setting correct. In the following screenshot I pressed *Tab* and got auto-completion in the console session:

Also notice that the current logged-in user is packtci.

Printing API endpoint Information

The endpoint command prints out the API endpoint that we are using. Notice that we are using the free and open source version of Travis API in the screenshot:

The PRO version of Travis uses the following endpoint at https://api.travis-ci.com/.

Conducting live monitoring with all the CI builds that are currently running

The travis monitor command will conduct live monitoring for all the CI builds in the logged-in account. In the following screenshot, there is no activity occurring in Travis CI at the moment:

```
┌→ multiple-languages git:(master) travis monitor
Monitoring travis-ci.org:
█
```

Let us add a unit test case for the `puppeteer-headless-chrome-travis-yml-script` repo (https://github.com/packtci/puppeteer-headless-chrome-travis-yml-script) and then push this change into the GitHub version control system. In the the following screenshot, we push up a change into the repository:

```
┌→ puppeteer-headless-chrome-travis-yml-script git:(master) x git add .
┌→ puppeteer-headless-chrome-travis-yml-script git:(master) x git log
┌→ puppeteer-headless-chrome-travis-yml-script git:(master) x git commit -m 'Add another test case into blog test.'
[master b7e91db] Add another test case into blog test.
 2 files changed, 10 insertions(+), 1 deletion(-)
┌→ puppeteer-headless-chrome-travis-yml-script git:(master) git push
Username for 'https://github.com': packtci
Password for 'https://packtci@github.com':
Counting objects: 4, done.
Delta compression using up to 8 threads.
Compressing objects: 100% (4/4), done.
Writing objects: 100% (4/4), 531 bytes | 531.00 KiB/s, done.
Total 4 (delta 3), reused 0 (delta 0)
remote: Resolving deltas: 100% (3/3), completed with 3 local objects.
To https://github.com/packtci/puppeteer-headless-chrome-travis-yml-script.git
   e838fc0..b7e91db  master -> master
┌→ puppeteer-headless-chrome-travis-yml-script git:(master) █
```

Now if we go back into the Terminal session where the Travis monitor is running, we will see that a build has been initiated and then it is passed:

```
┌→ multiple-languages git:(master) travis monitor
Monitoring travis-ci.org:
2018-06-29 12:19:01 packtci/puppeteer-headless-chrome-travis-yml-script#2 started Add another test case into blog test.
2018-06-29 12:19:01 packtci/puppeteer-headless-chrome-travis-yml-script#2.1 started Add another test case into blog test.
2018-06-29 12:19:56 packtci/puppeteer-headless-chrome-travis-yml-script#2 passed Add another test case into blog test.
2018-06-29 12:19:56 packtci/puppeteer-headless-chrome-travis-yml-script#2.1 passed Add another test case into blog test.
█
```

> We have a build job of `2.1`; in the `.travis.yml` file we did not specify any other build jobs so Travis CI bundled all of the build jobs into one build job.

You can read more about Travis CI build stages at https://docs.travis-ci.com/user/build-stages/.

Initiating a Travis CI API call

You can initiate a direct API call to the Travis API by using the `travis raw RESOURCE` command. Remember that we can always use the `travis help COMMAND` to find out how to use a particular command in Travis CLI. In the following screenshot, we run the `help` command for the `raw` command:

```
↳  multiple-languages git:(master) travis help raw
Makes an (authenticated) API call and prints out the result.
Usage: travis raw RESOURCE [OPTIONS]
    -h, --help                    Display help
    -i, --[no-]interactive        be interactive and colorful
    -E, --[no-]explode            don't rescue exceptions
        --skip-version-check      don't check if travis client is up to date
        --skip-completion-check   don't check if auto-completion is set up
    -e, --api-endpoint URL        Travis API server to talk to
    -I, --[no-]insecure           do not verify SSL certificate of API endpoint
        --pro                     short-cut for --api-endpoint 'https://api.travis-ci.com/'
        --org                     short-cut for --api-endpoint 'https://api.travis-ci.org/'
        --staging                 talks to staging system
    -t, --token [ACCESS_TOKEN]    access token to use
        --debug                   show API requests
        --debug-http              show HTTP(S) exchange
    -X, --enterprise [NAME]       use enterprise setup (optionally takes name for multiple setups)
        --adapter ADAPTER         Faraday adapter to use for HTTP requests
        --[no-]json               display as json
↳  multiple-languages git:(master) █
```

Now that we know how to run the `raw` command, let us issue a request to this endpoint in the Travis API:

```
GET /config
```

If you want to see the developer documentation for the Travis API, then you need to go to the following URL at `https://developer.travis-ci.com/`.

Make sure to log in and authorize Travis CI as a third-party application for GitHub. In the following screenshot, we authorize Travis CI for the `packtci` GitHub user:

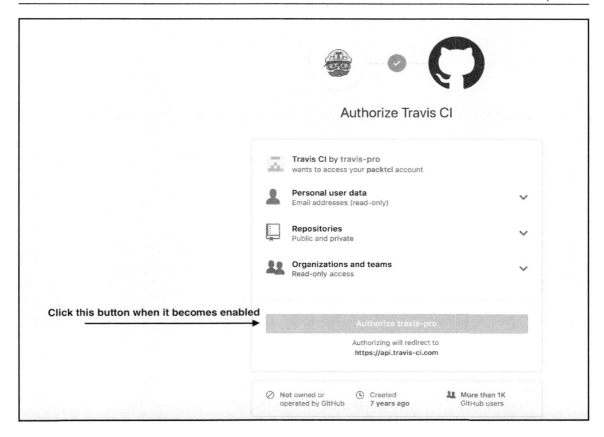

You can then view the API documentation for Travis CI at the URL: `https://developer.travis-ci.com/`. In the following screenshot, we make a GET request to the `/config` endpoint and use the following two different options in the `raw` command:

- `--json`
- `--debug`

```
↪ multiple-languages git:(master) travis raw /config --json --debug
** Loading
** GET "config"
** took 0.25 seconds
{"config":{"host":"travis-ci.org","shorten_host":"trvs.io","assets":{"host":"travis-ci.org"},"pusher":{"key":"5df8ac576dcccf4fd076"},"github":{"api_url":"htt
ps://api.github.com","scopes":["read:org","user:email","repo_deployment","repo:status","write:repo_hook"]},"notifications":{"webhook":{"public_key":"-----BEG
IN PUBLIC KEY-----\nMIIBIjANBgkqhkiG9w0BAQEFAAOCAQ8AMIIBCgKCAQEAvtjdLkS+FP+0fPC09j25\ny/PiuYDDivIT86COVedvlElk99B8YTrqNaJybxjXbIZlO6xFNhOY+iTcBr4E1zJu\ntizF3
Xi0V9tOuP/M8Wn4Y/1lCWbQKlWrNQuqNBmhovF4K3mDCYswVbpgTmp+JQYu\nBm9QMdieZMNry5s6aiMA9a5jDlNyedvS8NYo18F+NYg1J0C0JiPYTxheCb4optrl\n5xNzFKhAkuGs4XTOA5C7Q06GCKtDNf
44s/CVE30KODUxBi0MCKaxiXw/yy55zxXZ\n/YdGphIyQiA5i01986ZmZCLLW8udz9uhW5jUr3Jlp9LbmphAC61bVSf4ou2YsJaN\n0OIDAQAB\n-----END PUBLIC KEY-----"}}}
** Storing "/Users/jean-marcelbelmont/.travis/config.yml"
↪ multiple-languages git:(master) █
```

At some point in the near future, the Travis API plans on deprecating the V2 API and only the V3 API will be officially supported. You can use the API Explorer to make REST calls into the V3 API:

```
GET /owner/{owner.login}
```

In the following screenshot we make a REST call to the following endpoint using the API Explorer:

```
curl -H "Travis-API-Version: 3" -H "User-Agent: API Explorer" \
  -H "Authorization: token ███████████████████████ " \
  https://api.travis-ci.com/owner/packtci

{
  "@type":              "user",
  "@href":              "/user/863993",
  "@representation":    "standard",
  "@permissions":       {
    "read":             true,
    "sync":             true
  },
  "id":                 863993,
  "login":              "packtci",
  "name":               null,
  "github_id":          40322425,
  "avatar_url":         "https://avatars3.githubusercontent.com/u/40322425?v=4",
  "education":          false,
  "is_syncing":         false,
  "synced_at":          "2018-06-29T17:03:10Z"
}
```

You can go to the API Explorer at this url: https://developer.travis-ci.com/explore/. Then you input the resource in the input box that looks like this:

API Explorer

The API Explorer allows you to test endpoints.

Enter an endpoint in the box below:

```
/
```

API V3 REST call with curl

We will issue the travis token command so that we can copy the access token to the system clipboard:

```
travis token
```

Next we will run the travis endpoint command and copy the URL:

```
travis endpoint
API endpoint: https://api.travis-ci.org/
```

We will make a curl request in the following manner:

```
curl -X GET \
 -H "Content-Type: application/json" \
 -H "Travis-API-Version: 3" \
 -H "Authorization: token $(travis token)" \
https://api.travis-ci.org/repos
```

Notice that in this curl request we used the travis token cli command that will return a valid token for this particular HTTP Header. This HTTP request will return a JSON response payload which we will use to copy a particular repo ID to make the following REST call to find all the environment variables for the functional-summer repo (https:/
/github.com/packtci/functional-summer):

```
curl -X GET \
 -H "Content-Type: application/json" \
 -H "Travis-API-Version: 3" \
 -H "Authorization: token $(travis token)" \
https://api.travis-ci.org/repo/19721247/env_vars
```

In this GET request, we get all the environment variables from the functional-summer repository and receive a JSON response like the following:

```
{
  "@type": "env_vars",
  "@href": "/repo/19721247/env_vars",
  "@representation": "standard",
  "env_vars": [

  ]
}
```

Let us make a POST request to add an environment variable to the functional-summer repo:

```
curl -X POST \
  -H "Content-Type: application/json" \
  -H "Travis-API-Version: 3" \
  -H "Authorization: token $(travis token)" \
  -d '{ "env_var.name": "MOVIE", "env_var.value": "ROCKY",
"env_var.public": false }' \
  https://api.travis-ci.org/repo/19721247/env_vars
```

Now when we make a GET request for the environment variables, we see that we have an environment variable called MOVIE that has been set:

```
curl -X GET \
  -H "Content-Type: application/json" \
  -H "Travis-API-Version: 3" \
  -H "Authorization: token $(travis token)" \
  https://api.travis-ci.org/repo/19721247/env_vars
{
"@type": "env_vars",
"@href": "/repo/19721247/env_vars",
"@representation": "standard",
"env_vars": [
{
"@type": "env_var",
"@href": "/repo/19721247/env_var/1f64fa82-2cad-4270-abdc-13d70fa8faeb",
"@representation": "standard",
"@permissions": {
"read": true,
"write": true
},
"id": "1f64fa82-2cad-4270-abdc-13d70fa8faeb",
"name": "MOVIE",
"public": false
}
]
}
```

Printing out important system configuration information

The report command prints out important system configuration information, as you can see in the following screenshot:

```
⊢→  multiple-languages git:(master) travis report
System
Ruby:                    Ruby 2.4.1-p111
Operating System:        Mac OS X 10.13.5
RubyGems:                RubyGems 2.7.7

CLI
Version:                 1.8.8
Plugins:                 none
Auto-Completion:         no
Last Version Check:      2018-06-29 14:37:52 -0400

Session
API Endpoint:            https://api.travis-ci.org/
Logged In:               as "packtci"
Verify SSL:              yes
Enterprise:              no

Endpoints
org:                     https://api.travis-ci.org/ (access token, current)
pro:                     https://api.travis-ci.com/ (access token)

For issues with the command line tool, please visit https://github.com/travis-ci/travis.rb/issues.
For Travis CI in general, go to https://github.com/travis-ci/travis-ci/issues or email support@travis-ci.com.
⊢→  multiple-languages git:(master) █
```

Listing all the repositories that the currently logged in user has access to

The `repos` command will list repositories whether they are active or not and has a variety of options that can be used. In the following screenshot, we used the `-m` option to match all the repositories for the `packtci` GitHub user:

```
⊢→  multiple-languages git:(master) travis repos -m 'packtci/*'
packtci/docker-travis-ci-example (active: yes, admin: yes, push: yes, pull: yes)
Description: A travis ci yml script with a dockerfile example

packtci/functional-summer (active: yes, admin: yes, push: yes, pull: yes)
Description: A repository that calculates an average

packtci/multiple-languages (active: yes, admin: yes, push: yes, pull: yes)
Description: A repo with multiple languages in travis yml script

packtci/puppeteer-headless-chrome-travis-yml-script (active: yes, admin: yes, push: yes, pull: yes)
Description: A repo with a headless chrome travis yml script example
⊢→  multiple-languages git:(master) █
```

Initiating synchronization with Travis CI for any new or outdated repositories in GitHub

The sync command helps you update information about users and any new or modified repositories in GitHub. Let us add another repository to GitHub called functional-patterns (https://github.com/packtci/functional-patterns). In the following screenshot, we use the sync command so that Travis CI becomes aware of the new repository and then use the repos command to confirm that it shows up in the list of repos we have access to:

```
▸→  multiple-languages git:(master) travis sync
synchronizing: . done
▸→  multiple-languages git:(master) travis repos -m 'packtci/*'
packtci/docker-travis-ci-example (active: yes, admin: yes, push: yes, pull: yes)
Description: A travis ci yml script with a dockerfile example

packtci/functional-patterns (active: no, admin: yes, push: yes, pull: yes)     New Repo Added
Description: A library exploring functional patterns

packtci/functional-summer (active: yes, admin: yes, push: yes, pull: yes)
Description: A repository that calculates an average

packtci/multiple-languages (active: yes, admin: yes, push: yes, pull: yes)
Description: A repo with multiple languages in travis yml script

packtci/puppeteer-headless-chrome-travis-yml-script (active: yes, admin: yes, push: yes, pull: yes)
Description: A repo with a headless chrome travis yml script example
```

The sync command can replace the step we took in Chapter 9, *Installation and Basics of Travis CI*, where we clicked the **Sync account** button to synchronize all the repository information in our account.

lint - a Travis YML script

The lint command is very useful as it checks that you have the proper syntax in your Travis YML script. Let use create a Travis YML script in the functional-patterns repository (https://github.com/packtci/functional-patterns) that we just added to GitHub. We will add the following entry for the .travis.yml script:

```
language: blah

node_js: 8.11
```

Let us now run the lint command to check the syntax. In the following screenshot, Travis informs us that we are using an illegal value of blah and that it will default to ruby as the language:

```
↳  functional-patterns git:(master) x travis lint .travis.yml
Warnings for .travis.yml:
[x] in language section: illegal value blah, defaulting to ruby
[x] specified node_js, but setting is not relevant for ruby
↳  functional-patterns git:(master) x
```

Let us fix the language entry to use Node.js and then run the `lint` command again:

```
↳  functional-patterns git:(master) x travis lint .travis.yml
Hooray, .travis.yml looks valid :)
↳  functional-patterns git:(master) x
```

The `lint` command reports that we now have valid syntax in our `.travis.yml` script.

Obtaining current build information for the organization or user

The `whatsup` command lets you see activity that has recently occurred in Travis. When we ran this `whatsup` command, it gave us the most recent activity in Travis CI:

```
↳  functional-patterns git:(master) travis whatsup
packtci/puppeteer-headless-chrome-travis-yml-script passed: #2
packtci/docker-travis-ci-example passed: #3
packtci/multiple-languages passed: #2
packtci/functional-summer passed: #1
↳  functional-patterns git:(master)
```

In the `packtci` Travis account, there is only one user but you can have many users in a Travis CI account, and so it may be more useful to see only your repositories with the `whatsup` command. Remember that we can use the `help` command to find out more options for a particular command. As an exercise, use the `help` command to find the options to show only your own repositories.

Finding the currently logged-in user information

The `whoami` command is useful to find out the currently logged-in user for Travis CI account:

```
↳  functional-patterns git:(master) travis whoami
You are packtci
↳  functional-patterns git:(master)
```

The whoami command reports packtci as we would expect.

Repository commands

The repository commands have all the options that the API commands have and additionally you can specify the specific repository that you want to work with using the --repo owner/name option.

Displaying the most recent build information for each branch in Git version control

The branches command shows the most recent build information for each branch in version control:

```
 ↦  multiple-languages git:(master) travis branches
master:  #2     passed      Add go and node, tests and a travis yml script.
 ↦  multiple-languages git:(master) █
```

There could be more branches shown when you run this command.

Listing cache information for all the repositories

The cache command can list all the caches in a repository:

```
 ↦  puppeteer-headless-chrome-travis-yml-script git:(master) travis cache
Detected repository as packtci/puppeteer-headless-chrome-travis-yml-script, is this correct? |yes| yes
On branch master:
cache-linux-trusty-e3b0c44298fc1c149afbf4c8996fb92427ae41e4649b934ca495991b7852b855--node-8.11.tgz  last modified: 2018-06-23 13:22:58  size: 99.22 MiB

Overall size of above caches: 99.22 MiB
 ↦  puppeteer-headless-chrome-travis-yml-script git:(master) █
```

Deleting cache information for a given repository

The cache command can also delete the caches in the repository if you use the -d, --delete option:

```
 ↦  puppeteer-headless-chrome-travis-yml-script git:(master) travis cache --delete
DANGER ZONE: Do you really want to delete all caches? |no| yes
Deleted the following caches:

On branch master:
cache-linux-trusty-e3b0c44298fc1c149afbf4c8996fb92427ae41e4649b934ca495991b7852b855--node-8.11.tgz  last modified: 2018-06-23 13:22:58  size: 99.22 MiB

Overall size of above caches: 99.22 MiB
 ↦  puppeteer-headless-chrome-travis-yml-script git:(master) █
```

We received a warning message in red asking us for confirmation to delete the caches.

Enabling a repository in Travis CI

The enable command will activate Travis CI in your GitHub repository:

```
⊢→  functional-patterns git:(master) travis enable
packtci/functional-patterns: enabled :)
⊢→  functional-patterns git:(master) █
```

The enable command helps replace the manual step we took in Chapter 9, *Installation and Basics of Travis CI*, to activate a repository in Travis CI, where we clicked the slider button in the Travis web client to activate the repository.

Disabling a repository in Travis CI

The disable command will make the Travis CI in your GitHub repository inactive:

```
⊢→  functional-patterns git:(master) travis disable
packtci/functional-patterns: disabled :(
⊢→  functional-patterns git:(master) █
```

Cancelling the latest build in Travis CI

Let us enable the functional-patterns repo with the following command:

```
travis enable
```

Now let us push a commit to the repository by using the command:

```
git commit --amend --no-edit
```

The previous git command lets you reuse the previous git commit command that you used, but you will need to issue the following command:

```
git push -f
```

Let us look at the current state of the repositories in Travis CI; it may take a while for the build to be officially created in Travis CI:

```
▸ functional-patterns git:(master) travis whatsup
packtci/functional-patterns started: #1
packtci/puppeteer-headless-chrome-travis-yml-script passed: #2
packtci/docker-travis-ci-example passed: #3
packtci/multiple-languages passed: #2
packtci/functional-summer passed: #1
▸ functional-patterns git:(master) travis cancel 1
job #1.1 has been canceled
▸ functional-patterns git:(master) travis whatsup
packtci/functional-patterns canceled: #1
packtci/puppeteer-headless-chrome-travis-yml-script passed: #2
packtci/docker-travis-ci-example passed: #3
packtci/multiple-languages passed: #2
packtci/functional-summer passed: #1
▸ functional-patterns git:(master) 
```

In the previous screenshot, we issue the `whatsup` command to see the current status of the builds and notice that `packtci/functional-patterns` started job number 1. We then issued the `travis cancel` command and provided an argument of 1. This was not completely necessary as this was the current build, so we could have just issued the `travis cancel` command. When we run the `travis whatsup` command, the build is canceled.

Encrypting environment variables or deployment keys

The `encrypt` command lets you encrypt secret values stored in environment variables and/or deployment keys that you don't want to publicly expose:

```
▸ puppeteer-headless-chrome-travis-yml-script git:(master) travis encrypt SECRET_VALUE=SuperSecret12345
Please add the following to your .travis.yml file:

    secure: "DeeYuU76cFvBIZTDTTE+o+lApUlSlY9JZ97pGOixyJ7MCCVQD26m+3iGLCcos0TbvjfAjE+IKTKZ96CLJkf6DNTeetl3+/VDp9lOa2891meWSgL6ZoDLwG8pCvLxaIg2tAkC26hIT64YKmzEim
6QRQhLdUVUC1oz9BV8ygrcwtTo4Y9C0h7hMuYnrpcSlKsG9B8GfDdi7OSda4Ypn4aFOZ4/N3mQh/bMY7h6ai+tcAGzdCAzeocli0dw+xwIJ0P2Fg2KOy/d1CqoVBimWyHDxDoaXgmaaBeGIBTXM6birP09MHU
s2REpEB9b8Z1Q+DzcA+u5EucLrqsm8BYHmyuPhAnUMqYdD4eHPQApQybY+kJP18qf/9/tFTyO5mH3SLk6Oykc/bFaNCi7i4yAe708TI/Qyq3LPkHd1XEFDrHasmWwp/4k3m2p5ydDqsyyteJBHMO/wMDR7gb6
T6jVVVmDn0bmurb4CTmiSuzslBS9N5C9QRd5k4XFUbpqTAHm+GtNYOOzRFTTyVH3wSKBj8xhjPLGZzCXeUxuW72deJ+ofxpTgKs7DM9pcfUShk+Ngykgy6VGhPcuMSTNXQv2w7Mw5/ZOZJt36ndUNXT0Mc9ot
hq4bCVZBnRiDGoZuz9FSfXIK/kDKm2TjuVhmqZ7T//Y4AfNyQ/spaf8gjFZvW2ulCg="

Pro Tip: You can add it automatically by running with --add.
```

Adding environment variables in Travis CI

We will add this entry into our `.travis.yml` script in the `env` block. You can read more about using environment variables in Travis CI in this documentation at https://docs.travis-ci.com/user/environment-variables. In general, you can add environment variables by adding a block called `env` in your `.travis.yml` script.

I have added a sample snippet in the `.travis.yml` script:

```
env:
    DB_URL=http://localhost:8078
    global:
        secure:
"DeeYuU76cFvBIZTDTTE+o+lApU15lY9JZ97pGOixyJ7MCCVQD26m+3iGLCcos0TbvjfAjE+IKT
KZ96CLJkf6DNTeet13+/VDp91Oa2891meWSgL6ZoDLwG8pCvLxaIg2tAkC26hIT64YKmzEim6OR
QhLdUVUC1oz9BV8ygrcwtTo4Y9C0h7hMuYnrpcSlKsG9B8GfDdi7OSda4Ypn4aFOZ4/N3mQh/bM
Y7h6ai+tcAGzdCAzeoc1i0dw+xwIJ0P2Fg2KOy/d1CqoVBimWyHDxDoaXgmaaBeGIBTXM6birP0
9MHUs2REpEB9b8Z1Q+DzcA+u5EucLrqsm8BYHmyuPhAnUMqYdD4eHPQApQybY+kJP18qf/9/tFT
yD5mH3Slk60ykc/bFaNCi7i4yAe7O8TI/Qyq3LPkHd1XEFDrHasmWwp/4k3m2p5ydDqsyyteJBH
MO/wMDR7gb6T6jVVVmDn0bmurb4CTmiSuzslBS9N5C9QRd5k4XFUbpqTAHm+GtNYOOzRFTTyVH3
wSKBj8xhjPLGZzCXeUxuW72deJ+ofxpTgKs7DM9pcfUShk+Ngykgy6VGhPcuMSTNXQv2w7Hw5/Z
OZJt36ndUNXTOMc9othq4bCVZBhRiDGoZuz9FSfXIK/kDKm2TjuVhmqZ7T//Y4AfNyQ/spaf8gj
FZvW2u1Cg="
```

We added a public environment variable called `DB_URL` and a global variable by using the `global` block and then pasting the entry into it.

You can automatically add the entry by using the `--add` option if you want, although any comments you have in the `.travis.yml` script will be gone, as will the spacing, so be mindful of this when you run the `--add` option.

Encrypting a file

The `encrypt-file` command will encrypt an entire file using symmetric (AES-256) encryption and stores the secret in a file. Let us create a file called `secret.txt` and add the following entries into it:

```
SECRET_VALUE=ABCDE12345
CLIENT_ID=rocky123
CLIENT_SECRET=abc222222!
```

Now let us encrypt our secret file:

```
↦  puppeteer-headless-chrome-travis-yml-script git:(master) x travis encrypt-file secret.txt
encrypting secret.txt for packtci/puppeteer-headless-chrome-travis-yml-script
storing result as secret.txt.enc
storing secure env variables for decryption

Please add the following to your build script (before install stage in your .travis.yml, for instance):

    openssl aes-256-cbc -K $encrypted_74945c17fbe2_key -iv $encrypted_74945c17fbe2_iv -in secret.txt.enc -out secret.txt -d

Pro Tip: You can add it automatically by running with --add.

Make sure to add secret.txt.enc to the git repository.
Make sure not to add secret.txt to the git repository.
```

So now we will add this entry into our `.travis.yml` script:

```
before_install:
    - openssl aes-256-cbc -K $encrypted_74945c17fbe2_key -iv
$encrypted_74945c17fbe2_iv -in secret.txt.enc -out secret.txt -d
```

It can then decrypt the values in the secret text file for us.

Listing environment information

The `env` command can list all the environment variables set for the repository:

```
▸ multiple-languages git:(master) travis env list
# environment variables for packtci/multiple-languages
▸ multiple-languages git:(master)
```

We don't have any environment variables set for this repository.

Setting an environment variable

The `env` command can also set an environment variable from the repository:

```
▸ multiple-languages git:(master) travis env set API_URL http://localhost:8078
[+] setting environment variable $API_URL
▸ multiple-languages git:(master) travis env list
# environment variables for packtci/multiple-languages
API_URL=[secure]
▸ multiple-languages git:(master)
```

We set an environment variable of `API_URL` and that it shows up as an environment variable for the multiple languages repository now.

Deleting an environment variable

The `env` command can also remove an environment variable from the repository:

```
⊢→  multiple-languages git:(master) travis env unset API_URL
[x] removing environment variable $API_URL
⊢→  multiple-languages git:(master) travis env list
# environment variables for packtci/multiple-languages
⊢→  multiple-languages git:(master) ▯
```

The `travis env` list command now reports that we don't have any environment variables set for the multiple-languages repository which is what we expect.

Clearing out all environment variables

The `env` command can be used to clear out all of the environment variables that have been set in the repository:

```
⊢→  multiple-languages git:(master) travis env set API_URL http://localhost:8078
[+] setting environment variable $API_URL
⊢→  multiple-languages git:(master) travis env set MONGO_URL http://mongo:27017
[+] setting environment variable $MONGO_URL
⊢→  multiple-languages git:(master) travis env list
# environment variables for packtci/multiple-languages
API_URL=[secure]
MONGO_URL=[secure]
⊢→  multiple-languages git:(master) travis env clear
DANGER ZONE: Clear out all env variables for packtci/multiple-languages? |no| yes
[x] removing environment variable $API_URL
[x] removing environment variable $MONGO_URL
⊢→  multiple-languages git:(master) travis env list
# environment variables for packtci/multiple-languages
⊢→  multiple-languages git:(master) █
```

List history information for recent builds

The `history` command displays a repositories build history:

```
⊢→  multiple-languages git:(master) travis history
#2 passed:      master Add go and node, tests and a travis yml script.
#1 passed:      master Add go and node, tests and a travis yml script.
⊢→  multiple-languages git:(master) █
```

The `history` command will by default only display the last 10 builds, but you can limit or extend the number of builds by using the `--limit` option.

Initializing Travis CLI on a project

The init command will help you set up Travis CI in a project by generating a `.travis.yml` script for you. We have set up a new project in GitHub called `travis-init-command` (`https://github.com/packtci/travis-init-command`). We will use the init command to set up Golang in this repository:

```
↦  travis-init-command git:(master) travis sync
synchronizing: . done
↦  travis-init-command git:(master) travis enable
packtci/travis-init-command: enabled :)
↦  travis-init-command git:(master) travis init golang
unknown language golang
↦  travis-init-command git:(master) travis init go
.travis.yml file created!
packtci/travis-init-command: enabled :)
↦  travis-init-command git:(master) x cat .travis.yml
language: go
go:
- '1.0'
- '1.3'
↦  travis-init-command git:(master) x ▊
```

The steps in the process are as follows:

1. The first step is to use the `sync` command so that Travis CI is aware of this new repository
2. Next we will enable this new repository in Travis CI
3. Next we will try to create a `.travis.yml` script with Golang, but notice that it is not recognized, so we try again with Go and it succeeds
4. Lastly, we print out the contents of the new file and notice that it set the language to Go and used two different versions of Go

Printing out CI build log information

The `logs` command will print out the contents of the Travis CI log for the repository and by default it will print out the first job of the latest build. Here, we run the `logs` command in the recent repository that we created; it won't pass the CI build, however, since there aren't any buildable Go files in the repository yet:

```
travis logs

displaying logs for packtci/travis-init-command#1.1
Worker information
hostname: fb102913-2cd8-41fb-b69b-7e8488a0aa0a@1.production-1-worker-
org-03-packet
version: v3.8.2
https://github.com/travis-ci/worker/tree/c370f713bb4195cce20cdc6ce3e62f26b8
cf3961
instance: 22589e2 travisci/ci-garnet:packer-1512502276-986baf0 (via amqp)
startup: 1.083854718s
Build system information
Build language: go
Build group: stable
Build dist: trusty
Build id: 399102978
Job id: 399102980
Runtime kernel version: 4.4.0-112-generic
...
The command "go get -v ./..." failed and exited with 1 during .

Your build has been stopped.
```

Notice that the `build` failed, as we noted earlier, because there aren't any Go files to be built. The `logs` command can also be given a specific build number to run and you can also give them a specific branch to run. Run the `travis help logs` command for more options.

Opening the Travis web interface for the project

The `open` command will open the repository in the Travis CI web client:

```
travis open
```

Running `travis open` in the `travis-init-command` repository (https://github.com/packtci/travis-init-command) will take us to the following URL at https://travis-ci.org/packtci/travis-init-command.

You can use the `--print` option to print out the URL instead of opening it to the specific project view, as it does by default. Run the `travis help open` command for more options.

Printing out public key information for the repository

The `pubkey` command will print out the public SSH key for the repository:

```
travis-init-command git:(master) travis pubkey
Public key for packtci/travis-init-command:

ssh-rsa AAAAB3NzaC1yc2EAAAADAQABAAACAQCnW5SgB4jH2pHh37VRCP6uYvQeJk8PhlnMRP32SyA2gY9xVkQLTPsX0g5Py84GVv/chATSzazvFBFKKbOKRGVQvSu10ztfFBL5ReeXEj9Nb/bQlMaz70Ozu
aJvGpQf1jjNGo3v/l9rfYfj2xuu5T6YSOgreutRCeMlOOudaZXvrH5h0nm9himrni1UIGupIEniqowgWkCJNvj1xOK2Yjxdia/3pxsByn7RSRzx/qDOo8dckOweXjt6TK7LqynaLeGB1VC1SKWC4GA+TGZ8so
gA9EMPWwWy4FpsKEFMRV87FiNGKjhBbWMid89wFhTxMXqWNld8H5i/Vl2oH6h4vIipqUNFTW9RmOV9Ot0MOZSjTtSmXQLo24LEDansX/7IxuesDLNvnxilCxpRGORtdDS5lqpxhM7NGbxf8rCsR5Q4eAm2lRr
30LKCPk7s8wbWCrVQLLxlEuHlysWflpKBw9/rO3PPnuFrZwJOgOekQdx8WgrdXNz37jcoDW+dIAo5QsGoQS3lCn+Xwkp6xJM6LvNUwNasET4rUH7AtZ3v7iuOsEEaTOM1IhNUWVbeWq00Dqp29iShOVONJFJa
YG+c+a5UoRAj1pa/5eouQFLvbQpr9kuwOnp277AKWFiHG+gevOWxcICPYavyu2A0Un5wybZG1W3HUVwax5zdYVReny6u/w==
travis-init-command git:(master)
```

For security reasons, I removed the public key information. You can also display the key in different formats. For example, if you use the `--pem` option your key will display like this:

```
travis-init-command git:(master) travis pubkey --pem
Public key for packtci/travis-init-command:

-----BEGIN PUBLIC KEY-----
MIICIjANBgkqhkiG9w0BAQEFAAOCAg8AMIICCgKCAgEApluUoAeIx9qR4d+1UQj+
rmL0HiZPD4ZZzET99ksgNoGPcVZEC0z7F9IOT8vOBlb/3IQE0s2s7xQRSimzikRl
UL0rtdM7XxQS+UXnlxI/TW/20JTGs+9Ds7mibxqUH9Y4zRqN7/5fa32H49sbruU+
mEjoK3rrUQnjJTjrnWmV76x+YdJ5vYYpq54tVCBrqSBJ4qqMIFpAiTb49cTitmI8
XYmv96cbAcp+0Ukc8f6gzqPHXJDsHl47ekyuy6sp2i3hgdVQtUilguBgPkxmfLKI
APRDD1sFsuBabChBTEVfOxYjRio4QW1jInfPcBYU8TF6ljZXfB+Yv1ZdqB+oeLyI
qalDRU1vUZjlfTrdDDmUo07Upl0C6NuCxA2p7F/+yMbnrAyzb58YtQsaURjkbXQ0
uZaqcYTOzRm8XwawrEeUOHgJtpUa99Cygj5O7PMG1gq1UCy8ZRLh5crFn5aSvMPf
6ztzz57ha2cCToDnpEHcfFoK3Vzc9+43KA1vnSAKOULBqEEt5Qp/l8JKesSTOi7z
VMDWrBE+K1B+wLWd7+4rjrBBGkzjNSITVFlW3lqtNA6qdvYkoTldDSRSWmBvnPmu
VKEQI9aWv+XqLkBS720Ka/ZLsDp6du+wClhYhxvoHrzlsXCAj2Gr8rtgNFJ+cMm2
RtVtx1FcGsec3WFUXp8urv8CAwEAAQ==
-----END PUBLIC KEY-----
travis-init-command git:(master)
```

Run the `travis help pubkey` command to show more options for this command:

```
↳  travis-init-command git:(master) travis help pubkey
Prints out a repository's public key.
Usage: travis pubkey [OPTIONS]
    -h, --help                      Display help
    -i, --[no-]interactive          be interactive and colorful
    -E, --[no-]explode              don't rescue exceptions
        --skip-version-check        don't check if travis client is up to date
        --skip-completion-check     don't check if auto-completion is set up
    -e, --api-endpoint URL          Travis API server to talk to
    -I, --[no-]insecure             do not verify SSL certificate of API endpoint
        --pro                       short-cut for --api-endpoint 'https://api.travis-ci.com/'
        --com                       short-cut for --api-endpoint 'https://api.travis-ci.com/'
        --org                       short-cut for --api-endpoint 'https://api.travis-ci.org/'
        --staging                   talks to staging system
    -t, --token [ACCESS_TOKEN]      access token to use
        --debug                     show API requests
        --debug-http                show HTTP(S) exchange
    -X, --enterprise [NAME]         use enterprise setup (optionally takes name for multiple setups)
        --adapter ADAPTER           Faraday adapter to use for HTTP requests
    -r, --repo SLUG                 repository to use (will try to detect from current git clone)
    -R, --store-repo SLUG           like --repo, but remembers value for current directory
    -p, --pem                       encode in format used by pem
    -f, --fingerprint               display fingerprint
↳  travis-init-command git:(master) █
```

Restarting the latest CI build in Travis CI

The `restart` command will restart the latest build:

```
↳  travis-init-command git:(master) travis restart
build #1 has been restarted
```

Printing out current build requests in Travis CI

The `requests` command will list any build requests that Travis CI receives. We will run the `travis requests` command on the build we just triggered for the `travis-init-command` repository:

```
↳  travis-init-command git:(master) travis requests
push to master approved (validation pending)
    6609c39 - Add Travis CI to the project.
    received at: 2018-07-02 08:18:16
```

The build is still failing because there aren't any buildable Go files in it yet.

Printing out particular repository settings

The settings command will display repository settings for the repository:

```
↪  multiple-languages git:(master) travis settings
Settings for packtci/multiple-languages:
[-] builds_only_with_travis_yml    Only run builds with a .travis.yml
[+] build_pushes                   Build pushes
[+] build_pull_requests            Build pull requests
  0 maximum_number_of_builds       Maximum number of concurrent builds
↪  multiple-languages git:(master) █
```

Notice here that the minus (–) means it is disabled while the plus (+) means it is enabled.

The travis settings command can also be used to enable, disable, and set settings:

```
↪  multiple-languages git:(master) travis settings --enable builds_only_with_travis_yml
Settings for packtci/multiple-languages:
[+] builds_only_with_travis_yml    Only run builds with a .travis.yml
↪  multiple-languages git:(master) travis settings maximum_number_of_builds --set 1
Settings for packtci/multiple-languages:
  1 maximum_number_of_builds       Maximum number of concurrent builds
↪  multiple-languages git:(master) travis settings
Settings for packtci/multiple-languages:
[+] builds_only_with_travis_yml    Only run builds with a .travis.yml
[+] build_pushes                   Build pushes
[+] build_pull_requests            Build pull requests
  1 maximum_number_of_builds       Maximum number of concurrent builds
↪  multiple-languages git:(master) █
```

Configuring Travis CI add-ons

The setup command helps you configure Travis add-ons:

```
→  multiple-languages git:(master) travis setup sauce_connect
Sauce Labs user: jbelmont
Sauce Labs access key: ********
Encrypt access key? |yes| yes
```

You can see more Travis add-ons that are available in the Travis CLI user documentation (https://github.com/travis-ci/travis.rb#setup).

Displaying general information for the current CI build

The `show` command displays general information about the most recent CI build by default:

```
↦  multiple-languages git:(master) travis show
Job #2.1:  Add go and node, tests and a travis yml script.
State:        passed
Type:         push
Branch:       master
Compare URL:  https://github.com/packtci/multiple-languages/compare/6ef2a990401f...8e6d3ca20e01
Duration:     38 sec
Started:      2018-07-02 08:59:33
Finished:     2018-07-02 09:00:11
Allow Failure: false
Config:       os: linux, env: NODE_VERSION="6"
↦  multiple-languages git:(master) travis show 1
Job #1.1:  Add go and node, tests and a travis yml script.
State:        passed
Type:         push
Branch:       master
Compare URL:  https://github.com/packtci/multiple-languages/compare/fb4329d77f2e...6ef2a990401f
Duration:     1 min 2 sec
Started:      2018-06-23 11:23:07
Finished:     2018-06-23 11:24:09
Allow Failure: false
Config:       os: linux, env: NODE_VERSION="6"
↦  multiple-languages git:(master) 
```

The first command, `travis show`, displayed the most recent build and in the next run we provided a specific build number.

Listing SSH key in Travis CI

The `sshkey` command will check if there is a custom SSH key set up:

```
travis sshkey
```

> This command only works with Travis's Pro version, and if there is no SSH key it will report that no custom SSH key is installed.

You can read about more options in this command in the user documentation (https://github.com/travis-ci/travis.rb#sshkey).

Displaying status information for the current build

The status command outputs a one-line message about the project's last build:

```
▸→  multiple-languages git:(master) travis status
build #3 errored
▸→  multiple-languages git:(master) █
```

Travis CI options for Pro version and Enterprise version

By default, the general API commands hit the api.travis-ci.org endpoint. The Travis Pro version has some additional features and options that a regular Travis account does not have such as using the sshkey command and more. You can read more about the options in the user documentation (https://github.com/travis-ci/travis.rb#pro-and-enterprise).

Option to display the information for Pro version

If you use the --pro option with the general API command, then you will hit the Travis Pro endpoint at https://api.travis-ci.com/. So for example if we make the following request using the --pro option we will hit Travis Pro API:

```
▸→  travis-init-command git:(master) travis raw /config --pro
{"config"=>
  {"host"=>"travis-ci.com",
   "shorten_host"=>"trvs.io",
   "assets"=>{"host"=>"travis-ci.org"},
   "pusher"=>{"key"=>"59236bc0716a551eab40", "private"=>true},
   "github"=>
   {"api_url"=>"https://api.github.com",
    "scopes"=>["user:email", "repo", "read:org"]},
   "notifications"=>
   {"webhook"=>
    {"public_key"=>
     "-----BEGIN PUBLIC KEY-----\n" +
     "MIIBIjANBgkqhkiG9w0BAQEFAAOCAQ8AMIIBCgKCAQEAnQU2j9lnRtyuW36arNOc\n" +
     "dzCzyKVirLUi3/aLh6UfnTVXzTnx8eHUnBn1ZeQl7Eh3J3qqdbIKl6npS27ONzCy\n" +
     "3PIcfjpLPaVyGagIL8c8XgDEvB45AesC0osVP5gkXQkPUM3B2rrUmp1AZzG+Fuo0\n" +
     "SAeNnS71gN63U3brL9fN/MTCXJJ6TvMt3GrcJUq5uq56qNeJTsiowK6eiiWFUSfh\n" +
     "e1qapOdMFmcEs9J/R1XQ/scxbAnLcWfl8lqH/MjMdCMe0j3X2ZYMTqOHsb3cQGSS\n" +
     "dMPwZGeLWV+0axjJ7TrJ+riqMANOgqCBGpvWUnUfo046ACOx7p6u4fFc3aRiuqYK\n" +
     "VQIDAQAB\n" +
     "-----END PUBLIC KEY-----"}}}}
▸→  travis-init-command git:(master) █
```

Notice here that the host is travis-ci.com which is Travis PRO.

Option to display information for Enterprise version

If you have Travis Enterprise set up, then you can use the `--enterprise` option so that you hit where your enterprise domain lives:

```
├→  multiple-languages git:(master) travis login --enterprise
Enterprise domain: ▐
```

 We don't have Travis Enterprise set up, but if you did then you would enter your domain here.

Summary

In this chapter, we have gone over how to install Ruby and Travis CLI RubyGem on the Windows operating system, macOS operating system, and Linux operating system. We went over each Travis CLI command in detail and discussed the various ways to use each command and some of the options that each command takes. We also showed you how to directly call the Travis API using the curl REST client. Finally, we looked at some of the features in the Travis Pro and Enterprise versions.

In the next chapter, we will go over some more advanced techniques to log out values and to debug with Travis CI.

Questions

1. What is the recommended way to install Ruby on the Windows OS according to the Travis docs?
2. What command should you use to print out the current version of Travis that is installed?
3. What command do you use to print out helpful information in Travis CLI?
4. How do you get an access token to work with the general API commands in Travis CLI?
5. What HTTP header do you need to use to work with Travis API Version 3?
6. How do you print out system configuration information?
7. What command checks the syntax of your Travis YML script?
8. What command helps you set up Travis in your project?

Further reading

You can further explore the Travis CLI options in the user documentation (`https://github.com/travis-ci/travis.rb`) and you can read more about using the Travis API in the API documentation (`https://developer.travis-ci.com/`).

11

Travis CI UI Logging and Debugging

This chapter will give an overview of the Travis job log and the various sections in the job log. This chapter will also explain how to debug a Travis build job in a couple of different ways, including building locally using Docker and then running a build in debug mode. We will go over all the different ways to get a job ID and how to enable debug mode in public repositories and then use the Travis API to start a build in debug mode. We will explain how to use **tmate**, which is a terminal multiplexor, and then we will talk about logging environment variables in the Travis Web Client. Finally, we will cover how to do deployments in Travis CI using Heroku and how to debug deployment failures.

The following topics will be covered in this chapter:

- Travis web client overview
- Debug build locally with Docker
- Running build in debug mode
- Travis Web UI Logging
- Travis CI deployment overview and debugging

Technical requirements

This chapter will require some basic Unix programming skills as well as some bash scripting knowledge. A basic understanding about how to make RESTful API calls would be helpful as we will be using curl as a REST client to make a call to the Travis API. It would be helpful to also have a basic understanding about Docker and containers as we will be running a local build using Docker as well.

Travis web client overview

We briefly went over the web dashboard for Travis CI in `Chapter 9`, *Installation and Basics of Travis CI*, but let us take another look at the different parts of the UI again.

Main dashboard overview

The Travis CI web client has several different parts that are necessary to understand:

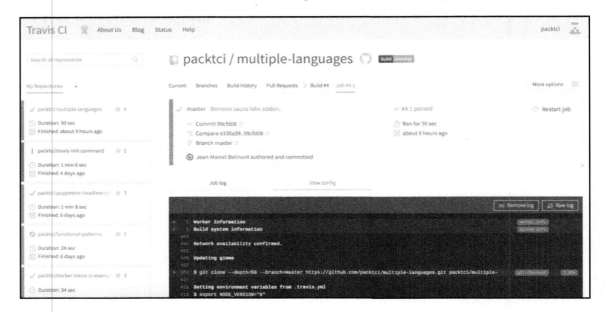

In the left divided section, you can individually click on each repository that you are interested in looking at. Additionally, you can search a repository by name as there could be many repositories that you or the organization that you belong to own. Also notice that there are details about the last build that was run in the project and whether it passed or failed as well as build detailed information about the duration and when the last build was run.

In the right divided section, you will find the main navigation components of the Travis web client. Notice here that you have several navigation links, such as the current build, which is the default link that is opened when you go to a repository. If you click the **Branches** link, you will see all the builds that have been triggered in all the different branches including pull requests. Let us push a new branch and create a pull request in the `multiple-languages` (`https://github.com/packtci/multiple-languages`) repository and see a new build in action:

Notice here that Travis CI created a new build for the new branch that we pushed called `add-test-case`:

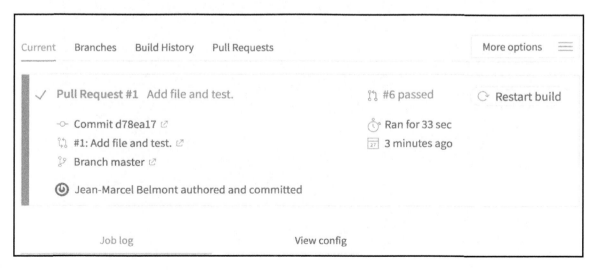

Additionally, any pull requests that you open will trigger a new build with Travis CI as well:

When you merge a pull request into another branch then another CI build is triggered in Travis CI.

Job log overview

The job log in Travis CI starts with build system configuration information:

```
 1  Build system information
 2  Build language: go
 3  Build group: stable
 4  Build dist: trusty
 5  Build id: 401101739
 6  Job id: 401101740
 7  Runtime kernel version: 4.14.12-041412-generic
 8  travis-build version: e2a995511
 9  Build image provisioning date and time
10  Tue Dec  5 20:11:19 UTC 2017
11  Operating System Details
12  Distributor ID: Ubuntu
13  Description:    Ubuntu 14.04.5 LTS
14  Release:       14.04
15  Codename:      trusty
16  Cookbooks Version
17  7c2c6a6 https://github.com/travis-ci/travis-cookbooks/tree/7c2c6a6
18  git version
19  git version 2.15.1
20  bash version
21  GNU bash, version 4.3.11(1)-release (x86_64-pc-linux-gnu)
22  gcc version
23  gcc (Ubuntu 4.8.4-2ubuntu1~14.04.3) 4.8.4
24  Copyright (C) 2013 Free Software Foundation, Inc.
25  This is free software; see the source for copying conditions.  There is NO
26  warranty; not even for MERCHANTABILITY or FITNESS FOR A PARTICULAR PURPOSE.
27
```

Notice here that the build language is set to `go` and that the build operation system is
Ubuntu Trusty 14.04:

```
$ git clone --depth=50 --branch=master https://github.com/packtci/multiple-languages.git packtci/multiple-    git.checkout    0.29s
languages
Cloning into 'packtci/multiple-languages'...
remote: Counting objects: 25, done.
remote: Compressing objects: 100% (22/22), done.
remote: Total 25 (delta 6), reused 17 (delta 3), pack-reused 0
Unpacking objects: 100% (25/25), done.

$ cd packtci/multiple-languages
$ git checkout -qf 2a663fc233d3ae3986fd99efc510369ded92ba94
```

Travis CI clones a fresh copy of the `multiple-languages` repository, which is an
important aspect of continuous integration. Remember that a CI build should build a fresh
copy on each build and there should be no assumed environment variables:

```
419  $ export GOPATH=$HOME/gopath
420  $ export PATH=$HOME/gopath/bin:$PATH
421  $ mkdir -p $HOME/gopath/src/github.com/packtci/multiple-languages
422  $ rsync -az ${TRAVIS_BUILD_DIR}/ $HOME/gopath/src/github.com/packtci/multiple-languages/
423  $ export TRAVIS_BUILD_DIR=$HOME/gopath/src/github.com/packtci/multiple-languages
424  $ cd $HOME/gopath/src/github.com/packtci/multiple-languages
425                                                                                          0.01s
426  $ gimme version
427  v1.5.0
428  $ go version
429  go version go1.10 linux/amd64
```

Notice that Travis CI sets some environment variables for us, including the `GOPATH` and
`PATH` environment variables. Travis CI runs the `go version` command as a verification
that Go version 1.10 is installed in the CI build:

In this step of the CI build, we install our secondary programming language of Node.js. This is optional but notice that Travis CI has a build label to the right of `before_install`, which is one of the build steps we discussed in Chapter 9, *Installation and Basics of Travis CI*, in the *Build customization* section. Also, notice that to the right of the build life cycle labels of `before_install` and `install`, there is a timestamp for how long the build step actually took which is in human readable format of 2.55 seconds and 2.88 seconds for the `before_install` and `install` life cycle events:

```
498  $ go test                                                          0.30s
499  PASS
500  ok      github.com/packtci/multiple-languages   0.001s
501
502
503  The command "go test" exited with 0.
504  $ npm test                                                         0.72s
505
506  > multiple-languages@1.0.0 test /home/travis/gopath/src/github.com/packtci/multiple-languages
507  > tape *.test.js
508
509  TAP version 13
510  # average should return the average of a list of numbers
511  ok 1 actual should equal expected
512  # sort should return a sorted list of names
513  ok 2 Should return sorted
514
515  1..2
516  # tests 2
517  # pass  2
518
519  # ok
520
521
522
523  The command "npm test" exited with 0.
524
525  Done. Your build exited with 0.
                                                                        Top ▲
```

Notice here that there is no build label for the script build life cycle as this is the main part of the CI build.

Any other life cycle events, such as the `after_success` and `after_script` life cycle events will have a build label and a timestamp.

Debugging build locally with Docker

You can debug a build locally by pulling down a Docker image that is held in the documentation link, Troubleshooting Locally in a Docker Image (`https://docs.travis-ci.com/user/common-build-problems/#Troubleshooting-Locally-in-a-Docker-Image`). You can find the instructions to install Docker in this link (`https://docs.docker.com/install/`).

1. Pull down the Go Docker image:

   ```
   docker pull travisci/ci-garnet:packer-1512502276-986baf0
   ```

   Notice that we run the `docker pull` command to actually pull down the Docker image

2. Start the interactive Docker session:

   ```
   ~ docker run --name travis-debug -dit travisci/ci-garnet:packer-1512502276-986baf0 /sbin/init
   f088669a10d42da9c10be963fa48bf4a7b9a282bd56d854b85763a4de1d4630b
   ~
   ```

   Notice here that we ran an interactive shell session in detached mode

3. Open a login shell in the running container:

   ```
   docker exec -it travis-debug bash -l
   ```

   This command starts an interactive shell session with the running Docker container using a Bash shell

4. Switch to the Travis user:

   ```
   su - travis
   ```

   In this command, we switch to the Travis user instead of the default root user

5. Clone the `multiple-languages` Git repository into the home directory:

   ```
   git clone --depth=50 --branch=master
   https://github.com/packtci/multiple-languages
   cd multiple-languages
   ```

   This command clones our `multiple-languages` repository locally onto the Docker container and then changes into this directory

6. Checkout the Git commit we want to test locally.

   Run the `git log` command and find the commit we want to checkout locally. Most probably it is the top level Git commit that we will check:

   ```
   git log
   git checkout 2a663fc233d3ae3986fd99efc510369ded92ba94
   ```

   In this step, we want to make sure that we test only the changes corresponding to the changes we want to test.

7. Install the library dependencies and the secondary programming language:

   ```
   NODE_VERSION="6"
   nvm install $NODE_VERSION
   npm install
   ```

   In this step, we install Node.js as the secondary programming language by using the **node version manager** (**nvm**) and then run `npm install` command to install all of our library dependencies

8. Run the script build steps.

   In the following screenshot, we run the `go test` and `npm test` command to simulate the script build life cycle event in our local Docker container:

   ```
   travis@62006c45d4e0:~/multiple-languages$ go test
   PASS
   ok      _/home/travis/multiple-languages        0.004s
   travis@62006c45d4e0:~/multiple-languages$ npm test

   > multiple-languages@1.0.0 test /home/travis/multiple-languages
   > tape *.test.js

   TAP version 13
   # average should return the average of a list of numbers
   ok 1 actual should equal expected
   # sort should return a sorted list of names
   ok 2 Should return sorted

   1..2
   # tests 2
   # pass  2

   # ok

   travis@62006c45d4e0:~/multiple-languages$
   ```

Running build in debug mode

Another technique to debug build time issues is by running a debug build in Travis CI. You need to email support@travis-ci.com to toggle this feature on for public repositories while private repositories have the debug mode enabled by default. The reason for this is that anyone can come across a log containing the SSH access and can then make a connection to the virtual machine and then potentially read out secret environment information, such as client IDs, secrets, and more.

Getting an API token from the profile page

To restart a job in debug mode via the API, you need to send a POST request to the job's debug endpoint. This request needs to be authenticated by adding your Travis CI API token to the authorization header. You can find your API token in your Travis CI Profile page for public projects.

You need to visit a URL, such as https://travis-ci.org/profile/packtci. Then you need to copy your API token in the profile page, which looks like this:

Next, you will need to hit the debug endpoint by using a REST client with your API token.

Getting access to a token using Travis CLI

You can use the Travis CLI to get an access token by running the following command:

```
travis token
```

Obtaining a job ID from the build log

You can obtain the job ID by expanding the `Build system information` tab and then looking for the label `Job id`. In the following screenshot, there is an arrow pointing to the `Job id`:

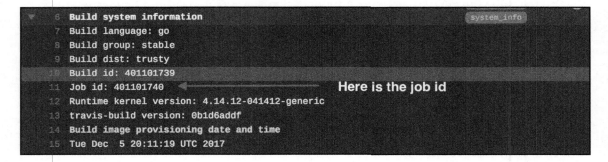

Obtaining the job ID from the URL in the View config button

If you click the **View config** button, the URL will change and you can copy the job ID from the URL. In the following screenshot, we clicked the **View config** button, which looks like this:

Then the URL changed to this config: `https://travis-ci.org/packtci/multiple-languages/jobs/401101740/config`.

The job ID is `401101740` in this URL.

Obtaining the job ID via an API call to the /builds endpoint

You can also obtain a job ID by calling the /builds endpoint in the Travis API. You will need to make a GET request and provide a valid access token in order to make the REST call. Here is a sample request using the curl REST client:

```
curl -s -X GET \
  -H "Content-Type: application/json" \
  -H "Accept: application/json" \
  -H "Travis-API-Version: 3" \
  -H "Authorization: token $(travis token)" \
  -d '{ "quiet": true }' \
  https://api.travis-ci.org/builds
```

This will fetch all the builds that are associated with the repository, which could potentially be a big JSON payload. You can use the **jq** (https://stedolan.github.io/jq/) command line JSON processor to filter out the job ID information. Here is the same REST call that pipes the JSON payload into the jq command-line utility to filter out only the job IDs that correspond to builds:

```
rust_dev curl -s -X GET \
  -H "Content-Type: application/json" \
  -H "Accept: application/json" \
  -H "Travis-API-Version: 3" \
  -H "Authorization: token $(travis token)" \
  -d '{ "quiet": true }' \
  https://api.travis-ci.org/builds | jq '.builds[] | .id'
401101739
401098459
401097385
400718369
399353691
395854355
399102978
398696669
398629798
398320277
395882387
395868343
395867634
395867021
395853670
393843388
rust_dev
```

API call to start a build job in debug mode

You can use any REST client to make a call to the Travis API as long as you have a valid access token.

Here is a sample REST call to the debug endpoint for the 40110174 job ID:

```
↦ rust_dev curl -s -X POST \
  -H "Content-Type: application/json" \
  -H "Accept: application/json" \
  -H "Travis-API-Version: 3" \
  -H "Authorization: token $(travis token)" \
  -d '{ "quiet": true }' \
  https://api.travis-ci.org/job/401101740/debug
{
  "@type": "pending",
  "job": {
    "@type": "job",
    "@href": "/job/401101740",
    "@representation": "minimal",
    "id": 401101740
  },
  "state_change": "created",
  "resource_type": "job"
}
↦ rust_dev ▮
```

Notice that in this screenshot, we added the Authorization HTTP header and used the Travis CLI to print out our access token by using Bash string interpolation like this:

```
Authorization: token $(travis token)
```

Also notice that we are using the public Travis endpoint of https://api.travis-ci.org.

Fetching an SSH session for the debug mode

If you travel back to the Travis web UI and look at the current job log, you will see the following:

```
459  Debug build initiated by packtci
460  Setting up debug tools.
461  Preparing debug sessions.
462  Use the following SSH command to access the interactive debugging environment:
463  ssh kPe2onBfAsOFdgwuk7DVWzjOu@ny2.tmate.io
464  This build is running in quiet mode. No session output will be displayed.
465  This debug build will stay alive for 30 minutes.
466  ...
                                                                              Top ▲
```

Now you simply go to a Command Prompt or Terminal session and enter the `ssh` command to start an interactive debug session with the current build:

```
↳ dev ssh 20Ds4n5a0wx5NuW54iEYzjzwF@ny2.tmate.io
```

The debug mode SSH session will only stay alive for 30 minutes and then you will need to make another API call to start another debug session:

```
Run individual commands; or execute configured build phases
with `travis_run_*` functions (e.g., `travis_run_before_install`).

For more information, consult https://docs.travis-ci.com/user/running-build-in-debug-mode/, or email support@travis-ci.com.

travis@travis-job-packtci-multiple-langu-401101740:~/gopath/src/github.com/packtci/multiple-languages$ ex^C
travis@travis-job-packtci-multiple-langu-401101740:~/gopath/src/github.com/packtci/multiple-languages$ tr
tr                        travis_fold                travis_run_before_cache    travis_run_install        travis_time_start
tracepath                 travis_internal_ruby       travis_run_before_install  travis_run_prepare        travis_wait
tracepath6                travis_jigger              travis_run_before_script   travis_run_reset_state    trial
traceroute6               travis_nanoseconds         travis_run_cache           travis_run_script         troff
traceroute6.iputils       travis_result             travis_run_checkout        travis_run_setup          true
trap                      travis_retry              travis_run_configure       travis_run_setup_cache    truncate
travis_assert             travis_run_after_failure   travis_run_debug           travis_run_setup_casher   try-from
travis_cmd                travis_run_after_script    travis_run_disable_sudo    travis_run_setup_filter
travis_debug.sh           travis_run_after_success   travis_run_export          travis_terminate
travis_download           travis_run_announce        travis_run_finish          travis_time_finish
travis@travis-job-packtci-multiple-langu-401101740:~/gopath/src/github.com/packtci/multiple-languages$ trav
```

Travis debug mode convenience Bash functions

Here is a list of convenience Bash functions that are available:

- `travis_run_before_install` corresponds to the **before_install** lifecycle event
- `travis_run_install` corresponds to the **install** lifecycle event
- `travis_run_before_script` corresponds to the **before_script** lifecycle event
- `travis_run_script` corresponds to the **script** lifecycle event
- `travis_run_after_success` corresponds to the **after_success** lifecycle event
- `travis_run_after_failure` corresponds to the **after_failure** lifecycle event
- `travis_run_after_script` corresponds to the **after_script** lifecycle event

In the following screenshot, we run the `travis_run_before_install` function:

```
travis@travis-job-packtci-multiple-langu-401101740:~/gopath/src/github.com/packtci/multiple-languages$ travis_run_before_install
$ nvm install $NODE_VERSION
Downloading and installing node v6.14.3...
Downloading https://nodejs.org/dist/v6.14.3/node-v6.14.3-linux-x64.tar.xz...
######################################################################## 100.0%
Computing checksum with sha256sum
Checksums matched!
Now using node v6.14.3 (npm v3.10.10)

travis@travis-job-packtci-multiple-langu-401101740:~/gopath/src/github.com/packtci/multiple-languages$
```

Remember that this is running what is specified in the `before_install` life cycle event, which has the following in the `multiple-languages` repository:

```
before_install:
  - nvm install $NODE_VERSION
```

Now we will run the `travis_run_install` convenience Bash function, which installs library dependencies that are specified in the Travis `install` life cycle event:

```
travis@travis-job-packtci-multiple-langu-401101740:~/gopath/src/github.com/packtci/multiple-languages$ travis_run_install
$ npm install
multiple-languages@1.0.0 /home/travis/gopath/src/github.com/packtci/multiple-languages
└── tape@4.9.1
    ├── deep-equal@1.0.1
    ├── defined@1.0.0
    ├── for-each@0.3.3
    │   └── is-callable@1.1.4
    ├── function-bind@1.1.1
    ├── glob@7.1.2
    │   ├── fs.realpath@1.0.0
    │   ├── inflight@1.0.6
    │   │   └── wrappy@1.0.2
    │   ├── minimatch@3.0.4
    │   │   └── brace-expansion@1.1.11
    │   │       ├── balanced-match@1.0.0
    │   │       └── concat-map@0.0.1
    │   ├── once@1.4.0
    │   └── path-is-absolute@1.0.1
    ├── has@1.0.3
    ├── inherits@2.0.3
    ├── minimist@1.2.0
    ├── object-inspect@1.6.0
    ├── resolve@1.7.1
    │   └── path-parse@1.0.5
    ├── resumer@0.0.0
    ├── string.prototype.trim@1.1.2
    │   ├── define-properties@1.1.2
    │   │   ├── foreach@2.0.5
    │   │   └── object-keys@1.0.12
    │   └── es-abstract@1.12.0
    │       └── es-to-primitive@1.1.1
    │           ├── is-date-object@1.0.1
    │           ├── is-symbol@1.0.1
    │           └── is-regex@1.0.4
    └── through@2.3.8
travis@travis-job-packtci-multiple-langu-401101740:~/gopath/src/github.com/packtci/multiple-languages$
```

We have the following entry in the `install` life cycle event in the `multiple-languages` repository Travis YML script:

```
install:
  - npm install
```

Notice that is exactly what is run when the `travis_run_install` convenience function is run.

Next, we run the `travis_run_script` convenience function, which runs any scripts that have been defined in the Travis `script` life cycle event:

```
travis@travis-job-packtci-multiple-langu-401101740:~/gopath/src/github.com/packtci/multiple-languages$ travis_run_script
$ go test
PASS
ok      github.com/packtci/multiple-languages   0.002s


The command "go test" exited with 0.
$ npm test

> multiple-languages@1.0.0 test /home/travis/gopath/src/github.com/packtci/multiple-languages
> tape *.test.js

TAP version 13
# average should return the average of a list of numbers
ok 1 actual should equal expected
# sort should return a sorted list of names
ok 2 Should return sorted

1..2
# tests 2
# pass  2

# ok


The command "npm test" exited with 0.
travis@travis-job-packtci-multiple-langu-401101740:~/gopath/src/github.com/packtci/multiple-languages$ █
```

We have the following entry in the `script` life cycle event in the `multiple-languages` repository Travis YML script:

```
script:
    - go test
    - npm test
```

If we had specified any other life cycle events, we could have used the remaining convenience Bash functions.

tmate shell session actions

The SSH shell session uses a fork of tmux (`https://github.com/tmux/tmux`) which is a Terminal multiplexor program called tmate (`https://tmate.io/`) and with it you can open Windows, scroll through history, and more.

- If you press *Control-b* [, you will be able to scroll up and down the history of your commands

- To quit the history scroll mode, you simply press the letter *q*.
- If you press *Control-b c*, you will create a new window that you can work with.

- If you press *Control-b [0..9]*, then you can toggle between any new windows that you have created. Notice here the brackets mean, for instance, Control-b 0, Control-b 1, and so on to toggle through window sessions.

Travis Web UI logging

You can certainly log out some environment variables in Travis CI but be careful that you do not log out secret information in your logs.

Steps that Travis CI takes to protect your environment-specific variables

Travis CI will, by default, hide any variables such as tokens and environment variables and simply display the string [secure] in their place.

If you go to build #3 https://travis-ci.org/packtci/puppeteer-headless-chrome-travis-yml-script/builds/398696669), you will see the following entry:

```
428  Setting environment variables from .travis.yml
429  $ export SECRET_VALUE=[secure]
```

Remember that we added the following encrypted environment variable in this repository in Chapter 10, *Travis CI CLI Commands and Automation*:

```
travis encrypt SECRET_VALUE=SuperSecret12345 --add
```

Notice that this command adds the following entry into the Travis YML script:

```
env:
    global:
        secure:
```

WLiuzi0CTx/ta5zuoU5K2LeZgzrAhWATUjngx++Azz7Tw4+XqbxeHZ/6ITymE1YLDRMxdIh8hIt
vkoNCbPmJ6q1To6bdirloWZq2r1Z5BPGYfVY3cuoUuxTAz1uhhfnngkqd76eJfB41BUfOIVNAg2
rpI7QFAQr1aiIKxjthiTms57fR4dusEi/efVO90I7yzFtyxEa0tLTgW9x+dPSt2ApmJ0EP9tftk
7M7Uw/F2Gm1/AzWpM1B1klm/iEHF3ZY6Ij/V+ZG2SCpfrF88m50a8nJF1a+KttZz/TTbwqA58dX
NokxcD30HB468/oaGMTJxYLFmG3QMfbXuP2wUkuinIEWQxGBEDh3uw11ZhypCGVNvE6vbRpdIIz
ywcVcX95G1px+Dgci1+c8AebO1wbW1DXMuWNQHC7JjdQspvLUtsLeyyei3LKshTY7LktvhJEG/+
sgd5sejeqnzFmLmC9TdbCazLMFWzqh1+SBcmQtFNVuqAGB1MF1T1154zFnZ17mixetVeBziuS7x
GG3XXm0BsYIQnkcJYxNGv8JrFMSoqBTdQV4C20UyyXAw8s+51u6dGziiMPSUK4KUSVPJ3hyeNiG
hLTBsJn4bnTPiJ5i1VdyNM8RD8X2EJRImT3uvGvuFqHraCBrBuZVaW4RtbGX0JYYtMMMr/P84jK
rNC3iFD8=

Remember that the Travis Job log only showed the string `[secure]` in place of this environment variable.

Travis CI deployment overview and debugging

We discussed Software Deployments in *Chapter 3, Basics of Continuous Delivery*, but to recap a Deployment is the end product of the software that is created by developers that your end users will use. A Deployment is typically done in the end of a successful CI/CD Pipeline has finished. Remember that a CI/CD pipeline can consist of a commit stage where any binaries are built and a Unit Test Suite is run followed by a 2nd stage where integration tests may be run, and then possibly followed by a 3rd stage consisting of Load Tests and/or Security Tests and then finally a 4th stage consisting of a suite of Acceptance Tests. If all of the stages of the CI/CD pipeline finish successfully then and only then should a Deployment pipeline be initiated.

Deployments in Travis CI are relatively easy/ Remember that you can use the Travis CLI to set up some deployment tools with ease in Travis CI.

Supported Providers in Travis CI

Here are some supported providers that you can use with Travis CI for deployments:

- AWS CodeDeploy (https://docs.travis-ci.com/user/deployment/codedeploy/)
- AWS Elastic Beanstalk (https://docs.travis-ci.com/user/deployment/elasticbeanstalk/)
- AWS Lambda (https://docs.travis-ci.com/user/deployment/lambda/)
- AWS S3 (https://docs.travis-ci.com/user/deployment/s3/)
- Azure Web App (https://docs.travis-ci.com/user/deployment/azure-web-apps/)
- Bluemix CloudFoundry (https://docs.travis-ci.com/user/deployment/bluemixcloudfoundry/)
- Chef Supermarket (https://docs.travis-ci.com/user/deployment/chefsupermarket/)
- CloudFoundry (https://docs.travis-ci.com/user/deployment/cloudfoundry/)

- GitHub Pages (https://docs.travis-ci.com/user/deployment/pages/)
- GitHub Releases (https://docs.travis-ci.com/user/deployment/releases/)
- Google App Engine (https://docs.travis-ci.com/user/deployment/google-app-engine/)
- Google Cloud Storage (https://docs.travis-ci.com/user/deployment/gcs/)
- Google Firebase (https://docs.travis-ci.com/user/deployment/firebase/)
- Heroku (https://docs.travis-ci.com/user/deployment/heroku/)
- OpenShift (https://docs.travis-ci.com/user/deployment/openshift/)
- npm (https://docs.travis-ci.com/user/deployment/npm/)
- Surge.sh (https://docs.travis-ci.com/user/deployment/surge/)

For the full list of supported providers, please go to the Travis user documentation (https://docs.travis-ci.com/user/deployment/#Supported-Providers).

Heroku setup in Travis CI

We can use the Travis CLI to help us set up Heroku (https://www.heroku.com/platform) in our multiple-languages (https://github.com/packtci/multiple-languages) repository.

The first step we need to do is to make sure that we are logged into Heroku by using the Heroku CLI, which you can download and install at https://devcenter.heroku.com/articles/heroku-cli#download-and-install. Once we are logged in, we will be given an access token that we can use:

```
▶→ multiple-languages git:(add-test-case) heroku login
heroku: Enter your login credentials
Email:
Password: ********************************
Logged in as
▶→ multiple-languages git:(add-test-case) heroku auth:token
  ›   Warning: token will expire
  ›   Use heroku authorizations:create to generate a long-term token

▶→ multiple-languages git:(add-test-case)
```

Notice here that we used the heroku auth:token command to print out our access token.

Now we simply need to use the `travis setup` command to get set up:

```
▶ multiple-languages git:(master) travis setup heroku
Heroku application name: |multiple-languages|
Deploy only from                         ? |yes|
Encrypt API key? |yes|
▶ multiple-languages git:(master) x git s
  M .travis.yml
```

Notice that we did not have to provide an access token as we already logged into Heroku and the `travis setup` command is smart enough to grab it for us.

The `travis setup` command automatically updates our Travis YML script with Heroku provider information and now our Travis TML script looks like this:

```
language: go

go:
 - '1.10'

env:
 - NODE_VERSION="6"

before_install:
 - nvm install $NODE_VERSION

install:
 - npm install

script:
 - go test
 - npm test

deploy:
 provider: heroku
 api_key:
  secure:
```

ueVMBom+3LHS4xhXXi9hbPR8FIIS/z01Z7NW4hngea4WRHq3gU8AY7Oxz25w/FshMPtaHeCUdZ9
0eDDvLF5/hwI+9zup/XI4gONiTTOpxpiY3EyHkP2frra0sdSQhYBHETsq4hEQxODE83ClQjx2jC
KM3LOTdzI6wrKXpI5UtoD73yIa7AbKCxl8IXGIeNePImyLe6Wl7ovfxq1zcXz5c6Tu6uIqO2Vwk
vILrQKB41Id6VQN1MpfY1kQMASuRwaiJQ8HCmi0NP8A067v0s83OM9bNVK+KXDTLsVyrovnpidU
nVS/Gk2QDNz0Or5xEIM2iXCsQDoa8jGNSCNfPcXq3aYtl2hjgDSVnz28EoxYRBmx365UxzwRVps
gdf1b+sCfd9FBJge7xZqTCGwimoBJvrQH0qvgYzQ855EvmtEyBU5t0JRmU8x/Z74KryO24YHD/h
SY0a1REPCnZqjBkBS5FHQprIJm5XQabwU/IOqPMdM1KvMYj34N+dxK0X92sf0TLSAv3/62oquQ7
Lkhjl4nAsEa05v+kQNMQdLemYFBZi8/Qf6a4YQPNmLXmKwis1FLTzicccwPE8qJ2H3wPQRQUUZV
```
```

```
YQxgjUkh5ni6ikqCkxmZRnNJgCbTWhw3ip1xaWjmm6jtvMhiWiUr6vDgIbvbty120ySBIe3k2P5
ARW77fOA=
```

```
app: multiple-languages
on:
repo: packtci/multiple-languages
```

Debug failure in Travis YML script

If we look at build 8.1 (`https://travis-ci.org/packtci/multiple-languages/jobs/403102478#L548`) for the `multiple-languages` project, we can see that it errored out, as the screenshot shows, because we don't actually have an app in Heroku called multiple-languages:

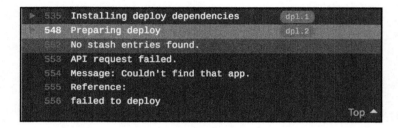

We simply need to create an app in Heroku with an app named `multiple-languages` like this:

Now let us restart the build in Travis using the `travis restart` command:

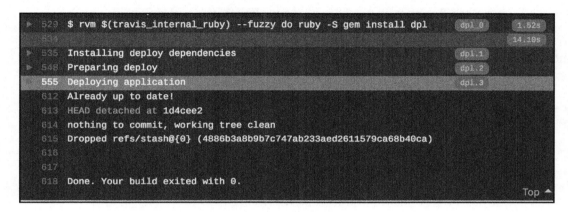

Now let us look at the job log for build 8.1 once more:

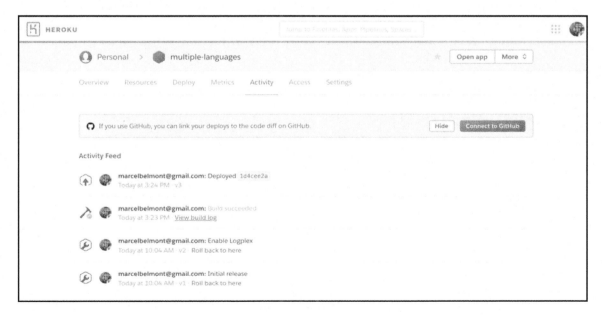

Now if we look at the Heroku dashboard, we can confirm that our application was successfully deployed to Heroku:

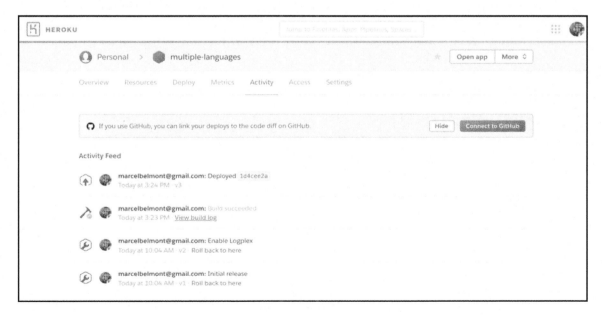

Summary

In this chapter, we presented an overview of the Travis job log and explained the different parts of the job log. We looked at running a build locally using Docker and learned how to enable a build in debug mode by using the Travis API as well. We then looked at the steps that Travis CI takes to secure your secrets and keys in the job log. Finally, we looked at how to deploy an application in Travis CI by using by using the Travis CLI and then looked at how to debug a build failure and get a successful deployment in Travis CI.

In the next chapter, we will explain how to get Circle CLI set up in a software project and then go over the basics of the Circle CI UI.

Questions

1. Does another build get kicked off when you merge a pull request in GitHub?
2. Does the Travis job log show a label when running any scripts in the script life cycle event?
3. How do we debug a build locally in Travis CI?
4. Is the debug build mode available for public repositories?
5. How would you use the Travis API to get a Job ID?
6. What is the convenience bash function that you can use for the before_install life cycle event when running a build in debug mode?
7. What Travis CLI command would you use to setup add-ons such as Heroku to do deployments?

Further reading

You can further explore debugging options and more advanced configuration information in the Travis user documentation: `https://docs.travis-ci.com/`.

12
Installation and Basics of CircleCI

In the previous chapter, we showed how to debug a Travis CI project locally and explained the Travis CI web interface in more detail. We also looked at how to do logging in Travis CI. This chapter will help you get set up with CircleCI and we will explain how to create a Bitbucket account and we will go over how to set up both GitHub and Bitbucket on a new CircleCI account. We will create a simple Java project in Bitbucket and run a CircleCI build for it. We will also discuss how to navigate the Bitbucket UI. We will then end the chapter by creating a new GitHub repository and discuss a CircleCI YML script that will install Golang via a Docker image and run our unit tests.

The following topics will be covered in this chapter:

- An introduction to CircleCI
- A comparison of CircleCI and Jenkins
- CircleCI prerequisites
- Setting up CircleCI in GitHub
- Setting up CircleCI in Bitbucket
- An overview of CircleCI configuration

Technical requirements

This chapter will require some basic programming skills and we will utilize some of the continuous integration/continuous delivery concepts that we will discuss in this chapter. It will be helpful if you try to create a Bitbucket account and a CircleCI account on your own. You can follow the steps in the *CircleCI prerequisites* section. We will create a basic Java application using Maven so it would be helpful to understand some basic programming concepts in Java, but if you know any programming language you should be able to follow along. Basic Git and Unix knowledge would be very helpful.

CircleCI

CircleCI is a hosted and automated solution for **continuous integration** (**CI**) builds. CircleCI uses an in application configuration file that uses YAML (http://yaml.org/spec/ 1.2/spec.html) syntax, such as Travis YML script, which we discussed in Chapter 9, *Installation and Basics of Travis CI*, to Chapter 11, *Travis CI UI Logging and Debugging*. Since CircleCI is hosted in the cloud, it has the advantage that it can be set up quickly in other environments as well as used in different operating systems without having to worry about setup and installation like you have to do with Jenkins CI. Because of this, CircleCI is much faster to set up than Jenkins.

Comparing CircleCI and Jenkins

Jenkins is a self-contained and open source automation server that is customizable and requires setup and configuration at the organization level. Remember in the Jenkins CI chapters, we spent some time installing Jenkins in the Windows, Linux, and macOS operating systems. We also had the ability to configure Jenkins however we wanted. While this is great for software companies with dedicated teams in operations, DevOps, and so on, it is not as great for open source projects where often lone developers are setting up environments for their personal projects.

CircleCI was designed around the principle of open source development and for ease of use. CircleCI can be set up within minutes of creating a project in the GitHub and Bitbucket platforms. Although CircleCI is not as customizable as Jenkins CI in this respect, it has the distinct advantage of having a quick setup. CircleCI uses an in application configuration file that uses YAML syntax and can be used in the GitHub (https://github.com/) platform as well as in the Bitbucket (https://bitbucket.org/) platform, unlike Travis CI.

CircleCI prerequisites

In order to get started with CircleCI, you will need to either create a GitHub account at https://github.com/ or a Bitbucket account at https://bitbucket.org/product.

Creating a GitHub account

We covered in detail how to create a GitHub account in Chapter 9, *Installation and Basics of Travis CI*, in the *Creating a GitHub account* section.

Creating a Bitbucket account

We will create a Bitbucket account and once again use the username of `packtci` for our user:

Once you click the green **Continue** button, you will be redirected to a page like this:

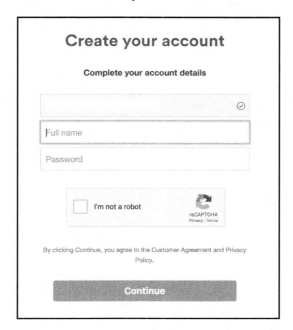

You will need to enter your **Full name** and a **Password** and the email address you provided in the previous page will already be set for you. Once you click the green **Continue** button, you will receive a verification email for your new Bitbucket account that looks like this:

Please verify your email address

Hi   ,

Please verify your email address so we know that it's really you!

Verify my email address

Cheers,
The Atlassians

Once you click the **Verify my email address** button, you will be redirected to the following page:

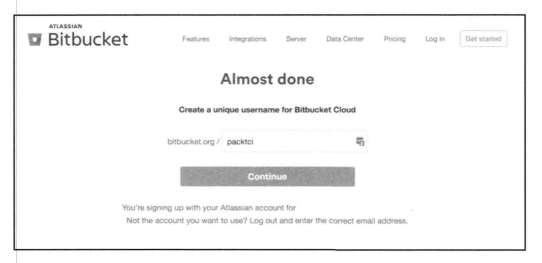

You must provide a unique username for your new Bitbucket account, as you cannot use any existing usernames. Once you click the **Continue** button, you will routed to the following page:

You can either skip this section by clicking the **Skip** button or you can enter your information and then click the **Submit** button and you will be routed to the following page:

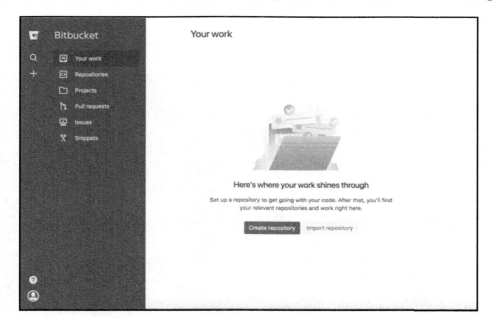

Creating a CircleCI account

You will need to create a CircleCI account in order to get started with CircleCI and you can either use your GitHub login credentials or your Bitbucket login credentials:

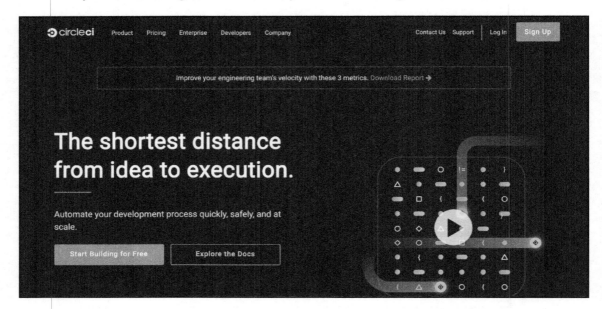

You will need to click the **Sign Up** button in order to create a new CircleCI account and you will be redirected to the following page:

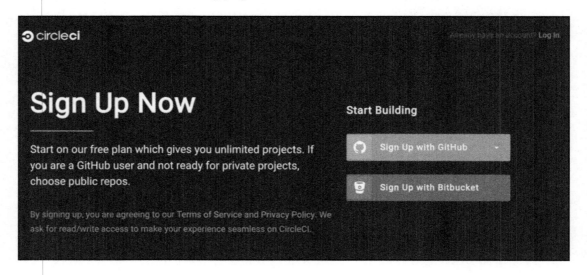

You can sign up with either but we will choose **Sign Up with Bitbucket.** Once you click the button, you will be redirected to the following page:

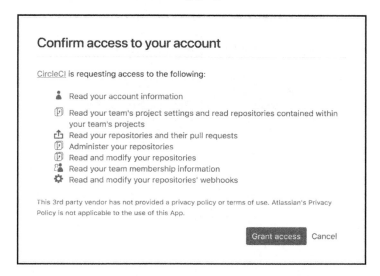

We will click the **Grant access** button and then we will be routed to the following page:

Notice that we have no projects set up to run in CircleCI and will need to add a project later on.

Even though we signed up our new Bitbucket account, we can still connect our GitHub account to our new CircleCI account. You will need to click on the avatar in the upper right corner of the screen and then click the **User settings** button:

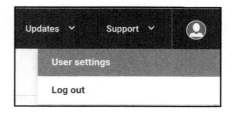

Once you click the **User settings** button, you will be routed to a page showing **Account Integrations**. We need to connect our GitHub account to CircleCI by clicking the **Connect** button:

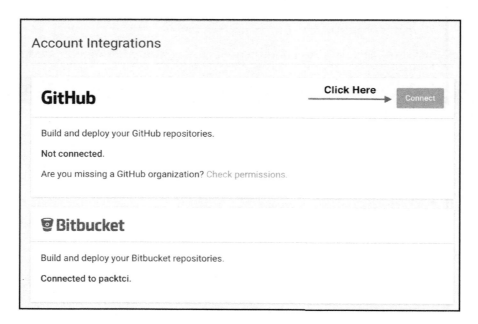

Once you click the **Connect** button, you will be redirected to an **Authorize CircleCI** application page that looks like this:

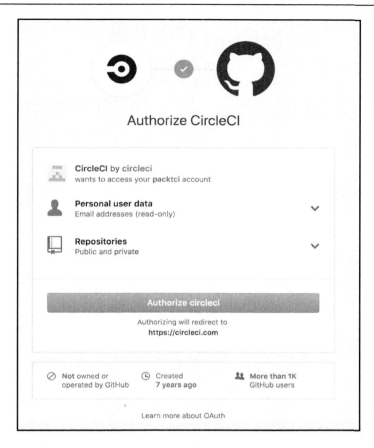

Once you click the **Authorize circleci** button, you will be redirected to the CircleCI dashboard page and you will now have two `packtci` accounts corresponding to your GitHub account and your Bitbucket account, respectively:

Setting up CircleCI in GitHub

Let us add a new project to CircleCI with our `functional-summer` (https://github.com/packtci/functional-summer) GitHub project using our `packtci` (https://github.com/packtci) GitHub account. The first thing we need to do is to click the **Add Projects** button for GitHub that looks like this in the dashboard:

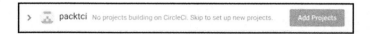

Once you click the **Add Projects** button you will be routed to a page like this:

We will click the **Set Up Project** button for the `functional-summer` GitHub repository and will be routed to a page like this:

CircleCI automatically picked **Node** as our language because we have a `package.json` file and because we have JavaScript files in this repository. We are not done yet, though. If you scroll further down this page, you will notice some next steps to get CircleCI started in our project:

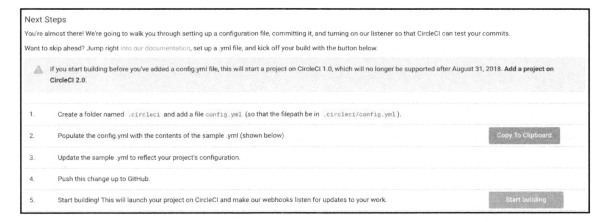

We need to create a folder called `.circleci` in the root of our project and add a file called `config.yml` in this folder. Let us create this folder and file by using the GitHub UI. We will go to the following URL: `https://github.com/packtci/functional-summer`. Then click the **Create new file** button:

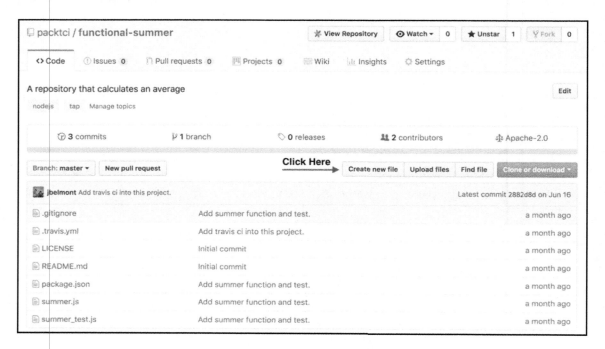

Once we click this button, we will be redirected to a page like this in the GitHub UI:

Enter the name of our folder as .circleci and then enter the / character and then name our file config.yml. Once you are done, it will look like this:

Now we need to enter contents for our config.yml file and .circleci provides us with a sample config.yml file with values that we can use for our new CircleCI project:

```
# Javascript Node CircleCI 2.0 configuration file
#
# Check https://circleci.com/docs/2.0/language-javascript/ for more details
#
version: 2
jobs:
 build:
    docker:
    # specify the version you desire here
    - image: circleci/node:7.10

    # Specify service dependencies here if necessary
    # CircleCI maintains a library of pre-built images
    # documented at https://circleci.com/docs/2.0/circleci-images/
    # - image: circleci/mongo:3.4.4

    working_directory: ~/repo

    steps:
        - checkout

        # Download and cache dependencies
        - restore_cache:
            keys:
            - v1-dependencies-{{ checksum "package.json" }}
            # fallback to using the latest cache if no exact match is
found
            - v1-dependencies-

        - run: yarn install

        - save_cache:
            paths:
                - node_modules
            key: v1-dependencies-{{ checksum "package.json" }}

        # run tests!
        - run: yarn testSetup Circle CI in Atlassian Bitbucket
```

We will explain the contents of this in more detail later but for now we will just copy and paste this into the GitHub UI Editor and then click the **Commit new file** button:

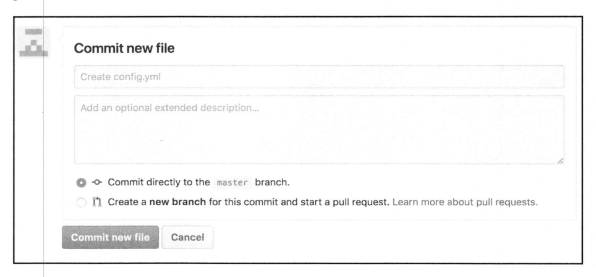

The last step that we need to do is to go back to the **Add Projects** page in CircleCI and click the **Start building** button to launch our newly configured project in CircleCI:

This also sets up a webhook with CircleCI so that CircleCI listens to any new code changes that we commit to GitHub.

Once we click the **Start building** button, we will be redirected to our first build job with our `functional-summer` repository with CircleCI:

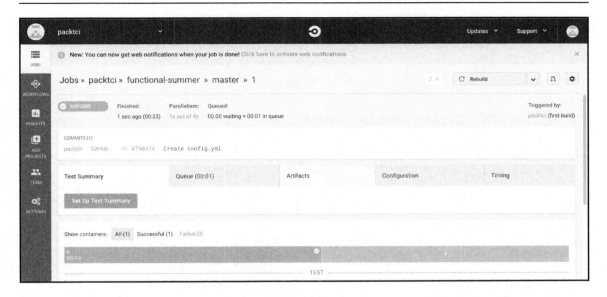

If we scroll further down, we will see each step of the build in the CircleCI application:

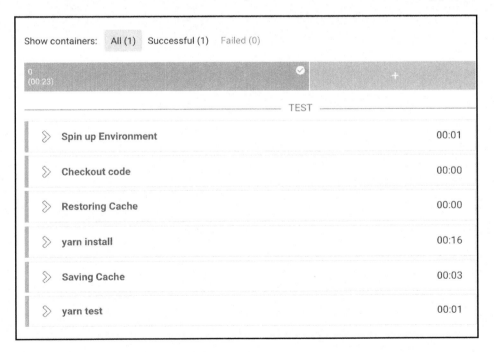

We will explain this in greater detail in later chapters but each step can be expanded to show the detail for that step. For example, if we click the **yarn test** step, we will see the following details:

```
♡  yarn test                                                                    00:01

$ #!/bin/bash -eo pipefail                                            Exit code: 0
  yarn test                                                                      ⊕

yarn test v0.24.4
$ tap summer_test.js
TAP version 13
# Subtest: summer_test.js
    # Subtest: summer function should return the sum of an array of numbers
        ok 1 - Should equal the sum of 15
        1..1
    ok 1 - summer function should return the sum of an array of numbers # time=7.075ms

    1..1
    # time=14.566ms
ok 1 - summer_test.js # time=348.891ms

1..1
# time=364.052ms
Done in 0.82s.
```

Setting up CircleCI in Bitbucket

Since we have just created a new Bitbucket account, we will need to upload our ssh keys into Bitbucket to be able to push changes to Bitbucket. We covered how to create SSH keys in Chapter 9, *Installation and Basics of Travis CI*, in the *Adding a SSH key to your new GitHub account* section, so please read that chapter if you do not have any SSH keys set up already. We already created an SSH Key in *Chapter 9, Installation and Basics of Travis CI* in the *Adding an SSH Key to your new GitHub Account* section. We just need to copy the public ssh key into our system clipboard, by running the following command:

```
pbcopy < ~/.ssh/id_rsa_example.pub
```

Once we have our public SSH key copied into our system clipboard, we need to go to the following page in Bitbucket:

We will need to click the **Add key** button. This will open a modal where we enter a label and the contents of our public key, which looks like this:

We then click the **Add key** button and now we are ready to push changes to our Bitbucket account.

Setting up a new Java project in Bitbucket with CircleCI build

We will create a new Java project in Bitbucket called `java-summer` by clicking on the plus button in the left navigation pane:

Next we will click the **Repository** button, which looks like this:

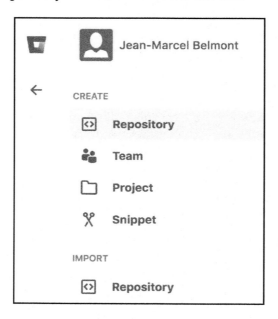

Next we will create a new repository by providing a **Repository name**, setting our **Version control system** to **Git**, and then finish by clicking the **Create repository** button:

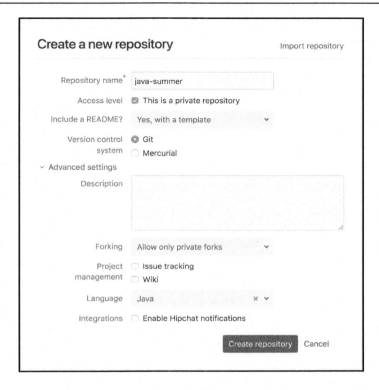

Notice here that we clicked the optional **Advanced settings** dropdown and set our **Language** to the **Java** programming language. Once we click the **Create repository** button, we will be redirected to a page that could look like this:

We will use the Maven build tool to create a new Java project that has a `src` directory with a main subdirectory and a test subdirectory. We explained in detail in Chapter 7, *Developing Plugins*, how to install and use the Maven build tool, so please reread the appropriate sections in Chapter 7, *Developing Plugins*, if you don't have Maven installed and don't know how to use it.

To create our new Java project with Maven, we will issue the following command:

```
mvn archetype:generate -DgroupId=com.packci.app -DartifactId=java-summer -
DarchetypeArtifactId=maven-archetype-quickstart -DinteractiveMode=false
```

We will first clone our repository by issuing the following command in a shell session:

```
git clone git@bitbucket.org:packtci/java-summer.git java-summer-proj
```

We will then copy the contents of the hidden `.git` directory in this cloned repository and paste it into our new `java-summer` folder that we created with the Maven build tool. Assuming that we have the correct path structure, we can issue the following command:

```
mv java-summer-proj/.git java-summer
```

We can then delete the `java-summer-proj` folder and then `cd` into the `java-summer` folder. We will then use the Java language sample configuration, which you can find at **language-java** (https://circleci.com/docs/2.0/language-java/) in CircleCI documentation. We will create a folder called `.circleci` and then create a file called `config.yml`.

We will commit our changes and push it to Bitbucket with the following command:

```
git push
```

Now if you look at the CircleCI application, we can switch to the **packtci** Bitbucket user account by clicking on the upper left of the application, which looks like this:

Next we need to click the **ADD PROJECTS** button in the left navigation pane, which looks like this:

We then need to click the **Set Up Project** button so that CircleCI knows about our `java-summer` repository in Bitbucket, which looks like this:

We will then be routed to the **Set Up Project** page where we need to pick our operating system, which defaults to **Linux** in CircleCI. Then we pick our build language, which should be Java in our case. For clarity, we will show this page once again in the following screenshot:

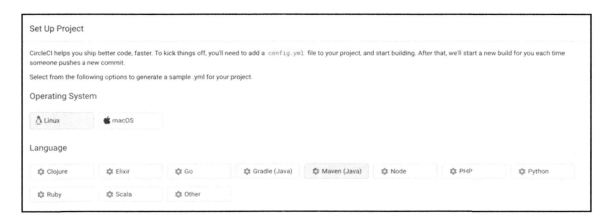

We will then copy the sample configuration file that CircleCI provided for us into the `.circleci/config.yml` file:

```
# Java Maven CircleCI 2.0 configuration file
#
# Check https://circleci.com/docs/2.0/language-java/ for more details
#
```

```
version: 2
jobs:
  build:
    docker:
      # specify the version you desire here
      - image: circleci/openjdk:8-jdk
      # Specify service dependencies here if necessary
      # CircleCI maintains a library of pre-built images
      # documented at https://circleci.com/docs/2.0/circleci-images/
      # - image: circleci/postgres:9.4

    working_directory: ~/repo

    environment:
      # Customize the JVM maximum heap limit
      MAVEN_OPTS: -Xmx3200m
    steps:
      - checkout

      # Download and cache dependencies
      - restore_cache:
          keys:
          - v1-dependencies-{{ checksum "pom.xml" }}
          # fallback to using the latest cache if no exact match is found
          - v1-dependencies-

      - run: mvn dependency:go-offline

      - save_cache:
          paths:
            - ~/.m2
          key: v1-dependencies-{{ checksum "pom.xml" }}
      # run tests!
      - run: mvn integration-test
```

Next we will commit the changes and push it up into Bitbucket version control system and then we need to scroll to the **Next Steps** section and simply click the **Start building** button, which looks like this:

5.	Start building! This will launch your project on CircleCI and make our webhooks listen for updates to your work.	Start building

This will trigger our first build for the `java-summer` project and get the webhook working for the repository. Once we click the **Start building** button, we need to click the **JOBS** button, in order to see our new build that was triggered:

Now to test that the webhooks are listening to code changes in Bitbucket, let us make a change to our `java-summer` file so that it actually has a function that sums up an array of values and add a unit test case with JUnit (https://junit.org/junit4/javadoc/latest/).

Let us add a static function like this in the app file:

```
public static int average(int[] numbers) {
    int sum = 0;
    for (int i = 0; i < numbers.length; i++) {
        sum += numbers[i];
    }
    return sum;
}
```

Then let us add a test case to test the average function like this with JUnit:

```
public void testaverage() {
    App myApp = new App();
    int[] numbers = {
            1, 2, 3, 4, 5
    };
    assertEquals(15, myApp.average(numbers));
}
```

We can test the changes locally with the `mvn package` command to make sure that nothing is broken and then commit our changes and push these changes up to the Bitbucket version control system. We should now notice a build that was automatically triggered with CircleCI because of our code change to the master branch.

If we go back to the CircleCI web application, we can see that a new build was triggered and that it passed:

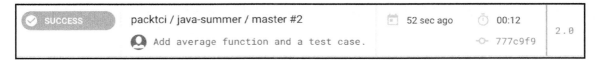

Notice that in the preceding screenshot, CircleCI shows that the second build was triggered. It also shows the commit SHA hash and the commit message and confirms that the build was a success.

CircleCI configuration overview

CircleCI uses YAML (http://yaml.org/spec/1.2/spec.html), which is a data serialization language, for its configuration language, as does Travis CI.

Concept overview of CircleCI configuration

We will discuss many more concepts and configuration options in CircleCI in later chapters but, as an overview, let us look at a basic config.yml file and explain some of its concepts. We will create a new repository in GitHub with our packtci (https://github.com/packtci) Github user. You can find the new repository at https://github.com/packtci/go-template-example-with-circle-ci. We will also create a function in Golang that parses a template. We will then write a test case that parses the template text and then create a CircleCI config.yml file. We will push these code changes up to GitHub and then finally set up this new project with CircleCI.

Adding source files to the new repository

In the new repository, we added a file called template.go and here is the function we will test:

```
func parseTemplate(soldier Soldier, tmpl string) *bytes.Buffer {
    var buff = new(bytes.Buffer)
    t := template.New("A template file")
    t, err := t.Parse(tmpl)
    if err != nil {
        log.Fatal("Parse: ", err)
        return buff
    }
    err = t.Execute(buff, soldier)
    if err != nil {
        log.Fatal("Execute: ", err)
        return buff
    }
    return buff
}
```

We added the following unit test case to test the `parseTemplate` function in the `template_test.go` file:

```go
func TestParseTemplate(t *testing.T) {
    newSoldier := Soldier{
        Name: "Luke Cage",
        Rank: "SGT",
        TimeInService: 4,
    }
    txt := parseTemplate(newSoldier, templateText)
    expectedTxt := `
Name is Luke Cage
Rank is SGT
Time in service is 4
`
    if txt.String() != expectedTxt {
        t.Error("The text returned should match")
    }
}
```

We then added the following CircleCI YML script to the repository:

```yaml
version: 2

jobs:
    build:
        docker:
            - image: circleci/golang:1.9
        working_directory: /go/src/github.com/packtci/go-template-example-
with-circle-ci
        steps:
            - checkout
            - run:
                name: "Print go version"
                command: go version
            - run:
                name: "Run Unit Tests"
                command: go test
```

The first thing to add in a CircleCI YML script is the version (https://circleci.com/docs/ 2.0/configuration-reference/#version) field. This is a required field to add, and at the moment **version 1** is still supported but will soon become deprecated so it is advised to use **version 2** of the CircleCI YML syntax. You can read more about this in the following CircleCI blog post: https://circleci.com/blog/sunsetting-1-0/.

The next thing we have in this `config.yml` script is the jobs (`https://circleci.com/docs/2.0/configuration-reference/#jobs`) field, which is comprised of one or more named jobs. In our case, we have one named job called build and this build job is required if we are not using the workflows field. We will discuss this in greater detail in later chapters.

We then have a field called `docker`, which has a language image for Golang. We can also have a service image to run a particular service, which we will discuss in later chapters.

We then have a field called `steps`, which defines the steps we want to execute in our CircleCI build. Notice that we have three field entries in the `steps` field, which are `checkout` and two `run` (`https://circleci.com/docs/2.0/configuration-reference/#jobs`) commands. The run commands have a name and a command but you can also omit a name and just give a command.

CircleCI build job for the new repository

The following screenshot shows that the CircleCI build passed:

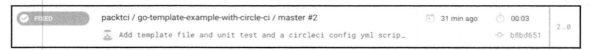

Here are the steps in the build job:

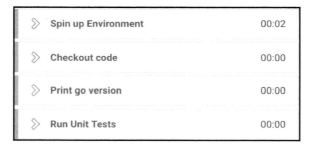

Notice here that there is an additional step called **Spin up Environment**. This step creates a new build environment and, for our build in particular, it creates a Golang Docker image and then sets some CircleCI-specific environment variables.

Summary

In this chapter, we covered the differences between CircleCI and Travis CI and covered the prerequisites of CircleCI. We created a new Bitbucket account and explained the basics of the Bitbucket UI and where to upload your SSH keys for repository access in Bitbucket. We then set up CircleCI in GitHub and Bitbucket and explained parts of the CircleCI web application and how to navigate around it. We finished by giving a brief overview of the CircleCI YAML configuration syntax. In the next chapter, we will go over the CircleCI commands and go over some more advanced topics in CircleCI, such as workflows.

Questions

1. What is the primary difference between Jenkins and Travis CI?
2. Can CircleCI work in both Bitbucket and GitHub?
3. Where do you set up a repository in CircleCI?
4. How do you view build jobs in CircleCI?
5. Which build tool did we use in the `java-summer` repository in Bitbucket?
6. Should you be using version 1 of the CircleCI syntax?
7. In what field do we enter our build language in CircleCI `config.yml` script?

Further reading

You can further explore concepts in CircleCI by looking at the official CircleCI documentation at `https://circleci.com/docs/2.0/`.

CircleCI CLI Commands and Automation

13

In the previous chapter, we covered how to get set up using CircleCI in Bitbucket and in GitHub and showed you how to navigate the Bitbucket UI and covered the basics of the CircleCI Web UI. In this chapter, we will cover how to install CircleCI CLI on macOS/Linux and show you how to get a nightly build from the CLI. We will go over each CircleCI CLI command in detail and explain how the workflows in CircleCI work. We'll show you how to get a more complicated workflow with a sequential jobs setup. We will finish by covering the CircleCI API and show you how to use the `jq` JSON command utility to transform JSON when using HTTP requests.

In this chapter, we will cover the following topics:

- CircleCI CLI installation
- CircleCI CLI commands
- Using workflows in CircleCI
- Working with the CircleCI API

Technical requirements

This chapter will require some basic Unix programming skills and we will build upon some of the **continuous integration** (**CI**) and **continuous delivery** (**CD**) concepts we have talked about in the previous chapters. It would be useful to be somewhat familiar with working with RESTful APIs as we will be using curl as a REST client at the end of the chapter.

CircleCI CLI installation

The first prerequisite to install CircleCI CLI is to have Docker (https://docs.docker.com/install/) installed. To install Docker on your OS, visit the Docker store at https://store.docker.com/search?type=editionoffering=community and click on the **Docker CE** link which is suitable for your OS or cloud service. Follow the installation instructions on their website.

Make sure that Docker is installed by checking the Docker version either on a Windows Command Prompt or an macOS/Linux Terminal application by running a command like this:

```
~ docker --version
Docker version 18.03.1-ce, build 9ee9f40
~
```

Here I have Docker version 18 installed.

Installing CircleCI CLI on macOS/Linux

You will need to run the following command to install CircleCI:

```
curl -o /usr/local/bin/circleci
https://circle-downloads.s3.amazonaws.com/releases/build_agent_wrapper/circleci && chmod +x /usr/local/bin/circleci
```

You will need to run this in a Terminal application shell session.

Installing nightly build versions of CircleCI through GitHub releases

You can install nightly versions of the CircleCI CLI at the GitHub releases page: https://github.com/CircleCI-Public/circleci-cli/releases. You will need to look at the **Assets** section, which looks like this:

We will pick the `circleci-cli_0.1.771_darwin_amd64.tar.gz` asset as we will be running the local CLI on the macOS OS.

Run the following commands in a Terminal shell session:

```
# Go to the Downloads Folder
cd ~/Downloads

# Unpack the compressed asset
tar -xvzf circleci-cli_0.1.771_darwin_amd64.tar.gz

# Go into the uncompressed directory
cd circleci-cli_0.1.771_darwin_amd64

# Move the circleci binary into the folder /usr/local/bin
mv circleci /usr/local/bin/circleci-beta

# Make sure that the binary is executable
chmod +x /usr/local/bin/circleci-beta

# Check that the binary version to make sure that it is working
circleci-beta help
```

We now have a newer version of the CircleCI CLI and can verify this:

```
⊢→  go-template-example-with-circle-ci git:(master) x circleci-beta version
0.1.771 (c46faa4)
⊢→  go-template-example-with-circle-ci git:(master) x ▊
```

 We have named this binary executable `circleci-beta`. This is so we can run the stable and nightly versions of CircleCI CLI. This is not something that you will have to do; we are doing this for illustration purposes only.

CircleCI CLI commands

The CircleCI CLI is not as fully featured as the Travis CI CLI in terms of feature parity with all the features that you can actually use in CircleCI. More commands will become available in the future, but at the moment you have six commands that you can use in CircleCI CLI, which are `build`, `config`, `help`, `step`, `tests`, and `version`, if you use the CircleCI CLI binary in AWS releases (https://circle-downloads.s3.amazonaws.com/releases/build_ agent_wrapper/circleci) from the official CircleCI documentation. We will be using both the stable build version and the nightly build version, which has several more commands than the stable version. Remember that we installed in the *Installing nightly build versions of CircleCI through GitHub releases* section of this chapter. The stable version of the command will be `circleci` and the nightly build will be `circleci-beta`.

In the following screenshot, we run the `help` command which shows the available commands and gives us a brief overview of what each command does:

```
⊢→  go-template-example-with-circle-ci git:(master) circleci help

The CLI tool to be used in CircleCI.

Usage:
  circleci [command]

Available Commands:
  build      Run a full build locally
  config     Validate and update the circleCI configuration file
  help       Help about any command
  step       Execute steps
  tests      Collect and split files with tests
  version    Output version info

Flags:
  -h, --help      help for circleci
      --verbose   enable verbose logging output

Use "circleci [command] --help" for more information about a command.
⊢→  go-template-example-with-circle-ci git:(master) ▊
```

Version command

The `version` command outputs the current version of the CLI that you have installed on your local system:

```
>→  dev circleci version

circleci version: 0.0.5894-01cdb92
Build Agent version: 0.0.5895-01cdb92
built: 2018-05-29T20:07:10+0000
>→  dev
```

You can also pass a flag/option to each command in the CLI and you can find the options that a command takes by running the `--help` flag:

```
>→  dev circleci version --help

circleci version: 0.0.5894-01cdb92
Output version info

Usage:
  circleci version [flags]

Flags:
  -h, --help   help for version

Global Flags:
      --verbose   enable verbose logging output
>→  dev
```

There is only one option we can pass to the `version` command, which is `-h, --help` as this is a very simple command.

Help command

The help command will show all the CLI commands, as we demonstrated at the beginning of this section, but it can also be used to explain how each command works and will display any flags/options that each command takes:

```
↪  dev circleci help help

Help provides help for any command in the application.
Simply type circleci help [path to command] for full details.

Usage:
  circleci help [command] [flags]

Flags:
  -h, --help   help for help

Global Flags:
      --verbose   enable verbose logging output
↪  dev
```

Here we ran help on the help command itself.

Config command

The config command validates and updates the CircleCI configuration YML script:

```
↪  functional-summer git:(master) circleci help config

Validate and update the circleCI configuration file

Usage:
  circleci config [command]

Available Commands:
  validate    validate config syntax.  Does not currently check workflows configuration.

Flags:
  -c, --config string   path to config file (default ".circleci/config.yml")
  -h, --help            help for config

Global Flags:
      --verbose   enable verbose logging output

Use "circleci config [command] --help" for more information about a command.
↪  functional-summer git:(master)
```

Here the `config` command also takes the `validate` command, which validates your config YML script file.

Let us validate the configuration script in the `functional-summer` repo (`https://github.com/packtci/functional-summer`):

```
↪  functional-summer git:(master) x circleci config validate

Error: 1 error occurred:

* Config file is invalid:
    at (root): (root): Must validate at least one schema (anyOf)
    at (root): workflows: workflows is required
    at jobs: jobs: Invalid type. Expected: object, given: null

↪  functional-summer git:(master) x █
```

Let us look at the configuration script again:

```
version: 2
jobs:
build:
    docker:
        # specify the version you desire here
        - image: circleci/node:7.10
    working_directory: ~/repo
    steps:
        - checkout
        - restore_cache:
            keys:
                - v1-dependencies-{{ checksum "package.json" }}
                - v1-dependencies-
        - run: yarn install
        - save_cache:
            paths:
                - node_modules
            key: v1-dependencies-{{ checksum "package.json" }}
        # run tests!
        - run: yarn test
```

This is actually a very subtle bug in the config YML script where we simply need to indent the `build` field because CircleCI thinks that we do not have any jobs in our script. To fix the issue, we simply need to indent the `build` field:

```
version: 2
jobs:
    build:
        ...
```

```
↳  functional-summer git:(master) x circleci config validate

.circleci/config.yml is valid
↳  functional-summer git:(master) █
```

When we ran the `validate` command, it reported that the config YML script is valid.

Build command

The `build` command helps you run a CircleCI build on your local machine and takes a variety of options as shown in the following screenshot:

```
↳  dev circleci help build

Run a full build locally

Usage:
  circleci build [flags]

Flags:
      --branch string           Git branch
      --checkout-key string     Git Checkout key (default "~/.ssh/id_rsa")
  -c, --config string           config file (default ".circleci/config.yml")
  -e, --env -e VAR=VAL          Set environment variables, e.g. -e VAR=VAL
  -h, --help                    help for build
      --index int               node index of parallelism
      --job string              job to be executed (default "build")
      --node-total int          total number of parallel nodes (default 1)
      --repo-url string         Git Url
      --revision string         Git Revision
      --skip-checkout           use local path as-is (default true)
  -v, --volume stringSlice      Volume bind-mounting

Global Flags:
      --verbose     enable verbose logging output
↳  dev █
```

Let us run the `go-template-example-with-circle-ci` (https://github.com/packtci/
go-template-example-with-circle-ci) GitHub repository that we created in Chapter 12,
Installation and Basics of CircleCI, and then run the `circleci build` command on our local
system.

Make sure that you go into the directory where your repository lives before you run the
build command as it needs to read the `config.yml` file inside of the `.circleci` folder:

```
▸→ functional-summer git:(master) circleci build

====>> Spin up Environment
Build-agent version 0.0.5895-01cdb92 (2018-05-29T20:07:10+0000)
```

The `build` command will execute the steps in the config YML script, starting by spinning
up an environment. If you have not pulled the language image specified in the config YML
script then the `circleci build` command will pull down the Docker image for you.

By default, the `circleci build` command will run the steps that are defined in the `build`
field in the `jobs` section, so if you want to run any other jobs than you will need to pass
the `--job string` option.

Here is the current `config.yml` script that we have in the `go-template-example-with-
circle-ci` GitHub project:

```
version: 2
jobs:
    build:
        docker:
            - image: circleci/golang:1.9
        working_directory: /go/src/github.com/packtci/go-template-example-
with-circle-ci

        steps:
            - checkout
            - run:
                name: "Print go version"
                command: go version
            - run:
                name: "Run Unit Tests"
                command: go test
```

If we want to use another job, we can use the `--job string` option, assuming that there is another job:

```
. . .
  build:
    . . .
  integration:
    docker:
        - image: cypress/base:8
            environment:
                TERM: xterm
    steps:
        - checkout
        - run: npm install
        - run:
            name: "Run Integration Tests"
            command: $(npm bin)/cypress run
```

Now let us validate our config YML script to make sure that it is still valid:

```
➜  go-template-example-with-circle-ci git:(master) ✗ circleci config validate
.circleci/config.yml is valid
➜  go-template-example-with-circle-ci git:(master) ✗
```

Now that we know our config YML script is still valid, we can run the new job using the `--job string` flag with the `build` command.

```
➜  go-template-example-with-circle-ci git:(master) ✗ circleci build --job integration
====>> Spin up Environment
Build-agent version 0.0.5895-01cdb92 (2018-05-29T20:07:10+0000)
Starting container circleci/node:8.11.3-stretch-browsers
  image cache not found on this host, downloading circleci/node:8.11.3-stretch-browsers
```

Here the CLI is downloading the Docker image because we have not pulled this particular Docker image into our local computer.

step command

The `step` command will execute a specific step in your config YML script that you have defined. At the moment, there is only one sub command of `halt`, which will halt the current execution.

Here is a sample run of the `step` command:

```
circleci step halt
```

configure command

The `configure` command is only available with the nightly build version of CircleCI and it helps you configure your credentials and the API endpoint you will hit:

```
↪ go-template-example-with-circle-ci git:(master) ✗ circleci-beta help configure
Configure the tool with your credentials

Usage:
  circleci configure [flags]

Flags:
  -h, --help   help for configure

Global Flags:
  -e, --endpoint string   the endpoint of your CircleCI GraphQL API (default "https://circleci.com/graphql-unstable")
  -t, --token string      your token for using CircleCI
  -v, --verbose           Enable verbose logging.
↪ go-template-example-with-circle-ci git:(master) ✗ 
```

We will run the `configure` command with no flags, which will set it to an interactive mode, and then we will set our API token and the API endpoint we wish to hit.

Setting an API token with CircleCI

You need to click on your user avatar in the upper-right side of the CircleCI web application, which looks like the following screenshot:

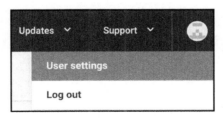

Once you click on the **User settings** link you will be redirected to the accounts API page which looks like this:

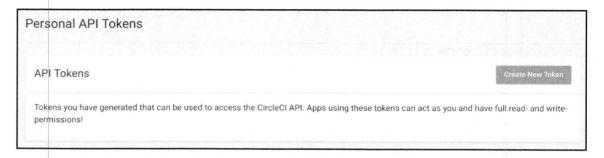

Next you will need to click on the **Create New Token** button, which pops up a modal like this:

Here we put in a token name of `PacktCI`. Then we simply click on the **Add API Token** button, which will generate a new API token for us. You need to copy the API token into a safe location as you can only use it once.

Setting the API token and API endpoint in interactive mode

We will run the `circleci-beta configure` command in a Terminal session and set our credentials and API endpoint:

```
→  go-template-example-with-circle-ci git:(master) ✗ circleci-beta configure
✔ CircleCI API Token:
API token has been set.
✔ CircleCI API End Point: https://circleci.com/api/v1.1/
API endpoint has been set.
Configuration has been saved.
→  go-template-example-with-circle-ci git:(master) ✗
```

Here we set the API token but the value is hidden for security purposes, and we set the API Endpoint to `https://circleci.com/api/v1.1/`.

 The `configure` command is only available in the nightly release and not the stable release.

Tests command

The `tests` command collects and splits files with tests:

```
▶→ go-template-example-with-circle-ci git:(master) circleci help tests

Collect and split files with tests

Usage:
  circleci tests [command]

Available Commands:
  glob        glob files using pattern
  split       return a split batch of provided files

Flags:
  -h, --help   help for tests

Global Flags:
      --verbose   enable verbose logging output

Use "circleci tests [command] --help" for more information about a command.
▶→ go-template-example-with-circle-ci git:(master) █
```

Let us use the `glob` subcommand to find all the Go test files in the `go-template-example-with-circle-ci` (https://github.com/packtci/go-template-example-with-circle-ci) GitHub repository:

```
▶→ go-template-example-with-circle-ci git:(master) circleci tests glob "**/*.go"

template_test.go
template.go
▶→ go-template-example-with-circle-ci git:(master) █
```

Using Workflows in CircleCI

Workflows in CircleCI are a way to run parallel `build` jobs and can be used to define a collection of jobs and to specify a job order. Let us add a workflows field to the `go-template-example-with-circle-ci` (https://github.com/packtci/go-template-example-with-circle-ci) configuration YML script:

```
version: 2
jobs:
    build:
        . . .
    integration:
        . . . .
workflows:
    version: 2
    build_and_integration:
        jobs:
            - build
            - integration
```

In this workflow, we create two parallel jobs called `build` and `integration` respectively. They are independent of each other and this will help speed up the build process.

Workflows in action in CircleCI Web UI

We can see the workflows in the CircleCI web UI if we click on the **Workflows** link in the left navigation pane. You then need to click on a specific project which in this case is `go-template-example-with-circle-ci` as shown in the following screenshot:

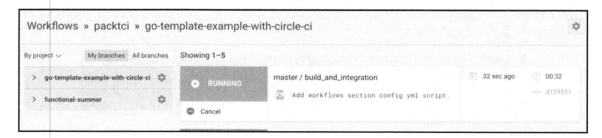

If you click on the **RUNNING** workflow, you will see the following page:

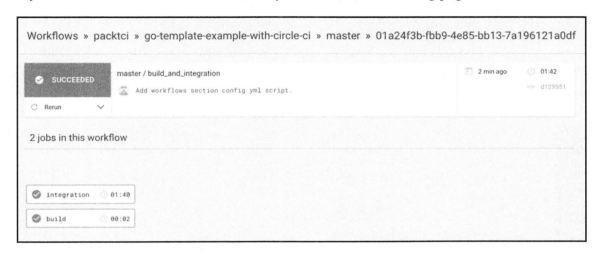

 The **build** job ran in 2 seconds but that the integration tests run for longer than the **build** job. It is better to separate these two jobs, as the workflows demonstrate, as they are not dependent on each other.

Sequential workflows example

The workflows example that we showed you previously contained two jobs that ran independent of each other, but we can also have jobs that require other jobs to finish in order to be run. Let us say that we have an acceptance test suite that only runs if the build is run, and then our application is only deployed if the acceptance test suite passes.

In our example, we run an end-to-end test using `cypress.io` (`https://www.cypress.io/`), which is an end-to-end JavaScript testing library. Assuming that our acceptance tests pass in the CI build we can then deploy our application to Heroku. We covered getting set up with Heroku in `Chapter 11`, *Travis CI UI Logging and Debugging*, in the *Heroku setup in Travis CI* section, so read that if you need more information on getting Heroku installed and set up and for creating an application in Heroku that you can deploy to. We will need to add our Heroku API key and app name as environment variables.

Adding environment variables to a project

In our CircleCI project, we first need to go to our project settings by clicking on the gear icon next to the `go-template-example-with-circle-ci` (https://circleci.com/gh/packtci/go-template-example-with-circle-ci) project. Make sure that you are in the **Jobs** or **Workflows** view and then you should see a gear icon:

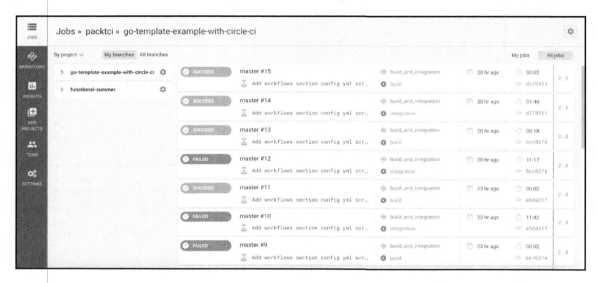

Once you click the gear icon, you will be redirected to the **PROJECT SETTINGS** page and you will need to click the **Environment Variables** link. Then your page will look like the following screenshot:

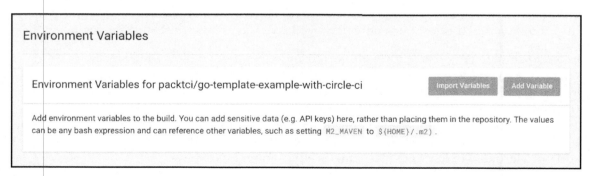

We are going to add two environment variables to our project by clicking on the **Add Variable** button, which pops up a modal like this:

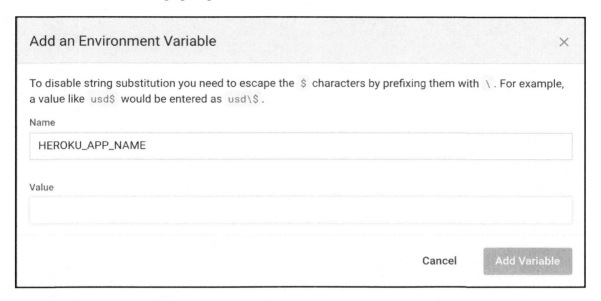

For security purposes, I have removed the contents of both the application name and the API token for the project, but once you click the **Add Variable** button, an environment variable is available in the project. We now have two environment variables we can use, namely HEROKU_API_KEY and HEROKU_APP_NAME. These environment variables will be available in our .circleci/config.yml script.

Updated workflows section and config YML script

Our config YML script now has a deploy jobs section and we have updated our workflows field like this:

```
...
deploy:
    docker:
        - image: buildpack-deps:trusty
    steps:
        - checkout
        - run:
            name: Deploy Master to Heroku
            command: |
                git push
```

```
https://heroku:$HEROKU_API_KEY@git.heroku.com/$HEROKU_APP_NAME.git master

workflows:
    version: 2
        build_integration_and_deploy:
            jobs:
                - build
                - integration:
                    requires:
                        - build
                - deploy:
                    requires:
                        -integration
```

The workflow for this change will look different now, as we have set up a sequential pipeline for the jobs:

In the preceding screenshot the **build** job ran first and then the **integration** job and finally the **deploy** job. Read the workflows documentation at `https://circleci.com/docs/2.0/workflows/` for information on more types of workflows.

Working with the CircleCI API

The CircleCI API documentation is available at `https://circleci.com/docs/api/v1-reference/`. To get started working with the API you will need to add an API token. We already set an API token in the *Setting an API token with CircleCI* section of this chapter, so read that section if necessary.

Test CircleCI API connection

We will use the `curl` command and our API token to test that we have a good CircleCI API connection:

```
↳ ~ curl -X GET \
--header "Accept: application/json" \
"https://circleci.com/api/v1.1/me?circle-token=$CIRCLECI_API_TOKEN_GITHUB"
{"enrolled_betas":[],"in_beta_program":false,"selected_email":"marcelbelmont+1@gmail.com","avatar_url":"https://avatars3.githubusercontent.com/u/40322425?v=4
","trial_end":"2018-08-04T18:24:11.355Z","admin":false,"basic_email_prefs":"smart","sign_in_count":2,"github_oauth_scopes":["user:email","repo"],"analytics_i
d":"ff6c7208-0c90-43e2-b71d-7755fc8885ec","name":null,"gravatar_id":null,"first_vcs_authorized_client_id":"1527434298464","days_left_in_trial":5,"parallelism
":1,"student":false,"bitbucket_authorized":true,"github_id":40322425,"bitbucket":{"id":"{e52ece0d-6c8c-4422-8313-94d59fbc1017}","login":null,"dev_admin":fal
se,"all_emails":["marcelbelmont+1@gmail.com","marcelbelmont+3@gmail.com"],"created_at":"2018-07-21T18:24:11.355Z","plan":null,"heroku_api_key":null,"identiti
es":{"github":{"avatar_url":"https://avatars3.githubusercontent.com/u/40322425?v=4","external_id":40322425,"id":40322425,"name":null,"user?":true,"domain":"g
ithub.com","type":"github","authorized?":true,"provider_id":"bcc68be8-ef10-4dd6-9b76-34f19e0db930","login":"packtci"},"bitbucket":{"avatar_url":"https://bitb
ucket.org/account/packtci/avatar/","external_id":"{e52ece0d-6c8c-4422-8313-94d59fbc1017}","id":"{e52ece0d-6c8c-4422-8313-94d59fbc1017}","name":"Jean-Marcel B
elmont","user?":true,"domain":"bitbucket.org","type":"bitbucket","authorized?":true,"provider_id":"752bbf0d-bea6-4c9c-9923-ce5936ca9be3","login":"packtci"}},
"projects":{"https://github.com/packtci/functional-summer":{"on_dashboard":true,"emails":"default"},"https://github.com/packtci/go-template-example-with-circle-ci":{"on_dashboard":true,"emails":"default"},"https://bitbucket.org/packtci/java-summer":{"on_dashboar
d":true,"emails":"default"},"https://github.com/packtci/go-template-example-with-circle-ci":{"on_dashboard":true,"emails":"default"}},"login":"packtci","orga
nization_prefs":{},"containers":1,"pusher_id":"3b04b2f60dcae08f877a6e67c74b815563c8cc38","num_projects_followed":3}
↳ ~ ∎
```

Here we did not get any response headers or a status code. In order for you to receive those, you need to use the `-i`, `--include` options with the `curl` command.

Using the CircleCI API to get build summary for a single Git repo

We will use the `GET /project/:vcs-type/:username/:project` API endpoint to get the build summary information. You can read the documentation for recent builds for a single project at `https://circleci.com/docs/api/v1-reference/#recent-builds-project`.

In the following screenshot, we use the `curl` command to make the REST call and use the `jq` (`https://stedolan.github.io/jq/`) JSON command-line processor to prettify the JSON output as shown in the following screenshot:

```
↳ go-template-example-with-circle-ci git:(master) curl -X GET \
--header "Accept: application/json" \
"https://circleci.com/api/v1.1/project/github/packtci/go-template-example-with-circle-ci?circle-token=$CIRCLECI_API_TOKEN_GITHUB" | jq
  % Total    % Received % Xferd  Average Speed   Time    Time     Time  Current
                                 Dload  Upload   Total   Spent    Left  Speed
100 15208  100 15208    0     0   8651      0  0:00:01  0:00:01 --:--:--  8650
[
  {
    "compare": "https://github.com/packtci/go-template-example-with-circle-ci/compare/7d7c87e2c35d...725e97cc7a24",
    "previous_successful_build": {
      "build_num": 4,
      "status": "success",
      "build_time_millis": 2938
    },
    "build_parameters": null,
    "oss": true,
    "all_commit_details_truncated": false,
    "committer_date": "2018-07-29T17:33:32-04:00",
```

Using the jq utility to compute some metrics of our CircleCI builds

Let us use the `jq` command-line utility in order to compute some metrics with information provided by the CircleCI API. One thing we may want to find is all the builds that have passed in the project. We can do this with the `jq` command by using the `map` and `select` built-in functions in jq (`https://stedolan.github.io/jq/manual/#Builtinoperatorsandfunctions`).

In the following screenshot, we get the build summary for the last 30 builds and then only show the build that actually passed:

Here, we run the `jq` utility with two different queries:

- The first query is `jq 'map(select(.failed == false)) | length'` and it maps over the array of objects and filters out the top-level attribute called `failed` when it is `false`.
- The second query is `jq '. | length'` and it simply computes the length of the array, which is 5.

We ran the second command to ensure that the first command did in fact filter out some entries in the response payload. From this, we can tell that one build did fail in the recent 30 builds for the `go-template-example-with-circle-ci` (`https://github.com/packtci/go-template-example-with-circle-ci`) GitHub repository.

Summary

In this chapter, we covered how to install CircleCI CLI in the macOS/Linux environments and showed you how to install a nightly build of the CLI. We showed you how to use each command in the CircleCI CLI and also showed you some command features that are available in the nightly build of CircleCI CLI. We explained why workflows are useful and how to use them in CircleCI. Finally, we showed you how to use the CircleCI API and how to gather useful metrics by using the `jq` command utility.

Questions

1. What is the primary prerequisite to installing the CircleCI CLI?
2. Where did we get the nightly build of CircleCI CLI from?
3. How many CLI commands exist for the CLI?
4. Which command in the CLI is useful to know what a specific command does and what options a given command takes?
5. How can we run parallel jobs in CircleCI?
6. Which command did we use to validate our CircleCI YML script?
7. What is the endpoint for the CircleCI RESTful API?

Further reading

You can further explore concepts in CircleCI by looking at the official CircleCI documentation at `https://circleci.com/docs/2.0/`.

14

CircleCI UI Logging and Debugging

In the previous chapter, we covered CircleCI CLI commands in depth and showed you some techniques to automate tasks in CircleCI. In this chapter, we will cover the Job Log in depth and explain the run steps in more detail. We will explain the workflows concept and show you how to use the CircleCI API to find the most recent builds for a project. We will look at how to debug a slow job by implementing caching in a build, and will finish by using some troubleshooting techniques to run a build with a local config YML script.

The following topics will be covered in this chapter:

- Job log overview
- Debugging slow builds in CircleCI
- Logging and troubleshooting techniques

Technical requirements

In this chapter, we cover some concepts about using RESTful APIs and will use the `curl` utility to make REST calls, so it would be good to understand what an API is and how to use a REST client such as `curl`. It would also be helpful to have a rudimentary understanding of the Unix programming environment and it would be beneficial to understand what scripting is and what a Bash environment is.

The code files for this chapter can be found at the following links:

- https://github.com/packtci/circleci-jobs-example
- https://github.com/packtci/go-template-example-with-circle-ci

Job log overview

The job log in CircleCI is different than in Travis CI, as each step in each job is run in a separate non-login shell and CircleCI sets some smart defaults for each step in the job.

Run steps in job with a default build job

We will create a new repository to demonstrate multiple jobs in the default build job. The repository will be called `circleci-jobs-example` (`https://github.com/packtci/circleci-jobs-example`) and will have multiple run declarations in the build job. We will be using Node.js as our programming language of choice for demonstration purposes. Remember that we need to add the new project to CircleCI so that it can become aware of our project. In the previous chapters, we added the projects using the CircleCI web UI, but let's use the CircleCI API to add our new project to CircleCI.

Adding a project to CircleCI via the API

We learned how to work with the CircleCI API in Chapter 13, *CircleCI CLI Commands and Automation*, so please read the *Working with the CircleCI API* section of that chapter for more details on working with the API. If you already read this, then you will already have an API token that you can use. The API endpoint to follow for new projects on CircleCI (`https://circleci.com/docs/api/v1-reference/#follow-project`) shows that you need to make a `POST HTTP` request and add your API token as a query string parameter.

Using curl as a REST client

We have already used `curl` as a REST client throughout the book, so you should be familiar with how to use it by now. We will be making a `POST` request to the following endpoint `https://circleci.com/api/v1.1/project/:vcs-type/:username/:project/follow?circle-token=:token`:

```
curl -X POST
"https://circleci.com/api/v1.1/project/github/packtci/circleci-jobs-example
/follow?circle-token=$CIRCLECI_API_TOKEN_GITHUB"
```

Here we use an environment variable called `CIRCLECI_API_TOKEN_GITHUB` that is set in our local environment, and we get the following response from the API:

```
{
  "following" : true,
  "workflow" : false,
```

```
"first_build" : {
  "compare" : null,
  "previous_successful_build" : null,
  "build_parameters" : null,
  "oss" : true,
  "committer_date" : null,
  "body" : null,
  "usage_queued_at" : "2018-08-04T21:36:26.982Z",
  "fail_reason" : null,
  "retry_of" : null,
  "reponame" : "circleci-jobs-example",
  "ssh_users" : [ ],
  "build_url" :
"https://circleci.com/gh/packtci/circleci-jobs-example/1",
  "parallel" : 1,
  "failed" : null,
  "branch" : "master",
  "username" : "packtci",
  "author_date" : null,
  "why" : "first-build",
  "user" : {
    "is_user" : true,
    "login" : "packtci",
    "avatar_url" :
"https://avatars3.githubusercontent.com/u/40322425?v=4",
    "name" : null,
    "vcs_type" : "github",
    "id" : 40322425
  },
  "vcs_revision" : "abc2ce258b44700400ec231c01529b3b6b8ecbba",
  "vcs_tag" : null,
  "build_num" : 1,
  "infrastructure_fail" : false,
  "committer_email" : null,
  "previous" : null,
  "status" : "not_running",
  "committer_name" : null,
  "retries" : null,
  "subject" : null,
  "vcs_type" : "github",
  "timedout" : false,
  "dont_build" : null,
  "lifecycle" : "not_running",
  "no_dependency_cache" : false,
  "stop_time" : null,
  "ssh_disabled" : true,
  "build_time_millis" : null,
  "picard" : null,
```

```
  "circle_yml" : {
    "string" : "version: 2\njobs:\n build:\n docker:\n - image:
circleci/node:8.11.3\n steps:\n - checkout\n - run:\n name: Install
Dependencies\n command: npm install\n - run:\n name: Run the Sort Test to
sort by first name\n command: $(npm bin)/tape sort_test.js\n - run:\n name:
Compute Standard Deviation\n command: $(npm bin)/tape
standard_deviation_test.js\n - run:\n name: Find the Text and Replace It\n
command: $(npm bin)/tape find_text_test.js\n - run: |\n echo \"Generate
Code Coverage\"\n npm test\n echo \"Show the coverage\"\n npm run
coverage\n "
  },
  "messages" : [ ],
  "is_first_green_build" : false,
  "job_name" : null,
  "start_time" : null,
  "canceler" : null,
  "platform" : "2.0",
  "outcome" : null,
  "vcs_url" : "https://github.com/packtci/circleci-jobs-example",
  "author_name" : null,
  "node" : null,
  "canceled" : false,
  "author_email" : null
  }
}
```

Parse build_url attribute from the JSON response

Let's save this response into a new file we call `circleci-jobs-example-follow.json` by using the cat utility in a Terminal shell session, like this:

```
cat > circleci-jobs-example-follow.json
# Paste the JSON Content from System Clipboard
# Press Enter
# Finally Press enter
```

Now let's use the jq (`https://stedolan.github.io/jq/manual/`) and find the `build_url` attribute in the JSON payload:

```
cat circleci-jobs-example-follow.json | jq '.first_build.build_url'
```

This command returns the following build URL: `https://circleci.com/gh/packtci/circleci-jobs-example/1`.

Now you can either open a browser and paste this URL in or you can use a command-line utility available on your operating system. We will use the `open` utility in macOS like this:

```
open https://circleci.com/gh/packtci/circleci-jobs-example/1
```

The preceding command will open the default browser in macOS and use the URL that you provide. In Linux, you might be able to use `xdg-open`, `gnome-open`, or `kde-open` depending on the OS that you have installed. Either way you can simply open a browser and paste the entry for the build URL.

CircleCI Web UI job log analysis

When we open the URL for the new job that we triggered via the API, the first part of the UI looks like this:

Notice here that the top part shows basic information such as the commit SHA hash, the contributor information, and other background information. If you scroll down further in the job log, you will see the steps run in each part of the job:

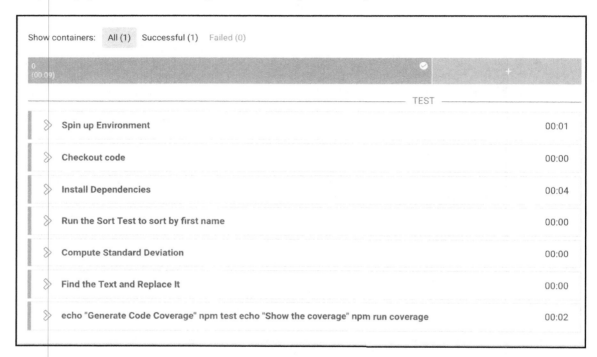

The build took 9 seconds to complete and notice here that each step in the build has its own section that is conveniently collapsed. You simply click on each section to get the details of the step. The names of each step correspond to the name field in the config YML script.

Notice that the name of the multi-line command used the name of the full command as its name.

This was the entry for the multi-line command:

```
. . .
- run: |
    echo "Generate Code Coverage"
    npm test
    echo "Show the coverage"
    npm run coverage
```

If we expand one of the steps we will see the following entries common to each:

```
♡  Find the Text and Replace It                          00:00

$ #!/bin/bash -eo pipefail                     Exit code: 0
  $(npm bin)/tape find_text_test.js                    ⊕

TAP version 13
# find and replace text
ok 1 Should be equal

1..1
# tests 1
# pass  1

# ok
```

The **Shebang** line `#!/bin/bash -eo pipefail` has set some sensible defaults for the non-login shell.

The Bash option `-e` means that the script should exit if a statement returns a non-true value. The Bash option `-o  pipefail` means use the error status of the first failure, rather than that of the last item in a pipeline. Instead of adding these options in the Shebang line, you could do the following:

```
#!/usr/bin/env bash

# Exit script if you try to use an uninitialized variable.
set -o nounset
# Exit script if a statement returns a non-true return value.
set -o errexit
# Use the error status of the first failure, rather than that of the last
item in a pipeline.
set -o pipefail
```

If we look at another step in the job, we see the same thing is done:

```
  ⬡  Compute Standard Deviation                                              00:00

    $ #!/bin/bash -eo pipefail                                      Exit code: 0
      $(npm bin)/tape standard_deviation_test.js                            ⬇

    TAP version 13
    # compute the standard deviation of a list of numbers
    ok 1 The standard devation should be 21.88

    1..1
    # tests 1
    # pass  1

    # ok
```

CircleCI does this in each step of a job because it helps us troubleshoot issues that occur when writing shell scripts, and it helps promote best practices when writing shell scripts.

Here is an example of a command that can fail that will report errors in the wrong spot of a build when using a Unix pipeline:

```
docker ps -a | grep -v "busybox:latest" | awk '{ print $1 }' - | grep -v
"CONTAINER"
```

In this pipeline, we list all the containers that are running, exited, or terminated for some reason and then pipe this into the `grep` utility and exclude any entries that have the text `busybox:latest` and then pipe this into the `awk` utility and only print the first column. We finally pipe this back into `grep` and exclude the text `CONTAINER`. This pipeline could fail at any chain of the pipeline but because we used the option `set -o pipefail` the script will fail on the first command that returns a non-true option. This is helpful because the default behavior is to report the last item in the pipeline.

Another aspect of the run declaration commands are that they are executed using non-login shells by default. This means that you must explicitly source any hidden files such as **dotfiles** as part of the command that is run, or else you risk not having environment variables ready to use as you might expect.

Here is an example to illustrate this:

```
# We source some environment variables here that we need
source ~/project/.env


npm run security-tests
```

Also, notice that the exit code is printed for each run declaration in the upper-right side:

Exit code: 0

You can also see a helpful button in the top-right corner, which will scroll you further down into the particular run step you are interested in seeing.

Best practices for environment variable safe usage

It is important that you do not add secrets inside of the `.circleci/config` YML script file. If you do, you may leak secret information on the job log that may be publicly accessible. The full text of the `config.yml` is visible to developers with access to your project on CircleCI, so instead store your secrets and/or keys in **Project** or **Context** settings in the CircleCI app. Running scripts within configuration may expose secret environment variables so be careful when using the `set -o xtrace` / `set -x` in your run steps as they might expose environment variables.

One thing to note is that all environment variables are encrypted using Hashicorp Vault (`https://www.vaultproject.io/`) and environment variables are encrypted using AES256-GCM96 and are unavailable to any CircleCI employees.

Run steps in job with workflows

According to the Circle CI Documentation on **workflows** (`https://circleci.com/docs/2.0/workflows/`), a workflow is a set of rules for defining a collection of jobs and their run order. Workflows support complex job orchestration using a simple set of configuration keys to help you resolve failures sooner.

We will use workflows in order to separate our jobs into more appropriate sections and then also to take advantage of the fact that some scripts are independent of each other and can be run separately. We can speed up our build process by using workflows in CircleCI.

Now let's think of the parts of the job that can be broken into separate steps in our build process. We can break the dependency step into a separate part of the build and then we can just collapse the individual steps we ran for the three tests into one step called test. Remember that the steps look like this in the config YML script:

```
. . .
- run:
  name: Run the Sort Test to sort by first name
  command: $(npm bin)/tape sort_test.js
- run:
  name: Compute Standard Deviation
  command: $(npm bin)/tape standard_deviation_test.js
- run:
  name: Find the Text and Replace It
  command: $(npm bin)/tape find_text_test.js
- run: |
  echo "Generate Code Coverage"
  npm test
  echo "Show the coverage"
  npm run coverage
. . .
```

In the last step, we have the command `npm test` and this command references the following command specified in the `package.json` file:

```
"scripts": {
    "test": "nyc tape *_test.js",
    "coverage": "nyc report --reporter=cobertura"
}
```

Notice that this command runs all the tests already and then reports coverage using the NYC code coverage utility. The last command generates a Cobertura XML report that we will use later in the chapter. We will now rewrite the series of steps into their own field called `test`, and it will look like this:

```
test:
    docker:
        - image: circleci/node:8.11.3
    steps:
        - checkout
        - run:
            name: Run Tests and Run Code Coverage with NYC
            command: |
                echo "Generate Code Coverage"
                npm test
                echo "Show the coverage"
                npm run coverage
```

Notice here that I gave a more appropriate name to the collapsed command and also notice that we can use a multi-line command in the `command` field itself using the pipe (|) operator.

We will add a deploy section like we did in Chapter 13, *CircleCI CLI Commands and Automation*, which will deploy our application into **Heroku** (https://dashboard.heroku.com/apps). If you don't understand what Heroku is then please read Chapter 11, *Travis CI UI Logging and Debugging*, and read the *Travis CI deployment overview and debugging* section for more details.

Adding a workflows section to the config YML script

We will add the `workflows` section to the bottom of our config YML script, but we could also add it to the beginning of our config YML script. Here is the updated config YML script:

```
...
workflows:
    version: 2
    build_test_and_deploy:
        jobs:
            - build
            - test:
                requires:
                    - build
            - deploy:
                requires:
                    - test
```

Once we finish updating the config YML script, we should ensure that our config YML script is still valid by using CircleCI CLI, like this:

```
↦ circleci-jobs-example git:(master) ✗ circleci config validate
Error: Error parsing config file: yaml: line 19: could not find expected ':'
↦ circleci-jobs-example git:(master) ✗ █
```

It looks like we have an issue in our config YML script in line 19:

```
...
- run:
    name: Run Tests and Run Code Coverage with NYC
    command: |
    echo "Generate Code Coverage"
```

```
npm test
echo "Show the coverage"
npm run coverage
```

This is actually a subtle bug in our config YML script because we did not properly indent the multi-line command and so CircleCI does not know where our multi-line command starts. Here is the updated config YML script section now:

```
...
- run:
name: Run Tests and Run Code Coverage with NYC
command: |
echo "Generate Code Coverage"
npm test
echo "Show the coverage"
npm run coverage
```

Now let's run the CircleCI CLI validation again:

```
↦ circleci-jobs-example git:(master) x circleci config validate

.circleci/config.yml is valid
↦ circleci-jobs-example git:(master) x
```

Our config YML script is valid, so now let's commit this into source control by issuing the following command:

```
↦ circleci-jobs-example git:(master) x git add .
↦ circleci-jobs-example git:(master) x git commit -m 'Update config yml script to different jobs and use workflows.'
[master 9ea4518] Update config yml script to different jobs and use workflows.
 2 files changed, 110 insertions(+), 25 deletions(-)
 rewrite .circleci/config.yml (68%)
 create mode 100644 circleci-jobs-example-follow.json
↦ circleci-jobs-example git:(master) git push
Username for 'https://github.com': packtci
Password for 'https://packtci@github.com':
Counting objects: 5, done.
Delta compression using up to 8 threads.
Compressing objects: 100% (4/4), done.
Writing objects: 100% (5/5), 1.64 KiB | 1.64 MiB/s, done.
Total 5 (delta 1), reused 0 (delta 0)
remote: Resolving deltas: 100% (1/1), completed with 1 local object.
To https://github.com/packtci/circleci-jobs-example.git
   abc2ce2..9ea4518  master -> master
↦ circleci-jobs-example git:(master)
```

Notice here that we gave a descriptive commit message which is good practice to do in version control if anything you are working with has a particular tag, such as JIRA for instance; you could add it like this for example:

```
git commit -m '[PACKT-1005] Update config yml script to different jobs and
use workflows.'
```

Using the CircleCI API to find the most recent build URL

We can certainly use the CircleCI web app and click the `workflows` section and find our most recent build, but let's use the CircleCI API instead and use `jq` to parse the JSON response payload as we have done before for other API endpoints.

Here is a command that will pipe output from the `/recent-builds` API endpoint to `jq` and return the first `build_url` from the array of objects, which will be the most recent build, and then pipe that into the system clipboard. We can see the shape of the JSON in the recent build project in the `https://circleci.com/docs/api/v1-reference/#recent-builds-project` documentation:

```
curl -X GET \
    --header "Accept: application/json" \
"https://circleci.com/api/v1.1/project/github/packtci/circleci-jobs-example
?circle-token=$CIRCLECI_API_TOKEN_GITHUB" | jq '.[0].build_url'
```

This returns the following URL to the Terminal: `https://circleci.com/gh/packtci/circleci-jobs-example/6`.

Now let's go to this URL and look at the recent build; we will notice that the build failed:

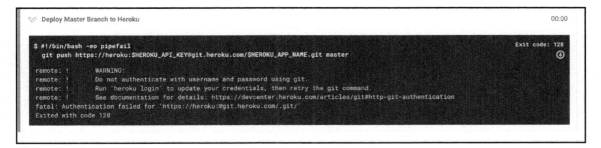

The build failed because we didn't set the necessary environment variables that our config YML script is referencing, namely HEROKU_API_KEY and HEROKU_APP_NAME. We covered how to set project-level environment variables in Chapter 13, *CircleCI CLI Commands and Automation*, but we only need to copy over the project environment-level variables. CircleCI has an easy way to do that if the environment variables are the same:

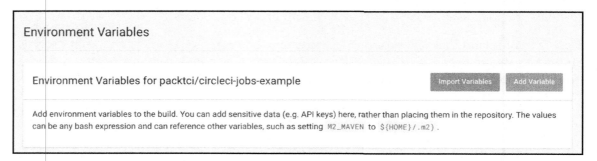

Click the **Import Variables** button and then enter the project you want to copy, like this:

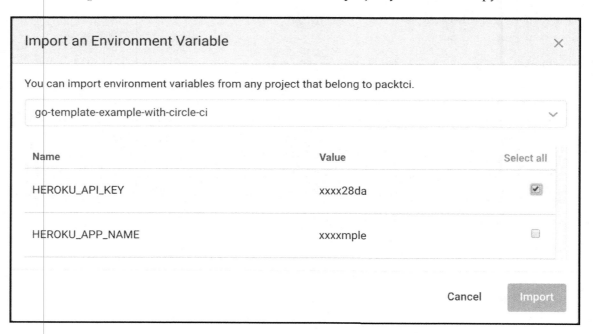

Notice here that I only checked the HEROKU_API_KEY environment variable, and I will manually set the HEROKU_APP_NAME as it will be different for the circleci-jobs-example (https://github.com/packtci/circleci-jobs-example) project:

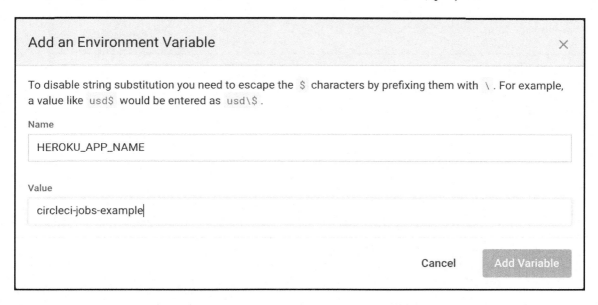

Now, with these environment variables set, let's retry the same build using the Retries the build, returns a summary of the new build https://circleci.com/docs/api/v1-reference/#retry-build API endpoint. We will use curl to make a call to the endpoint like this:

```
curl -X POST
https://circleci.com/api/v1.1/project/github/packtci/circleci-jobs-example/
6/retry\?circle-token\=$CIRCLECI_API_TOKEN_GITHUB | jq '.build_url'
```

Now we can verify that the build was fixed by copying the build_url value that is returned to standard output, which is https://circleci.com/gh/packtci/circleci-jobs-example/7:

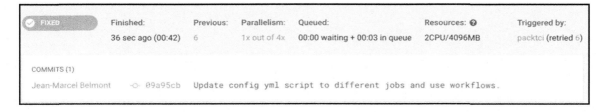

Debugging slow builds in CircleCI

A build may be slow in CircleCI due to a myriad of reasons. Let's look at a workflow example for `go-template-example-with-circleci` (`https://circleci.com/workflow-run/533ee47a-a990-4679-826b-7b24221df2ca`):

In particular, notice that the integration job took over a minute to finish and the deploy job took over a minute to finish as well, which is making the build take 3 minutes and 20 seconds to complete. If we click on the integration job, we see the following steps in the job:

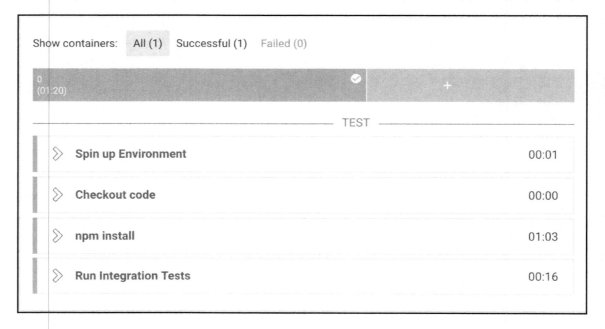

Notice here that the `npm install` took 1 minute and 3 seconds to finish. Let's open up the run step call `npm install` for further details:

```
$ #!/bin/bash -eo pipefail                                    Exit code: 0
  npm install                                                     ⊕


> cypress@3.0.2 postinstall /root/project/node_modules/cypress
> node index.js --exec install

Installing Cypress (version: 3.0.2)

[22:22:57]  Downloading Cypress      [started]
[22:23:04]  Downloading Cypress      [completed]
[22:23:04]  Unzipping Cypress        [started]
[22:23:51]  Unzipping Cypress        [completed]
[22:23:51]  Finishing Installation   [started]
[22:23:51]  Finishing Installation   [completed]

You can now open Cypress by running: node_modules/.bin/cypress open

https://on.cypress.io/installing-cypress

added 197 packages from 167 contributors and audited 326 packages in 62.145s
found 2 low severity vulnerabilities
  run `npm audit fix` to fix them, or `npm audit` for details
```

The only dependency we have is for `cypress.io`, but we are not caching this dependency so it will run this step every time. CircleCI has a way for us to cache our node dependencies by utilizing two field declarations called `save_cache` (`https://circleci.com/docs/2.0/configuration-reference/#save_cache`) and `restore_cache` (`https://circleci.com/docs/2.0/configuration-reference/#restore_cache`) respectively. Let's update the config YML script to use this caching strategy for the integration build:

```
integration:
  docker:
    - image: cypress/base:8
      environment:
      ## this enables colors in the output
      TERM: xterm
  steps:
    - checkout
    # special step to restore the dependency cache
    - restore_cache:
        key: v2-{{ checksum "package.json" }}
    - run: npm install
```

```
      # special step to save the dependency cache
    - save_cache:
        key: v2-{{ checksum "package.json" }}
        paths:
            - ~/.npm
            - ~/.cache
    - run:
        name: "Run Integration Tests"
        command: npm test
```

Notice here that we have placed the restore_cache step before the npm install and then placed the save_cache step after the npm install step. We also use a key field in both fields. The key value is immutable and we are using a prefix of v2 as a way to version our cache key values and then getting the checksum for the package.json file. If we want to invalidate the cache for any changes, we can simply increment the cache value value by one, v3 for example. Also notice that we have a paths field and we specify the paths to be the ~/.npm and ~/.cache directories. The cypress test runner expects the binary to be saved into a directory like this, or else it will throw an error. Let's push this change up to source control and trigger a new build and look at the job log. Now let's use a call to the recent builds API endpoint and copy the URL and see how the build went:

```
curl -X GET \
--header "Accept: application/json" \
"https://circleci.com/api/v1.1/project/github/packtci/go-template-example-w
ith-circle-ci?circle-token=$CIRCLECI_API_TOKEN_GITHUB" | jq
'.[0].build_url'
```

We will need to copy the build_url entry that gets printed onto standard output and paste the URL into a browser. The build_url will open the current build, and from this page we can easily navigate to the workflow for that particular job by clicking a link that looks like this:

We can click on the build_integration_and_deploy link under the **Workflow** label to get to the workflow. We now have the following steps in the integration build:

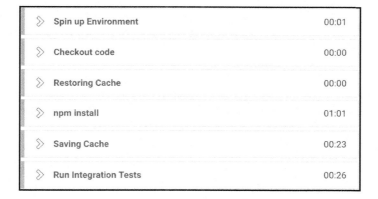

If we expand the **Restoring Cache** dropdown we can see the following:

 Notice here that no cache was found, which is expected since this is the first run of the build with this step added.

If we expand the **Saving Cache** button we can see the following:

Notice here that a cache archive was created and stored in the `node_modules` path as we specified the paths field in the config YML script.

Let's make a simple text change in the `README.md` file and commit the change to trigger a new build. We will find the latest build using the API as we have been doing. Now let's look at the new job log for the integration job:

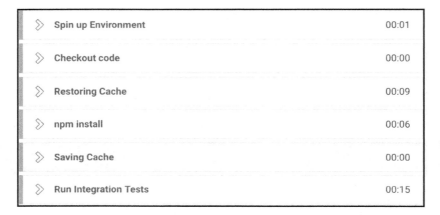

Notice that the build went from 1 minute 20 seconds to 33 seconds. If we open the **Restoring Cache** dropdown, we see the following:

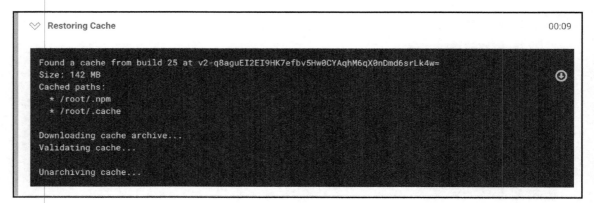

Now let's look at the **Saving Cache** step:

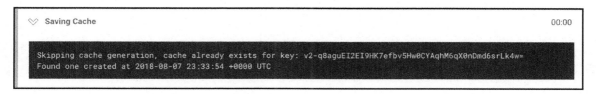

Notice here that it skipped the cache generation as it was able to find the cache that we saved from the previous build.

Logging and troubleshooting techniques

We can troubleshoot a problematic config YML script without having to make Git commits by using the CircleCI API. One technique that we can do is to create another folder and place a duplicate of our config YML script into it and then use this YML script as our debugging script. Once we can verify that the YML script is working correctly we can update the original YML script. This is useful since we won't be clogging up the Git history with troubleshooting commits but instead we will hit the CircleCI API directly.

Running a build using a local config YML script to troubleshoot

Let's say that we want to experiment with storing build artifacts, such as code coverage on a project. At the moment we are generating a coverage report but it is not being saved during the builds for us to view a coverage report. This is a good use case of creating a separate config YML script to test this new functionality. Let's store the coverage artifacts from the `circleci-jobs-example` (https://github.com/packtci/circleci-jobs-example) project and let's also update the test job to cache the node dependencies, as we learned how to do in the previous section.

Run this command to copy the contents of the `.circleci` directory and create a new directory in the shell:

```
cp -r .circleci store_and_cache_experiment
```

Now we will use the `store_and_cache_experiment` folder to run our local config YML script experiments. Here are the changes that we are going to make for the config YML script in the `store_and_cache_experiment` folder:

```
test:
    docker:
        - image: circleci/node:8.11.3
    steps:
        - checkout
        # special step to restore the dependency cache
        - restore_cache:
            key: v2-{{ checksum "package.json" }}
        # special step to save the dependency cache
        - run:
            name: Install Dependencies
            command: npm install
        - save_cache:
            key: v2-{{ checksum "package.json" }}
            paths:
                - ~/.npm
                - ~/.cache
        - run:
            name: Run Tests and Run Code Coverage with NYC
            command: |
                echo "Generate Code Coverage"
                npm test
                echo "Show the coverage"
                npm run coverage
        - store_artifacts:
            path: coverage
            prefix: coverage
```

We added the `save_cache` and `restore_cache` declaration changes and also added the `store_artifacts` declaration changes. Let's verify that the config YML script is still valid with the `circleci config validate` command. Now, in order to test these changes in our local configuration without having to make a Git commit, we can use the CircleCI API and provide our local config YML script in the body of our request and reference a recent Git commit. We can get the latest Git commit by running this command:

```
↪  circleci-jobs-example git:(master) x git log --pretty=oneline | head -1 | cut -c 1-40
09a95cb11914fe8cf4058bfe70547b0eec0656bc
↪  circleci-jobs-example git:(master) x ▊
```

So now we have a revision number that we can use for the API call that we are going to make. Here is the command that we will use to debug the changes in our new config YML script:

```bash
#! /bin/bash

curl --user ${CIRCLECI_API_TOKEN_GITHUB}: \
    --request POST \
    --form revision=09a95cb11914fe8cf4058bfe70547b0eec0656bc \
    --form config=@config.yml \
    --form notify=false \
https://circleci.com/api/v1.1/project/github/packtci/circleci-jobs-example/
tree/master | jq '.build_url'
```

The first option, `--user`, takes our API token that is saved in an environment variable and then the `:` after it means that there is no password that follows. The next option, `--request`, is the `HTTP POST` verb that we are specifying. The next option of `--form` revision is where we put the Git revision number that we got earlier and then in the next option we specify the `config.yml` script. We specify a form value of false for notify and then we provide the URL. Here we specify the version control system provider of GitHub and then our `packtci` username, followed by the project name, and then tree and then finally our branch name. Then we pipe this into the `jq` utility and parse out the `build_url`. Here is the API endpoint for clarity:

POST: /project/:vcs-type/:username/:project/tree/:branch

After we make the REST call, we should get a JSON response that gives us a build URL for us to look at, and here is the build URL that we get: `https://circleci.com/gh/packtci/circleci-jobs-example/8`. If we look at this new build in the CircleCI Web UI, we see that it passed:

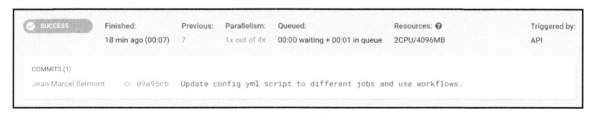

Let's remove the troubleshooting directory and config YML script and shell script and copy over the config YML script into the `.circleci` directory, like this:

```bash
cp store_and_cache_experiment/config.yml .circleci
rm -r store_and_cache_experiment
git add .
```

```
git commit -m 'Cache and Store artifacts.'
git push
```

Now if we click on the current build and then go to the **workflows** link, we will see that the step **Uploading artifacts** was added to the job; this is what it looks like:

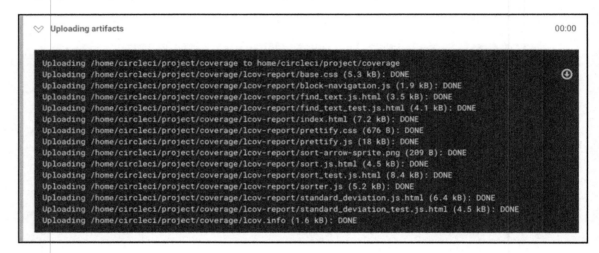

We can now scroll up and click on the **Artifacts** tab and see that an artifact has been saved on the build, like this:

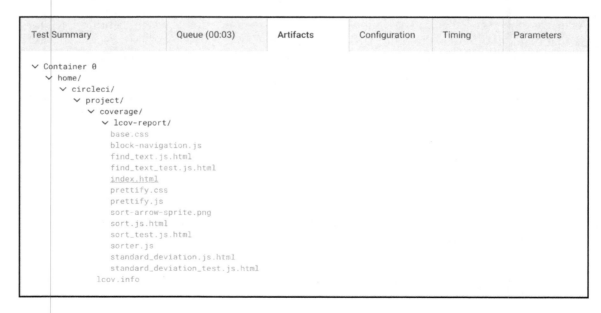

If we click on `index.html`, we will be redirected to a nice coverage report that looks like this:

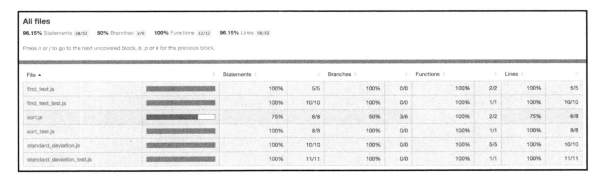

File ▲		Statements			Branches			Functions			Lines		
find_text.js		100%	5/5		100%	0/0		100%	2/2		100%	5/5
find_text_test.js		100%	10/10		100%	0/0		100%	1/1		100%	10/10
sort.js		75%	6/8		50%	3/6		100%	2/2		75%	6/8
sort_test.js		100%	8/8		100%	0/0		100%	1/1		100%	8/8
standard_deviation.js		100%	10/10		100%	0/0		100%	5/5		100%	10/10
standard_deviation_test.js		100%	11/11		100%	0/0		100%	1/1		100%	11/11

All files
96.15% Statements 50/52   **50%** Branches 3/6   **100%** Functions 12/12   **96.15%** Lines 50/52

Press *n* or *j* to go to the next uncovered block, *b*, *p* or *k* for the previous block.

Summary

In this chapter, we covered the job log in depth and showed you how to use the CircleCI API to add projects. We showed you how to analyze the job log and explained in more detail what a workflow is in CircleCI. We looked at how to use the CircleCI API to find the most recent build. We then looked at how to debug slow builds in Circle CI and wrapped up by showing you how to use a local config YML script to experiment with new changes to the CircleCI YML script.

In the next chapter, we will look at some best practices with continuous integration/continuous delivery and look at some patterns of configuration management, in particular secrets management, and present some checklists when implementing CI/CD in software companies.

Questions

1. What was the API endpoint that we used to follow new projects in CircleCI?
2. Can the cat utility be used to create new files?
3. How would you run a multi-line command in the CircleCI config YML script?
4. Are there any security vulnerabilities when using the set -x or execution tracing in scripts in CircleCI?
5. What was the CLI command we used to validate our config YML script?
6. Can environment variables be imported from other projects in CircleCI?
7. What declarations did we use to cache our dependencies in CircleCI?

Further reading

To find out more about debugging and troubleshooting, and other useful information, please read the official CircleCI documentation: https://circleci.com/docs/2.0/.

15
Best Practices

In the last chapter, `Chapter 14`, *CircleCI UI Logging and Debugging*, we covered more advanced debugging and logging techniques using CircleCI and went over more options using the CircleCI API. In the last chapter of the book, we will go over best practices for different types of testing, such as unit testing, integration testing, system testing, and acceptance testing. We will go over best practices with password management and use the Vault library as an example. Lastly, we will go over best practices in deployments in CI/CD and write a custom Go script to create a GitHub release.

The following topics will be covered in this chapter:

- Best practices for different types of testing in CI/CD
- Best practices in password and secrets storage
- Best practices in deployment

Technical requirements

This chapter will require some basic programming skills, as we will discuss some programming language-specific material in the deployment script and in the unit test example as well. It would be very helpful to have some familiarity with Unix programming and what a Bash shell is.

Best practices for different types of testing in CI/CD

In Chapter 3, *Basics of Continuous Delivery*, we went over acceptance testing and spoke briefly about how an acceptance test suite can serve as a regression test suite. In this section, we will talk about different types of software testing that you can do and formulate some best practices with each type of test. We will go over the following types of tests:

- Smoke testing
- Unit testing
- Integration testing
- System testing
- Acceptance testing

Smoke testing

Smoke tests are a special kind of test that help verify basic functionality in your application. Smoke tests will assume some basic implementation and environmental setup. Smoke tests are typically run at the beginning of a test cycle that behave as a sanity check before starting a complete test suite.

The main idea behind a smoke test is to catch glaring problems when working on new features in a software system. Smoke tests are not meant to be exhaustive but instead are meant to run very quickly. Let's say that a software company follows agile software development practices and there are 2 week sprints where new features are added to the product. When a new feature is merged into the release, meaning the main trunk of the software, a smoke test fails, and this should immediately raise a red flag that the new feature may have broken existing functionality.

You can create smoke tests that are context-specific when testing a new functionality in a system that will employ some basic assumptions and that can assert that the requirements are being met. You can create smoke tests that are run before any integration testing is done and before any deployments are done for staging environments, and these smoke tests will check different conditions on each staging environment.

Smoke test example

We will use an existing application that I have built that shows a list of users in a table. The application is called `containerized-golang-and-vuejs` (`https://github.com/jbelmont/containerized-golang-and-vuejs`) and it shows how to use the containers, Golang and Vue.js for reference purposes. The first thing we will do is to make sure that the application is running using a `makefile` task called `make dev`. This command does the following:

```
docker-compose up frontend backend db redis
```

To summarize, this command spins up four Docker containers and, when it is up and running, we should be able to hit `http://localhost:8080`. Now, in reality, a smoke test would hit a live running application but this is just for demonstration purposes for a smoke test. We will use an end-to-end testing library called **Cypress** (`https://www.cypress.io/`) but we could just as easily use another library for this.

We will write the following simple smoke test using JavaScript:

```javascript
describe('The user list table is shown and buttons', function () {
    it('successfully loads table', function () {
        cy.visit('/')
        cy
        .get('.users-area-table')
        .find('tbody tr')
        .first()
        .screenshot()
    })
})
```

You can read more about Cypress in the **Getting Started** (`https://docs.cypress.io/guides/getting-started/writing-your-first-test.html#`) documents but this test is essentially verifying that the page is loading with data and Cypress takes screenshots so we can visually verify the page.

Here is the screenshot that the Cypress library took:

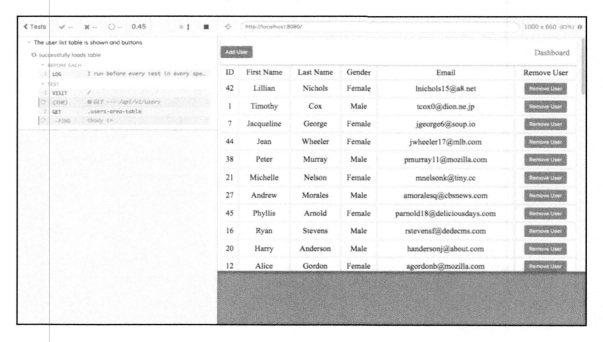

For this simple application, we can be sure that the application is roughly working, but a more complete smoke test may go through a login screen and then do a basic action that the application is expected to do.

Another nice feature of Cypress is that it can take videos of the tests showing all the steps that the test is taking, which can further verify that the application is meeting the basic requirements.

Unit testing

Unit tests can be considered the foundation of software testing in that unit tests test individual blocks of code, such as a function or a class/object. With a unit test, you are testing the functionality of functions and/or classes on their own. Because of this fact, unit tests typically stub out or mock out any external dependencies so that that the test can focus entirely on the function and/or class in question.

Unit tests are fundamental to testing a system in terms of correctness of behavior of individual components. The fact that unit tests are limited in this respect means that it is easier to isolate where defects have occurred at. Unit tests are often used to test code branches and how a function may handle different types of input. Unit tests are typically the first tests that developers will run in a build while QA engineers may run smoke tests first and then follow that with any unit tests.

Individual developers will run unit tests on their workstations prior to submitting changes to version control projects, such as GitHub. With that being said, continuous integration servers, such as Jenkins, Travis CI, and CircleCI, will run unit tests before running any integration tests, as we have seen in the previous chapters.

Unit test example

We will look at a previous project called `circleci-jobs-example` (`https://github.com/packtci/circleci-jobs-example`) that has several unit tests that have been written to test individual functions. In the repository, we have a file called `sort.js` that has the following function in it:

```
/ Takes an array of objects and sorts by First Name
function sortListOfNames(names) {
    return names.sort((a, b) => {
        if (a.firstName < b.firstName) {
            return -1;
        }
        if (a.firstName > b.firstName) {
            return 1;
        }
        if (a.firstName === b.firstName) {
            return 0;
        }
    });
}
```

This function takes an array of objects and sorts the objects by the `firstName` attribute. For our unit test, we simply want to test that the `sortListOfNames` function will sort the first name in alphabetical order. Here is the unit test that we have written in the `tape.js` (`https://github.com/substack/tape`) testing library:

```
test('Test the sort function', t => {
    t.plan(1);

    const names = [
        {
```

```
            firstName: 'Sam',
            lastName: 'Cooke'
        },
        {
            firstName: 'Barry',
            lastName: 'White'
        },
        {
            firstName: 'Jedi',
            lastName: 'Knight'
        }
    ];
    const actual = sort.sortListOfNames(names);
    const expected = [
        {
            firstName: 'Barry',
            lastName: 'White'
        },
        {
            firstName: 'Jedi',
            lastName: 'Knight'
        },
        {
            firstName: 'Sam',
            lastName: 'Cooke'
        }
    ];
    t.deepEqual(actual, expected, 'The names should be sorted by the first
name.')
});
```

You can see here that the unit test is able to isolate and test only the behavior of the sortListOfNames function, which is very useful because, if the sortListOfNames function were to have any issues, we can quickly isolate where the regression is occurring. Now, granted this function is very basic and simple, but you can see that unit tests serve an important purpose in a continuous integration build's job in catching regressions in software.

Integration testing

Integration tests will test groups of software components as they work with each other. While unit tests can help validate the functionality of a block on code in isolation, integration tests help test blocks of code as they interact with one another. Integration tests are useful because they can help catch different types of issues that arise when software components interact.

While unit tests may be run in a developer's workstation, integration tests are usually run when code is checked into source control. A CI server will check out the code, perform build steps, and then follow with any smoke tests and then run unit tests and then integration tests.

Since integration tests are a higher level of abstraction and test software components interacting with each other, they help protect the health of a code base. When developers introduce new features to a system, the integration tests can help ensure that the new code is working with other blocks of code as expected. Integration tests can help ensure that new features in a system can safely be deployed to an environment. Integration tests are usually the first types of tests that are done outside of a developer's workstation and help show whether they may be environmental dependency breakages and whether newer code is behaving properly with external libraries and external services and/or data.

Integration test example

We will look at a public API, such as CircleCI, and write an integration test that hits the API endpoint and verifies that the status code and the body of the request are what we would expect. This would typically be a local API that you are working on and want verification of correct behavior but, as an example, we will hit the CircleCI for illustration purposes only. We will create a new repository in GitHub using our `packtci` user and call it `integration-test-example` (https://github.com/packtci/integration-test-example). We will use several libraries including supertest (https://github.com/visionmedia/supertest), a Node.js library, `baloo` (https://github.com/h2non/baloo), a Golang library to hit API endpoints, and , finally, just `curl` and `bash`. It does not matter which library that you use; I am using these libraries for demonstration purposes only.

API testing example using the supertest Node.js library

In this integration test example, we hit the `GET /projects` (https://circleci.com/docs/api/v1-reference/#projects) endpoint in CircleCI. Here is the code testing this endpoint:

```
'use strict';

const request = require('supertest');
const assert = require('assert');

const CIRCLECI_API = {
    // List of all the projects you're following on CircleCI, with build
information organized by branch
    getProjects: 'https://circleci.com/api/v1.1'
```

```
};

describe('Testing CircleCI API Endpoints', function() {
    it('the /projects endpoints should return 200 with a body', function()
{
        return request(CIRCLECI_API.getProjects)
            .get(`/projects?circle-
token=${process.env.CIRCLECI_API_TOKEN_GITHUB}`)
            .set('Accept', 'application/json')
            .expect(200)
            .then(response => {
                assert.ok(response.body.length > 0, "Body have
information")
                assert.equal(response.body[0].oss, true);
            });
    });
});
```

Here, we test that the endpoint returns a 200 HTTP response and that it has a body and that there is an attribute in the array of objects of oss.

API testing example with the baloo Golang library

In this integration test, we hit the GET /user (https://developer.travis-ci.com/resource/user#User) endpoint in the Travis API. Here is the code testing this endpoint:

```
package main

import (
    "errors"
    "net/http"
    "os"
    "testing"
    "gopkg.in/h2non/baloo.v3"
)

var test = baloo.New("https://api.travis-ci.com")

func assertTravisUserEndpoint(res *http.Response, req *http.Request) error
{
  if res.StatusCode != http.StatusOK {
    return errors.New("This endpoint should return a 200 response code")
  }
  if res.Body == nil {
    return errors.New("The body should not be empty")
  }
  return nil
```

```
}

func TestBalooClient(t *testing.T) {
    test.Get("/user").
    SetHeader("Authorization", "token
"+os.Getenv("TRAVIS_PERSONAL_TOKEN")).
    SetHeader("Travis-API-Version", "3").
    Expect(t).
    Status(200).
    Type("json").
    AssertFunc(assertTravisUserEndpoint).
    Done()
}
```

Here, we test that the response is a `200` and that the body has values.

API testing example with curl, bash, and jq

In this integration test example, we will hit `GET: /project/:vcs-type/:username/:project` (https://circleci.com/docs/api/v1-reference/#recent-builds-project), a recent build endpoint in the CircleCI API. Here is the code testing this endpoint:

```
#! /bin/bash

GO_TEMPLATE_EXAMPLE_REPO=$(curl -X GET \
    --header "Accept: application/json" \
"https://circleci.com/api/v1.1/project/github/packtci/go-template-example-w
ith-circle-ci?circle-token=$CIRCLECI_API_TOKEN_GITHUB" | jq
'.[0].author_name' | tr -d "\n")

if [[ -n ${GO_TEMPLATE_EXAMPLE_REPO} ]]; then
    echo "The current owner was shown"
    exit 0
else
    echo "No owner own"
    exit 1
fi
```

Here, we test that we received an `author_name` attribute from the endpoint that should be returned in the JSON payload.

System testing

System tests are typically broader integration tests that extend integration tests. System tests will aggregate groups of functionality in an application and so are even wider in scope than integration tests. System tests will usually be run after integration tests as they are testing larger behaviors in an application and will take longer to run.

System test example

System tests can include:

- **Usability testing**: A type of test that tests the ease of use in the system and the overall ability of the system to meet its proposed functionality
- **Load testing**: A type of test that will measure the behavior of a system under real-world load
- **Regression testing**: A type of test that checks that the system is behaving normally whenever newer features are added to a system

There are other types of system testing but we have only included some common types of system tests.

Acceptance testing

We have gone over acceptance tests throughout the book but, to reiterate, an acceptance test is a formal verification of the behavior of an application. Acceptance tests will typically be the last types of tests that you will write in a CI/CD pipeline as they are longer running and more involved in terms of the verification aspect of acceptance tests as a whole.

Acceptance tests can also serve as a regression test suite since they provide assurances that the application is behaving as it should. There are some libraries that use a formal domain-specific language called **Gherkin** (https://docs.cucumber.io/gherkin/reference/). This has specific files that write down what is called **acceptance criteria.** These stipulate what the new feature needs to do and it is not uncommon for a software company to write an acceptance test that is failing at the beginning of the sprint and that will pass once the acceptance criteria have been met when the feature is implemented correctly.

Acceptance test example

We can look at a very simple example of an acceptance test in my repository called `cucumber-examples` (`https://github.com/jbelmont/cucumber-examples`), which has a Gherkin file that checks that our acceptance criteria is met for a simple calculator program:

```
# features/simple_addition.feature
Feature: Simple Addition of Numbers
    In order to do simple math as a developer I want to add numbers

    Scenario: Easy Math Problem
      Given a list of numbers set to []
      When I add the numbers together by []
      Then I get a larger result that is the sum of the numbers
```

Notice here that the Gherkin syntax is human-readable and is meant to be read as a list of declarations for the new functionality. Here, we state that we want to be able to do a simple math addition operation and then provide a scenario to fulfill this. Here is the code that implements this functionality:

```
const { setWorldConstructor } = require('cucumber')

class Addition {
  constructor() {
    this.summation = 0
  }

  setTo(numbers) {
    this.numbers = numbers
  }

  addBy() {
    this.summation = this.numbers.reduce((prev, curr) => prev + curr, 0);
  }
}

setWorldConstructor(Addition)
```

This file is a JavaScript class that does simple addition and here is another class that has a list of scenarios that add a list of numbers up:

```
const { Given, When, Then } = require('cucumber')
const { expect } = require('chai')

Given('a list of numbers set to []', function () {
    this.setTo([1, 2, 3, 4, 5])
```

```
});

When('I add the numbers together by []', function () {
    this.addBy();
});

Then('I get a larger result that is the sum of the numbers', function () {
    expect(this.summation).to.eql(15)
});
```

 This is a very simple acceptance test but it is meant to illustrate the fact that an acceptance test is a formal verification that the new feature is behaving as it is should be.

Best practices for running different tests in a CI/CD pipeline

We described the the following stages in Chapter 3, *Basics of Continuous Delivery*:

1. The first stage of a CI/CD pipeline will typically encompass a build and commit stage. This is where you build any artifacts needed for the rest of the pipeline and run your unit test suite in the build. The first stage is meant to be very fast running as developers need to have a short feedback loop or else you risk developers bypassing this stage.

2. The second stage of a CI/CD pipeline will typically run integration tests as they are longer running types of tests and can be run after the first stage of the pipeline runs and passes. The second stage is a layer of assurance that any new functionality has broken integrated components of a system.

3. The third stage of a CI/CD pipeline might consist of a suite of load tests and or regression tests and or security tests and will be much longer running than the first two stages of the CI/CD pipeline.

4. The fourth stage can be where the acceptance tests are run, although I have personally seen companies that run an acceptance test suite in tandem with integration tests and so they only had three stages in their CI/CD pipeline. The stages we have laid out in this chapter are not hard and fast rules but merely some suggestions, as each application is unique in its behavior.

Best practices in password and secrets storage

As we have seen throughout the chapters covering Jenkins, Travis CI, and CircleCI, each continuous integration server has a way to store secure information such as passwords, API keys, and secrets. It is dangerous to run certain actions in the CI server, such as execution tracing with Bash by using the set -x option in Bash. It is better to either use the CI server's functionality to securely store passwords and secrets, such as the context settings for each project in CircleCI ,which cannot be seen by anyone other than a project owner. You can also use a tool such as **Vault** (https://www.vaultproject.io/intro/index.html) to securely store your passwords and that can be retrieved using a RESTful API or use something like the **Amazon Key Management Service** (https://aws.amazon.com/secrets-manager/). We will briefly look at using Vault for password needs in a local development environment and make calls to Vault's RESTful API.

Vault installation

Installing Vault (https://www.vaultproject.io/) can be done at the **Install Vault** (https://www.vaultproject.io/intro/getting-started/install.html) link. Once you download Vault, you will need to move the single binary into a PATH that your OS will be able to find. Here is a sample run that I did on my local machine:

```
echo $PATH
## This prints out the current path where binaries can be found

mv ~/Downloads /usr/local/bin
```

The last command will move the binary called `vault` into the <u>/usr/local/bin</u> directory that is in my path and I should now be able run the `vault` command and see the help menu like this:

```
↦  ~ vault
Usage: vault <command> [args]

Common commands:
    read            Read data and retrieves secrets
    write           Write data, configuration, and secrets
    delete          Delete secrets and configuration
    list            List data or secrets
    login           Authenticate locally
    agent           Start a Vault agent
    server          Start a Vault server
    status          Print seal and HA status
    unwrap          Unwrap a wrapped secret

Other commands:
    audit           Interact with audit devices
    auth            Interact with auth methods
    kv              Interact with Vault's Key-Value storage
    lease           Interact with leases
    operator        Perform operator-specific tasks
    path-help       Retrieve API help for paths
    plugin          Interact with Vault plugins and catalog
    policy          Interact with policies
    secrets         Interact with secrets engines
    ssh             Initiate an SSH session
    token           Interact with tokens
↦  ~ ▮
```

Notice here that the `vault` command has `Common commands` and `Other commands` that can be run.

Starting the dev server for Vault

We need to run the vault server `-dev` command to start the dev server:

```
|→ ~ vault server -dev
==> Vault server configuration:

             Api Address: http://127.0.0.1:8200
                     Cgo: disabled
         Cluster Address: https://127.0.0.1:8201
              Listener 1: tcp (addr: "127.0.0.1:8200", cluster address: "127.0.0.1:8201", max_request_duration: "999999h0m0s", max_request_size: "33554432",
tls: "disabled")
               Log Level: info
                   Mlock: supported: false, enabled: false
                 Storage: inmem
                 Version: Vault v0.10.4
             Version Sha: e21712a687889de1125e0a12a980420b1a4f72d3

WARNING! dev mode is enabled! In this mode, Vault runs entirely in-memory
and starts unsealed with a single unseal key. The root token is already
authenticated to the CLI, so you can immediately begin using Vault.

You may need to set the following environment variable:

    $ export VAULT_ADDR='http://127.0.0.1:8200'

The unseal key and root token are displayed below in case you want to
seal/unseal the Vault or re-authenticate.

Unseal Key: IV9awH9ADjBa2ujSf6QKC1CMpf2GSMEo9TQp3taXcBs=
Root Token: 2e18f4d9-1a12-72be-14ff-600522a519af

Development mode should NOT be used in production installations!
```

Notice here that we get a list of instructions to set up our local dev environment.

> Keep in mind that this is just for demonstration purposes and that the dev
> mode is not meant for a production instance.

Checking the status of the Vault server

In the following screenshot, we check the status of the dev Vault server:

```
|→  ~ export VAULT_ADDR='http://127.0.0.1:8200'
|→  ~ vault status
Key                    Value
---                    -----
Seal Type              shamir
Sealed                 false
Total Shares           1
Threshold              1
Version                0.10.4
Cluster Name           vault-cluster-344c2648
Cluster ID             2b7e1355-6417-e1b0-9f67-31cd47284b97
HA Enabled             false
|→  ~ █
```

The first thing we did was export the VAULT_ADDR environment variable in a new shell, as
we will be using this command, and then we checked the status of our dev Vault server.

Setting an API secret in Vault

In the following screenshot, we set an API secret and then retrieve it with Vault:

```
↦  ~ vault kv put secret/api_key API_SECRET_VAL=supersecret
Key              Value
---              -----
created_time     2018-08-14T23:46:43.354473608Z
deletion_time    n/a
destroyed        false
version          1
↦  ~ vault kv get secret/api_key
====== Metadata ======
Key              Value
---              -----
created_time     2018-08-14T23:46:43.354473608Z
deletion_time    n/a
destroyed        false
version          1

========= Data =========
Key              Value
---              -----
API_SECRET_VAL   supersecret
↦  ~ ▮
```

We can also list out all the secrets in the Vault like this:

```
↦  ~ vault secrets list
Path          Type          Accessor              Description
----          ----          --------              -----------
cubbyhole/    cubbyhole     cubbyhole_432ec7ce     per-token private secret storage
identity/     identity      identity_836258ce      identity store
secret/       kv            kv_6d4daef7            key/value secret storage
sys/          system        system_267150b4        system endpoints used for control, policy and debugging
↦  ~ ▮
```

Using the Vault RESTful API

Remember that we are running a dev Vault server instance and so we can run `curl` as a REST client to the Vault API on our local machine. Let's us run the following `curl` command to check whether our Vault instance has been initialized, which it should be at this point:

```
curl http://127.0.0.1:8200/v1/sys/init
```

We need to create a file called `config.hcl` in order to bypass TLS defaults for Vault with the following content:

```
backend "file" {
 path = "vault"
}

listener "tcp" {
 tls_disable = 1
}
```

We will need to unseal the Vault and log in, as the following screenshot shows:

```
~ vault operator unseal kO8heI6I3pVcWfqkQpoeCbMjoTEb11DmFNxfjYM7hoc=
Key                Value
---                -----
Seal Type          shamir
Sealed             false
Total Shares       1
Threshold          1
Version            0.10.4
Cluster Name       vault-cluster-6dad2aa4
Cluster ID         c9656933-787c-9e38-786f-3a51e3f1055b
HA Enabled         false
~ vault login 3507d8cc-5ca2-28b5-62f9-a54378f3366d
Success! You are now authenticated. The token information displayed below
is already stored in the token helper. You do NOT need to run "vault login"
again. Future Vault requests will automatically use this token.

Key                 Value
---                 -----
token               3507d8cc-5ca2-28b5-62f9-a54378f3366d
token_accessor      e8a71f5d-d35f-29cc-cbf0-6b23f6d8f65d
token_duration      ∞
token_renewable     false
token_policies      ["root"]
identity_policies   []
policies            ["root"]
~
```

Notice here that we get a token, which is what we will need to make requests to the RESTful API using the following HTTP header: `X-Vault-Token:` `3507d8cc-5ca2-28b5-62f9-a54378f3366d`.

Vault RESTful API endpoint GET /v1/sys/raw/logical

Here is a sample `curl GET` request for the endpoint:

```
↦  ~ curl -X GET \
>  --request LIST \
>  --header "X-Vault-Token: 3507d8cc-5ca2-28b5-62f9-a54378f3366d" \
>  http://127.0.0.1:8200/v1/sys/raw/logical | jq
  % Total     % Received % Xferd  Average Speed   Time    Time     Time  Current
                                  Dload  Upload   Total   Spent    Left  Speed
100   208  100   208    0     0   185k      0 --:--:-- --:--:-- --:--:--  203k
{
  "request_id": "c466b833-7f33-7524-0f6e-20d2f42d825d",
  "lease_id": "",
  "renewable": false,
  "lease_duration": 0,
  "data": {
    "keys": [
      "8384b95a-56c0-7939-6e6b-0c23a69f6689/"
    ]
  },
  "wrap_info": null,
  "warnings": null,
  "auth": null
}
↦  ~ ▮
```

Notice here that we used the token that was printed from the standard output after we ran the Vault login ROOT_KEY command. This endpoint returns the list of keys for the given path, which in this case is `/sys/raw/logical`.

Overall best practices for secrets management

As we have stated before throughout the book, it is not good practice to commit raw passwords and secrets into source control and you will need to have a way to safely retrieve passwords when running CI/CD pipelines. You can use the CI server itself to store passwords and secrets and then retrieve them using environment variables or you can use services such as Vault to securely store your passwords. Remember that it can be unsafe to use execution tracing in shell scripts in CI environments so be mindful when debugging builds and using the `set -x` flag in Bash.

Best practices in deployment

In Chapter 3, *Basics of Continuous Delivery*, we went over what a deployment is, explained the deployment pipeline, and spoke about test gates in a deployment pipeline. We also spoke about deployment scripting and about the deployment ecosystem.

Let's highlight some other good strategies when doing deployments:

- Creating a deployment checklist
- Releasing automation

Creating a deployment checklist

Every company will have unique constraints and so it is not possible to create a deployment checklist that satisfies the constraints of every company but, in general, here are some guidelines that may be helpful throughout all deployments.

Collaboration among developers and operations

There should be communication between the development team and operations to properly coordinate a deployment. This is critical because miscommunications are bound to happen and so close communication should be happening during a deployment to avoid outages and lost of data.

Releasing automation

Manual processes are error-prone and so a deployment should be automated as much as possible to avoid human error. Manual processes are not repeatable and are not sustainable, as deployments become more complicated. It is better to have automation scripts that take human error out of the equation.

Deployment script example

There are many different options in terms of where software can be deployed. In this way, a deployment script can vary greatly depending on whether a project is open source, private, or enterprise. Many open source projects simply create a GitHub release (`https://help.github.com/articles/creating-releases/`) for each new release and automate the process by using a Bash script. Some companies may use **Heroku** (`https://devcenter.heroku.com/start`) as their provider or some may use **AWS CodeDeploy** (`https://aws.amazon.com/codedeploy/`) but, in the end, you want to automate your deployment process so that there is a standard and automated way to deploy your software. It is also good to have a deployment script that will collate version control commits and be able to display new features and bug fixes in each software release.

Automated GitHub release example

We will use the following endpoint in the GitHub API to automate the release strategy: `POST /repos/:owner/:repo/releases`. The documentation for this endpoint can be found at `https://developer.github.com/v3/repos/releases/#create-a-release`. We will create a Golang script in the `multiple-languages` (`https://github.com/packtci/multiple-languages`) GitHub repository that will create a new GitHub release.

Golang script example

We will use Golang to make an HTTP request and give the Go script some command-line arguments. These will be used to formulate the following `request` body that will have the following shape:

```
{
"tag_name": "v1.0.0",
"target_commitish": "master",
"name": "v1.0.0",
"body": "Description of the release",
"draft": false,
"prerelease": false
}
```

Here is the first part of the deployment script:

```go
package main
import (
    "bytes"
    "encoding/json"
    "flag"
    "log"
    "net/http"
    "os"
)
var (
    tagName         = flag.String("tagName", "", "Please provide a tag name for the release")
    targetCommitish = flag.String("targetCommitish", "", "Please provide a targetCommitish value namely master")
    name            = flag.String("name", "", "A name for the Github Release")
    body            = flag.String("body", "", "Provide a description of the release")
)
func checkArgs() {
    if *tagName == "" {
        flag.PrintDefaults()
        os.Exit(2)
    }
    if *targetCommitish == "" {
        flag.PrintDefaults()
        os.Exit(2)
    }
    if *name == "" {
        flag.PrintDefaults()
        os.Exit(2)
    }
    if *body == "" {
        flag.PrintDefaults()
        os.Exit(2)
    }
}
```

In this part of the script, we declare our package of main and then get some command-line arguments that we will need to make our HTTP request. We need to parse them and check if they are are set, which is what the checkArgs function does when it gets called in the main function, as shown in the following screenshot:

```go
func main() {
    flag.Parse()
    checkArgs()
    body := struct {
        TagName         string `json:"tag_name"`
        TargetCommitish string `json:"target_commitish"`
        Name            string `json:"name"`
        Body            string `json:"body"`
        Draft           bool   `json:"draft"`
        Prerelease      bool   `json:"prerelease"`
    }{
        *tagName,
        *targetCommitish,
        *name,
        *body,
        false,
        false,
    }
    postBody, err := json.Marshal(body)
    if err != nil {
        log.Fatalln("An issue occurred marshalling this data ", err)
    }
    client := http.Client{}
    req, err := http.NewRequest(
        "POST",
        "https://api.github.com/repos/packtci/multiple-languages/releases",
        bytes.NewBuffer(postBody),
    )
    req.Header.Set("Content-Type", "application/json")
    req.Header.Set("Authorization", "token "+os.Getenv("PACKTCI_PERSONAL_TOKEN"))
```

Now, in this second part of the script, we are in our `main` function and here we parse the command-line arguments and then invoke our `checkArgs` function. Next, we create an anonymous struct that we will use to create our `request` body and then we set up the HTTP request and set our HTTP headers. In the last part of the script, we make our request and print out the release URL:

```go
if err != nil {
    log.Fatalln(err)
}

resp, err := client.Do(req)
if err != nil {
    log.Fatalln(err)
}
if resp.StatusCode != http.StatusCreated {
    log.Fatalln("Should receive a status code of 201 created")
}

var result map[string]interface{}

json.NewDecoder(resp.Body).Decode(&result)

log.Println(result)
log.Println(result["url"])
}
```

Let us show a run in a Terminal session for this deployment script:

```
→  scripts git:(master) ✗ go run deploy.go -tagName="v1.0.0" -targetCommitish="5883ea0c0177bc0f5b9072488f8ff33cb0671d1f" -name="First Release of Multiple Lan
guages for PacktCI" -body="A collection of code files exploring travis ci with multiple languages"
2018/08/15 19:24:50 map[draft:false prerelease:false tarball_url:https://api.github.com/repos/packtci/multiple-languages/tarball/v1.0.0 upload_url:https://up
loads.github.com/repos/packtci/multiple-languages/releases/12424724/assets{?name,label} node_id:MDc6UmVsZWFzZTEyNDI0NzI0 name:First Release of Multiple Langu
ages for PacktCI tag_name:v1.0.0 created_at:2018-08-15T23:15:45Z published_at:2018-08-15T23:24:50Z url:https://api.github.com/repos/packtci/multiple-language
s/releases/12424724 assets_url:https://api.github.com/repos/packtci/multiple-languages/releases/12424724/assets html_url:https://github.com/packtci/multiple-
languages/releases/tag/v1.0.0 id:1 2424724 target_commitish:5883ea0c0177bc0f5b9072488f8ff33cb0671d1f author:map[subscriptions_url:https://api.github.com/
users/packtci/subscriptions type:User login:packtci followers_url:https://api.github.com/users/packtci/followers starred_url:https://api.github.com/users/pac
ktci/starred{/owner}{/repo} site_admin:false node_id:MDQ6VXNlcjQwMzIyNDI1 gists_url:https://api.github.com/users/packtci/gists{/gist_id} html_url:https://git
hub.com/packtci following_url:https://api.github.com/users/packtci/following{/other_user} organizations_url:https://api.github.com/users/packtci/orgs repos_u
rl:https://api.github.com/users/packtci/repos avatar_url:https://avatars3.githubusercontent.com/u/40322425?v=4 url:https://api.github.com/users/packtci event
s_url:https://api.github.com/users/packtci/events{/privacy} received_events_url:https://api.github.com/users/packtci/received_events id:4.0322425e+07 gravata
r_id: assets:[] zipball_url:https://api.github.com/repos/packtci/multiple-languages/zipball/v1.0.0 body:A collection of code files exploring travis ci with
multiple languages]
2018/08/15 19:24:50 https://api.github.com/repos/packtci/multiple-languages/releases/12424724
→  scripts git:(master) ✗
```

Notice here that we provided the four command-line arguments after `go run deploy.go` and the script printed out a release URL at the end.

Let us go to the **Releases** tab in the `multiple-languages` (`https://github.com/packtci/multiple-languages/releases`) repository and click on our new release, which looks like this:

Best practices for a deployment script

It is best to automate the deployment process when releasing new software for your consumers. It is not necessary to create a custom deployment script as we have done here as their are great libraries that you can use that are more structured and feature rich than this small script that we wrote. For example, you can use the **GoReleaser** (`https://goreleaser.com/`) automation release script that works fantastically for Go projects. There are many libraries available that are language-specific as well as options in CI providers, such TravisCI ,that will deploy your software to providers, such as the Google App Engine (`https://docs.travis-ci.com/user/deployment/google-app-engine/`) and more.

Summary

In this last chapter, we covered best practices for different types of tests in a CI/CD pipeline, including unit tests, integration tests, system tests, and acceptance tests. We provided code examples and showed ways of how to test an API endpoint using Node.js, Golang, and a shell script. We covered best practices in password management and showed how to use the Vault library to securely manage secrets and showed how to use the Vault API. We finished the chapter by showing some best practices regarding deployment. We talked about a deployment checklist, release automation, and we wrote a custom release script in Golang to create a GitHub release.

This is the end of the book and I hope that you have learned a lot about CI/CD, testing and automation, and using Jenkins CI, CircleCI, and Travis CI.

Questions

1. Why is it important to separate integration tests from unit tests?
2. What is a commit stage?
3. Name a type of system test.
4. What was the name of the password management tool that we used?
5. Why should you be careful with execution tracing in a shell script?
6. Name one item that we mentioned in the deployment checklist.
7. What was the name of the deployment tool that we mentioned for Golang?

Further reading

You should check out the book called *Continuous Integration, Delivery, and Deployment* (https://www.packtpub.com/application-development/continuous-integration-delivery-and-deployment) by Packt Publishing to learn more about best practices with CI/CD.

Assessments

Chapter 1: CI/CD with Automated Testing

1. A manual process is any process that is repetitive and capable of being automated.
2. Automation is a process where you enable an action to be done automatically via a script or some kind of action.
3. It is important to open communication between departments in order to find manual processes.
4. Continuous Integration / Continuous Delivery
5. Automation scripts are useful because they help automate manual tasks.
6. A company intranet can help empower other departments share information and link disconnected information.
7. Other departments should share data because it helps bridge information across departments and increases the chances of using data in interesting ways.

Chapter 2: Basics of Continuous Integration

1. A Software Build can consist of just compiling software components. A build can consist of compiling and running automated tests, but in general the more processes you add to the build the slower the feedback loop becomes on a build.
2. A staged build is a build that is broken down into a smaller build. For example in the first build you can do your compilation step and run all the unit tests. A secondary build can be used to run longer running tests such as end to end tests.
3. Make is a widely used scripting tool that can be used for many different types of programming languages. Maven is a scripting tool used by the Java community.
4. It is better to follow a naming convention because it helps organize a code base better and helps developers quickly understand what is going on a source file. Following a particular folder structure can help you quickly setup a new project.
5. CI has many things of value but in particular a CI system helps decouple environment configuration and setup into an isolated environment where developers can run all the tests in a codebase and do important tasks such as reporting and call other 3rd party services in an automated fashion.

Chapter 3: Basics of Continuous Delivery

1. What we mean by delivering software is that the actual software product has been delivered to the intended user and not just that the software product has been approved by the QA department. In other words the intended users are actually using the software.

2. Deploying software manually is an antipattern as well as manual software configuration.

3. Some benefits of automation when delivering software is team empowerment (teams feel empowered to make decisions), error reduction as you eliminate errors that creep up due to manual processes as well as stress reduction.

4. Configuration Management is the process by which all software artifacts that are pertinent to each given project as well as any relationships among the software artifacts are retrieved, stored, identified and modified.

5. Writing descriptive and meaningful commit messages helps developers quickly track the issue that is worked on and helps developers understand the work that you actually did.

6. A deployment pipeline can thought of as the process for getting software that is written by developers into the hands of your users.

7. The deployment should be done the same in each environment so that you get reliably know that it is being tested the same in each environment and avoid possible configuration mismatches.

Chapter 4: The Business Value of CI/CD

1. It is difficult for developers to work on a new feature without having all the requirements up front. It can be a great hindrance for a developers ability to finish assigned work without all the necessary requirements.

2. Pain driven development is about improving processes that are causing you pain. The main point being that the pain that you feel will help point you into areas of improvement.

3. Developers will eventually ignore messages if they are bombarded with too many alerts. It is best if the alerts are meaningful and not just noise.

4. By rotating team members into different teams you help shape their perspective and give a broader understanding of development practices and increase their product knowledge.

5. It is beneficial because not all development practices are valuable, it could be that a development practice is being done because something better has not been thought of, sometimes asking why something is done will help bring changes necessary for an organization.

6. Metrics and reporting are a great way to convince your stakeholders on the value of CI/CD. Remember that a picture is worth a thousand words sometimes.

7. Leadership may not understand what automation means and understand the impact that automation can have on an organization. You may need to educate them by doing a lunch and learn or make a company presentation.

Chapter 5: Installation and Basics of Jenkins

1. Chocolatey
2. Java
3. `curl -X POST -u <user>:<password> http://<jenkins.server>/restart`
4. `sudo ufw allow 8080`
5. Homebrew
6. In the Jenkins Dashboard, click Manage Jenkins and then click Manage Plugins
7. In the Jenkins Dashboard, click Manage Jenkins and then click Configure System, then you need to scroll down into the global properties and the necessary environment variables.

Chapter 6: Writing Freestyle Scripts

1. The question mark symbol is handy when you need to know the details about a build configuration option.
2. It is a Crontab syntax that you can use for polling your version control system.
3. Yes, you can use more than one language, for instance you may have a go script and a Node.js script that you need to run in your environment.
4. It is a Unix environment that you are operating in and a lot of Unix commands are available for use like `sed` and `awk`.

5. A global property will be available throughout all the build jobs you add while a project level environment variable will only be available in the specific project you add them in. This is enabled by the EnvInject Plugin.

6. It is useful to see the command executed and/or the output of the command so that you can more easily debug issues that occur with each command that is run in the CI environment.

7. The post build action is useful for things like reporting and gathering metrics but also for any additional action that you deem important outside of the main build script actions.

Chapter 7: Developing Plugins

1. We used the Maven Build tool.
2. We used the Chocolatey Package Manager in Windows.
3. We used the Homebrew Package Manager in macOS.
4. The `settings.xml` file for the Maven Build Tool.
5. You can go to the url {{domain}}/pluginManager/advanced to manage plugins.
6. The command `mvn install` is used to both build and install Jenkins Plugins.
7. Maven creates a file called `pluginname.hpi` where plugin name can be any name you gave for the actual plugin.

Chapter 8: Building Pipelines with Jenkins

1. Yes you can, it is actually one of the suggested plugins that you can install when you use the Docker Install of Jenkins.
2. By using the Pipeline Editor you can get helpful debugging and visualize stages in a pipeline.
3. The Blue Ocean View is still under active development so any type of Administrative task needs to be done in the classic view.
4. Yes if you click on a node of the pipeline and then click the popdown you will get a detailed view of that particular build stage.
5. No not yet.
6. The stages keyword contains a sequence of one or more stage directives, the stages section is where the bulk of the "work" described by a Pipeline will be located.
7. Yes it does need to be wrapped.

Chapter 9: Installation and Basics of Travis CI

1. Jenkins allows for full customization because it must be installed and setup by a Jenkins Administrator while Travis CI is much easier to setup because it uses an in application YML script and is only used in the GitHub, which is a web-based hosting service for version control that uses Git.
2. No.
3. You need to go to your profile in Travis and then click the sync button and then toggle your newly synced repository on.
4. Scalars are ordinary values meaning they can be numbers, strings, booleans.
5. Lists in YAML are just collections of elements.
6. Anchors serve as a way to reuse items in YML files.
7. Yes, you add a secondary programming language in the **before_install** block.
8. You enable docker by adding docker in the services block in the YML script.

Chapter 10: Travis CI CLI Commands and Automation

1. The Travis CLI User Documentation (`https://github.com/travis-ci/travis.rb#windows`) recommends that you use the RubyInstaller (`https://rubyinstaller.org/`) to install the latest version Ruby on the Windows OS.
2. You should use the `travis version` command.
3. You use the `travis help` command. For example to print out information about the token command you run the following command: `travis help token`.
4. You will need to run the `travis login` command and then enter your GitHub username and password.
5. You will need to pass the following HTTP Header: `Travis-API-Version: 3`.
6. The `travis report` command prints out system configuration information.
7. The `travis lint` command will check the syntax and validity of your Travis yml script.
8. The `travis init` command helps you setup Travis in your project, and for example to setup go in your project run the following command: `travis init go`.

Chapter 11: Travis CI UI Logging and Debugging

1. Yes whenever you merge a pull request in GitHub, Travis CI will automatically kick off another build.

2. No it doesn't, but you will see labels for the before_install and install lifecycle events as well as some other lifecycle events.

3. You will need to use Docker to pull down an image and you can find the full list of Docker images here (https://docs.travis-ci.com/user/common-build-problems/#Troubleshooting-Locally-in-a-Docker-Image).

4. Yes, but you will need to email support@travis-ci.com and then request whatever specific repositories you want to have debug mode enabled for. Additionally you will need to make a call to Travis API with the corresponding job id to trigger a build in debug mode.

5. You will need to make an API call to the Travis API by doing a GET request to the /builds endpoint. Here is a sample request using the curl REST client:

```
curl -s -X GET \
   -H "Content-Type: application/json" \
   -H "Accept: application/json" \
   -H "Travis-API-Version: 3" \
   -H "Authorization: token $(travis token)" \
   -d '{ "quiet": true }' \
  https://api.travis-ci.org/builds
```

6. `travis_run_before_install` is the convenience bash function that you would use.

7. You would use the travis setup SERVICE cli command, and here is an example command to setup Heroku in Travis CI: `travis setup heroku`.

Chapter 12: Installation and Basics of CircleCI

1. Jenkins allows for full customization because it must be installed and setup by a Jenkins Administrator while Circle CI is much easier to setup but doesn't allow for the customization that you can get with Jenkins. With that being said all you have to do is declare an environment that you want to work with which is Linux by default and declare the build language that you are going to use in the yml script such as Java.
2. Yes, Circle CI works with both Bitbucket and GitHub.
3. You simply have to click the Add Projects button in the Circle CI Application and then click the Setup Project button for the repository that you want to setup.
4. You click on the JOBS link in the left navigation pane and then click on the repository that you are working with and then look at the most recent job that completed.
5. We used the `https://maven.apache.org/` Maven build tool.
6. No, you should be using version 2 of the Circle CI Syntax because version 1 is deprecated.
7. You put the build language as a key in the ^{image} field that inside of the `docker` field. Here is a snippet of what it looks like:

```
jobs:
   build:
      docker:
          # specify the version you desire here
          - image: circleci/node:7.10
```

Chapter 13: Circle CI CLI Commands and Automation

1. You need to have Docker installed in order to use the Circle CI CLI.
2. We got the nightly build from GitHub Releases (`https://github.com/CircleCI-Public/circleci-cli/releases`).
3. There are currently 6 command in the CLI but more commands may be added in the future.
4. The `help` command is useful because it explains how to use each command what the command does.

5. The workflows field is how you can run parallel jobs in Circle CI.
6. We used the command `circleci config validate`.
7. The API Endpoint is `https://circleci.com/api/v1.1/`.

Chapter 14: Circle CI UI Logging and Debugging

1. The API Endpoint was
   `POST https://circleci.com/api/v1.1/project/:vcs-type/:username/:project/follow?circle-token=:token`.

2. Yes the cat utility can be used to create new files you can do the following:

```
cat > somefile
# input
input
Press Control D
```

3. You would use the vertical Pipe operator (|) to create a multi-line command like this for example:

```
- run:
    name: Run Tests and Run Code Coverage with NYC
    command: |
        echo "Generate Code Coverage"
        npm test
        echo "Show the coverage"
        npm run coverage
# or simply
- run: |
    echo "Generate Code Coverage"
    npm test
    echo "Show the coverage"
    npm run coverage
```

4. Yes if you run the `set -x` option in a script and are setting secrets they may leak into standard output so instead store secrets or keys in project or context settings in the CircleCI app.

5. The CLI command to validate your config yml script is `circleci config validate`.

6. Yes they can if you go the project settings and look at Environment Variables and use the Import Variables button.

7. We used the save_cache and restore_cache declarations.

Chapter 15: Best Practices

1. It is important because the first stage in a CI/CD pipeline is meant to run fast.

2. The commit stage in a CI/CD pipeline is typically the first stage in a pipeline where you build your artifacts and run your unit tests.

3. A load test.

4. Vault

5. You should be careful because you could accidentally expose a password.

6. Collaboration among developers and operations.

7. goreleaser (`https://goreleaser.com/`)

Other Books You May Enjoy

If you enjoyed this book, you may be interested in these other books by Packt:

Learning Continuous Integration with Jenkins - Second Edition
Nikhil Pathania

ISBN: 9781788479356

- Get to know some of the most popular ways to set up Jenkins
- See all the new features introduced in the latest Jenkins, such as pipeline as code, Multibranch pipeline, and more
- Manage users, projects, and permissions in Jenkins to ensure better security
- Leverage the power of plugins in Jenkins
- Learn how to create a CI pipeline using Jenkins Blue Ocean
- Create a distributed build farm using Docker and use it with Jenkins
- Implement CI and CD using Jenkins
- See the difference between CD and Continuous Deployment
- Understand the concepts of CI

Continuous Delivery with Docker and Jenkins
Rafał Leszko

ISBN: 9781787125230

- Get to grips with docker fundamentals and how to dockerize an application for the Continuous Delivery process.
- Configure Jenkins and scale it using Docker-based agents.
- Understand the principles and the technical aspects of a successful Continuous Delivery pipeline.
- Create a complete Continuous Delivery process using modern tools: Docker, Jenkins, and Ansible
- Write acceptance tests using Cucumber and run them in the Docker ecosystem using Jenkins.
- Create multi-container applications using Docker Compose.
- Managing database changes inside the Continuous Delivery process and understand effective frameworks such as Cucumber and Flyweight
- Build clustering applications with Jenkins using Docker Swarm
- Publish a built Docker image to a Docker Registry and deploy cycles of Jenkins pipelines using community best practices

Leave a review - let other readers know what you think

Please share your thoughts on this book with others by leaving a review on the site that you bought it from. If you purchased the book from Amazon, please leave us an honest review on this book's Amazon page. This is vital so that other potential readers can see and use your unbiased opinion to make purchasing decisions, we can understand what our customers think about our products, and our authors can see your feedback on the title that they have worked with Packt to create. It will only take a few minutes of your time, but is valuable to other potential customers, our authors, and Packt. Thank you!

Index

Printed in Great Britain
by Amazon

82947982R00237